Routledge Revivals

The Development of the British Army, 1899–1914

Originally published in 1938, this book was the first to be written which dealt with the history of Army Development during the confused years which followed the South African War. The period 1899–1914 marked the change from Victorian scarlet and pipeclay to the service dress of the Expeditionary Force of 1914. Similarly, it saw the growth of the Volunteer Rifle Corps of the nineteenth century into the Territorial Force of the Haldane Scheme. The writer, sometime history scholar of St John's College Cambridge, himself a Territorial of twenty-three years' service, was at the time one of the T.A. officers recently appointed to newly created posts at the War Office.

The Development of the British Army, 1899–1914

From the Eve of the South African War to the
Eve of the Great War, with Special Reference
to the Territorial Force

John K. Dunlop

First published in 1938
by Methuen

This edition first published in 2022 by Routledge
4 Park Square, Milton Park, Abingdon, Oxon, OX14 4RN

and by Routledge
605 Third Avenue, New York, NY 10017

Routledge is an imprint of the Taylor & Francis Group, an informa business

© 1938 John K. Dunlop

All rights reserved. No part of this book may be reprinted or reproduced or utilised in any form or by any electronic, mechanical, or other means, now known or hereafter invented, including photocopying and recording, or in any information storage or retrieval system, without permission in writing from the publishers.

Publisher's Note
The publisher has gone to great lengths to ensure the quality of this reprint but points out that some imperfections in the original copies may be apparent.

Disclaimer
The publisher has made every effort to trace copyright holders and welcomes correspondence from those they have been unable to contact.

A Library of Congress record exists under LCCN: 38019904

ISBN: 978-1-032-22429-9 (hbk)
ISBN: 978-1-003-27255-7 (ebk)
ISBN: 978-1-032-22431-2 (pbk)

Book DOI 10.4324/9781003272557

THE DEVELOPMENT OF THE BRITISH ARMY
1899–1914

FROM THE EVE OF THE SOUTH AFRICAN WAR
TO THE EVE OF THE GREAT WAR, WITH SPECIAL
REFERENCE TO THE TERRITORIAL FORCE

by

COLONEL JOHN K. DUNLOP
O.B.E., M.C., T.D., Ph.D.

With a Foreword by
MAJOR-GENERAL SIR FREDERICK MAURICE
K.C.M.G., C.B., LL.D.

METHUEN  LONDON

36 ESSEX STREET STRAND W.C.2

First published in 1938

PRINTED IN GREAT BRITAIN

FOREWORD

By MAJOR-GENERAL SIR FREDERICK MAURICE
K.C.M.G., C.B., LL.D.

THIS book fills a definite gap in the history of the British Army. The period between the South African War and the Great War saw the creation of the General Staff, extended later to comprise the whole Empire, the organization of the Regular Army at home in the formations in which it would fight in the event of war, and a complete change in our attitude towards the auxiliary forces of the Crown. These developments involved many enquiries and much controversy. The greatest of them was the reorganization of the inchoate mass of Yeomanry, Militia and Volunteers, which had no higher commands, no transport and none of those services, which enable an army to take the field, into the Territorial Army of to-day.

This book appears at an opportune moment, for the Territorial Army is now at long last represented on the Army Council and Colonel Dunlop has just been appointed to the Staff of the Director-General to assist in carrying on the good work of development and progress. The Territorial Army is to-day charged with highly important functions in the defence of our coasts, and in anti-aircraft defence, while it is the recognized means of expansion of the regular forces in the event of a great national emergency. The story of how these changes came about is appropriately told by an officer who has devoted his life to the Territorial Army and has had practical experience in command of a famous battalion of that army. It is presented to us here with very complete documentation and is not only a valuable historical record but also an useful guide to those who have to deal with the problems of the Territorial Army of to-day.

F. MAURICE

November 1937

AUTHOR'S FOREWORD

A LIST of some of the authorities consulted will be found in a Bibliography at the end of this work.

Much of the most interesting information has, however, been derived from discussion and correspondence with those who themselves played important parts in the period covered by the book. It is not possible to include all the names of those who have thus helped, but I should wish to pay special tribute to some whose advice and guidance have been of particular value. First to Major-General Sir Frederick Maurice, K.C.M.G., C.B., to whose encouragement the book owes its very origin; then to the Rt. Hon. the Earl of Midleton, K.P. (who, as Mr. St. John Brodrick, was Secretary of State for War from 1902–1906), to Lieut.-General Sir Gerald Ellison, K.C.B., K.C.M.G., to Sir Charles Harris, G.B.E., K.C.B., and to Mr. A. E. Widdows, C.B., especially for their information on the Haldane period; to Colonel A. S. Barham, C.M.G., V.D., J.P., Colonel A. D. Bayliffe, C.M.G., T.D., who, together with the late Colonel H. F. Coldicott, V.D., T.D., were my authorities on the subject of 'the Volunteers of 1899'.

I should also wish to express my thanks to my wife and to Mrs. John Bruford and Miss H. V. Webb, for their great help in transcribing and checking references.

CONTENTS

PART I
THE STATE OF THE BRITISH ARMY ON THE EVE OF THE SOUTH AFRICAN WAR

CHAPTER		PAGE
1	INTRODUCTION	3
2	ORGANIZATION FOR WAR	11
3	THE REGULAR ARMY	25
4	THE AUXILIARY FORCES	42

PART II
THE MOBILIZATION AND EXPANSION OF THE BRITISH ARMY DURING THE SOUTH AFRICAN WAR, 1899–1902

5	THE MOBILIZATION OF THE REGULAR ARMY	69
6	THE EMPLOYMENT OF THE AUXILIARY FORCES	89

PART III
1900–1905. A PERIOD OF ATTEMPTED REFORMS

7	MR. BRODRICK AS SECRETARY OF STATE FOR WAR	121
8	THE END OF THE WAR—REFORMS AND COMMISSIONS	146
9	MR. ARNOLD-FORSTER TAKES OFFICE	165
10	THE FORMATION OF THE ARMY COUNCIL AND COMMITTEE OF IMPERIAL DEFENCE	198
11	RETROSPECT	218

PART IV
THE HALDANE REFORMS

12	MR. HALDANE BECOMES SECRETARY OF STATE FOR WAR	231
13	THE FORMATION OF THE EXPEDITIONARY FORCE	251

xii THE DEVELOPMENT OF THE BRITISH ARMY

CHAPTER PAGE
14 THE TERRITORIAL AND RESERVE FORCES ACT . . . 266

15 THE CREATION OF THE IMPERIAL GENERAL STAFF AND THE
TRAINING OF THE ARMY 291

CONCLUSION 305

APPENDICES 307

BIBLIOGRAPHY 325

INDEX 331

PART I

THE STATE OF THE BRITISH ARMY ON THE EVE OF THE SOUTH AFRICAN WAR

CHAPTER 1

INTRODUCTION

IN the summer of 1899 the British Army consisted, according to the terms of the Army Estimates, of the Regular Army and the Auxiliary Forces. Included in the Regular Army was the Army Reserve; included in the Auxiliary Forces were the Militia, the Yeomanry, and the Volunteers.

Within the compass of forty years each of these component parts had experienced very important changes. The Volunteers in their present form had sprung into existence in the year 1859. The Militia, after the post-Waterloo quiescence, had revived but not in the old character. As for the Regular Army, the military reforms associated with the names of Mr. Cardwell and Mr. Childers, the reforms of the years 1870 to 1882, were regarded by Sir John Fortescue, in his classic 'History of the Army' as so complete in their purview, so revolutionary in their scope, that they marked the end of a military age. The Old Army, that had endured from Stuart times had passed away and a New Army was to take its place. Three sentences from his final volume will show how vital, in the opinion of this judge, were the alterations effected by this series of legislation. 'Two relics of the old system alone remained, long service for soldiers, and purchase for officers. The former was swept away in 1870, the latter in 1871; and therewith the knell of the Old British Army was rung. . . . Some other hand must record the vicissitudes of the New Army which grew up after. . . .'[1]

This conception of a complete change was also present in

---

[1] These sentences are taken from the end of one chapter and the commencement of the next.—Fortescue, vol. xiii, pp. 560–1.

the minds of the authors of a work 'The Army Book of the British Empire' which was published in 1893. In a chapter entitled 'The Modern System in Britain' they made clear the prevalent feeling that the introduction of short service, the dependence upon an army largely composed of reservists, was a complete revolution which rendered comparison with the past difficult, if not impossible.[1]

The great series of new legislation had commenced with 'The Army Enlistment Act' of 1870. This measure had authorized enlistment for short service, such service to be partly with the Colours and partly with the Reserve.[2] This was followed, in the following year, by the Royal Warrant of July 20, 1871, which abolished purchase of commissions, and the New Warrant of October 30th of the same year, which laid down the new conditions for first commissions and for subsequent promotion.[3]

In 1872, as a result of the Report of General MacDougall's Committee on Military Organization, a scheme for the Territorial localization of the Army was laid before the House of Commons. Therein the Duke of Cambridge, as Commander-in-Chief of the Army, sketched out the new plan for the organization of the land forces.

The plan had provided, in brief, for the linking in pairs of all single battalion regiments of Infantry, and for the 'localization' of regular infantry by associating each regiment with a definite part of the country and with the militia battalions, already, so to speak, attached to the soil.[4] The Brigade

[1] 'The condition of our military forces fifty years ago can probably hardly be realized by whose who have only come to observe these things in more recent years.'—Major-General Sir E. F. Ducane, K.C.B., 'R.U.S.I. Journal', xlii, p. 159.

[2] 'Chronology', p. 19.

[3] 'Chronology', p. 21. It may be worth mentioning that the system of purchase only applied to the cavalry and infantry. In the two 'Ordnance Corps' of Artillery and Engineers promotion was by seniority, and there was no purchase.—Fortescue, vol. xiii, p. 550

[4] The Foot Guards, the 60th Rifles, and the Rifle Brigade were not included in the 'localization' scheme.

INTRODUCTION 5

depot was established as the territorial nerve centre of the regiment.

In 1881, Mr. Childers carried the scheme to its logical conclusion by amalgamating the linked battalions.[1]

The last of the major reforms initiated by Mr. Cardwell had been to bring together, under the one roof of the War Office, the department of the Secretary of State for War, and the department of the Commander-in-Chief. At the same time, all the reserve forces as they were then called, the Militia, the Yeomanry, and the Volunteers, were brought under the control of the War Office.[2]

In 1899 these important changes were within the memory of many officers still serving. There were many in the senior ranks who had entered the Army in the days of purchase and a long service soldiery. It was perhaps inevitable that there had been controversy over the introduction of such far-reaching reforms. Even in 1899 echoes of the arguments were heard. 'Lord Cardwell's Reforms vital as they were to the well-being of the Army disturbed prejudices and interests in many quarters, and left behind them a long trail of grievances of which the War Office has been made the legatee.'[3]

The very controversies however had forced the Army to take itself seriously. Discussions at the Royal United Service Institution, and in the Service journals showed that a great weight of serious military opinion was in favour of the short service system with the Army Reserve. In any event the change was bound to come. The lesson of the Crimean War was perfectly clear. To engage upon a wasteful campaign with

[1] The Cameron Highlanders remained a single-battalion regiment till a second battalion was raised in 1897. The actual change was ordered by G.O. 41 of April 1881. Sir C. H. Ellice's Committee on the Formation of Territorial Regiments had contributed recommendations to this effect.— A.R.C. No. 240 of 1881.

[2] Clause 7, Military and Reserve Forces Circular, 1872. 'Chronology', p. 23.

[3] Mr. St. John Brodrick. Cf. also Major-General R. L. Dashwood at the R.U.S.I. February 9, 1898: 'If these battalions are unlinked—which I sincerely hope they will be.'

no system of reserves for the supply of regimental drafts was clear folly.

Lord Wolseley was a powerful advocate of the short service system, and he placed the evidence in its favour quite fairly when he said: 'This at least is certain, that an Army Reserve of 80,000 men places us in a military position that for either offence or defence we have never before attained to in this country. . . . When that Army Reserve rejoins the colours, the home Army would then be immeasurably superior to any Army we have had in England for 100 years.'[1]

Some parts of the new system had already been tested on the battle-field. The short service soldiers had been engaged in a series of small wars. At a later period the Esher Committee spoke of the years between 1870 and 1899 as a 'period of immunity from real stress, when the provision of relatively small expeditionary forces to operate against unorganized and ill-armed peoples has been the principal occupation of the War Office apart from its multifarious duties of purely peace routine'.[2] Indeed during the last half of the nineteenth century the British Army had been almost continuously at War.[3] In South Africa had come in rapid succession the Kaffir War of 1877, the Zulu War of 1878-9, the Basuto War of 1879-80 and the Boer War of 1880-1.

In North Africa, the period had commenced with Sir Garnet Wolseley's decisive Egyptian campaign of 1882. To that had succeeded a period of almost continuous warfare against Mahdism. There had been disasters as well as victories, but the end had recently come with the crushing defeat of the Khalifa's Army at Omdurman.[4] In West Africa had been the expedition to Ashanti of 1873-4.

[1] Quoted in Military Notes, 'R.U.S.I. Journal', vol. xlii, p. 336.
[2] Report of the War Office (Reconstitution) Committee (Command Paper 1932 of 1904), p. 8, para. 7.
[3] 'Our Army is almost always at War.'—Wolseley at R.U.S.I., November 17, 1897.
[4] The official Battle Honours covering these Egyptian and Sudan campaigns are: Tel-el-Kebir, Egypt 1882, Abu Klea, Kirbekan, Tofrek, Egypt 1884, Nile 1884-5, Suakim 1885, Atbara, Khartoum.

Further East had been the hard-fought Second Afghan War of 1878–80 made memorable by General Roberts' occupation of Kabul and march to Kandahar. Also on the frontiers of India had been the campaigns of the Tirah and Chitral in 1897–8 and the Burmese War of 1885–7.

The only occasion on which reservists had been used overseas had been the Egyptian campaign of 1882, but the working of the new system had also been tested in 1885 at the time of the Pendjeh incident. The Army Reserve of one cavalry regiment and fifteen regiments of infantry had been called out. A total of 4,681 reservists rejoined the colours and served from April till August.[1]

Thus the British Army had, in the course of some thirty years, gained great experience of warfare of various kinds, and most of the high commands were filled with men who had seen active service, and had given proof of fighting ability and personal courage of a high order.

Internationally there was reason enough for considering the strength of the Army. Though it had been the success of Prussian militarism in the wars of 1864, 1866 and 1870 that had shocked Great Britain into Army Reform, so long as Bismarck retained power Germany was careful and friendly in her policy to this country. It was the France of Napoleon III which in 1859 had caused the formation in England of hundreds of Volunteer Rifle Corps, and the France of the Third Republic was very jealous of English activities in Egypt. Russia, also, was beginning to threaten. When Disraeli called out the Reserve as a challenge to the Treaty of San Stefano, and brought troops from India to the Mediterranean, he was indulging in a policy which led directly to the Second Afghan War.

However these distant scares of wars with great powers

---

[1] 'Chronology', p. 43. Mobilization arrangements were not well developed at this stage. Neither clothing nor accoutrements were available for the Reservists when first they reached barracks, and there was a good deal of drunkenness till the men settled down.—Ellison, chap. vii.

had paled before the very real tension of the Fashoda question. In the summer of 1899, that crisis was recent history. The French press was still strongly Anglophobe, while, in this country it was France that was the enemy in all war stories of the popular press.

One result of this long period of small wars and continental scares had been a very definite improvement in the attitude of the public towards the Army. There were several reasons for this. The Diamond Jubilee of 1897 had been the occasion of a great and very genuine outburst of affection and respect for a venerated sovereign. Her Majesty's regard for the Army, particularly for her beloved Highland Regiments, was well known, and set a fashion. The Romanticism of the late Victorian age was well suited to admire deeds of heroism. Lady Butler's pictures and Caton Woodville's drawings were popular.

Though the disasters of Maiwand and Isandlwana shook the popularity of Lord Beaconsfield's ministry in 1880, the populace reacted to the stories of heroism in those fights. The Berkshire Lion at Reading typified local feeling, while the self-sacrifice of Lieutenants Coghill and White at Isandlwana endeared the British Army to many in these islands who had previously thought little of such things. When the Queen placed a wreath of immortelles on the Queen's colour of the 1/24th Foot it was a gesture attuned to the spirit of the day.

At Dargai, on the North-West Frontier, a young Highland piper, wounded in both ankles, had sat down on a rock and played forward his comrades.

Sir Evelyn Wood tells that he had to exercise his personal influence with the management of the Alhambra to cut short the appearance on the stage of this Piper Findlater, V.C.[1] Though decorum would reasonably have disliked such advertisement, a student of national psychology would, perhaps, have had different views. At all events, one of the main

[1] 'From Midshipman to Field-Marshal', vol. ii, p. 240. May 28, 1898.

tableaux of the year at Madame Tussaud's Exhibition had represented Piper Findlater playing forward a spirited group of Gordon Highlanders. In similar vein 'Major Wilson's Last Stand' had been the central episode in a Wild West Show at Olympia. The Military Tournament, first founded by the Volunteers, had been taken over by London District, and provided a medium for public interest in the Army.

This improvement in public interest in the army did not necessarily indicate much greater comprehension of military matters,[1] nor did it indicate any great improvement in recruiting. It was however becoming the fashion to regard 'Tommy Atkins' as a kind of domestic pet.

The army continued to draw its officers from a rather narrow circle, and its rank and file from a low stratum of society; 'from the froth and scum of the nation' as had been said. On the other hand the Volunteer Movement, in spite of many defects and deficiencies, had at least been means whereby the middle classes gained a certain knowledge of military affairs. 'If the Volunteers had never done anything else, we owe them a debt of gratitude for one thing, that they have brought military knowledge to the people much more than it was before they existed.'[2]

Such popular appreciation was improved by the latest battle news. The Sudan Campaign of 1898 had been excellently organized. The two battles had been definite victories, Omdurman[3] itself being one of the most crushing defeats ever inflicted on a numerically much superior foe. British casualties had been very low. 'Even the ranks of Tusculum could scarce forbear to cheer.' In the debate in the House of Commons on a grant to Lord Kitchener the Radical opposition could

---

[1] 'In counties where the sporting rights are leased to non-residents manœuvres are, in the present state of Public feeling in the United Kingdom, impossible without an Act of Parliament.'—'From Midshipman to Field-Marshal', vol. ii, p. 221.

[2] Captain W. H. James, R.U.S.I. Institution, March 10, 1898.

[3] September 2, 1898.

find nothing to criticize in the conduct of the operations. Comments centred on the desecration of the Mahdi's tomb, or the great slaughter of Dervishes. It was suggested that the very ease and cheapness of the victory might prove a temptation to further facile colonial conquests.

CHAPTER 2

ORGANIZATION FOR WAR

THE STANHOPE MEMORANDUM

THE Military Intelligence Department of the War Office had been established on April 1, 1873.[1] Incidentally it was at 18, Queen Anne's Gate, half a mile away from the War Office at Pall Mall. In 1886, Major-General Henry Brackenbury as head of this Intelligence Division had been instructed by Lord Wolseley, the Adjutant-General, to 'prepare a scheme for the mobilization of two Army Corps and the necessary lines of communication troops for war outside Great Britain and Ireland'.[2] Brackenbury prepared his report and stated, 'there is no want of either infantry or cavalry officers and men, for the formation of two Army Corps, but that for the mobilization of one Army Corps there are not sufficient men available to fill up the cadres of the Medical Staff Corps, the Commissariat and Transport Corps, the Ordnance Store Department and the Veterinary Department, and nearly 8,000 horses would have to be purchased'.[3]

It was as a direct result of this Memorandum from General Brackenbury that a Mobilization Department was formed, at first at Queen Anne's Gate. A year later, in 1889, it was transferred to Pall Mall and became the Mobilization Sub-Division of the Adjutant-General's Division (A.G.7) under Colonel Ardagh, C.B., R.E.[4]

[1] 'Chronology', p. 23. It was first a branch of the Quartermaster-General's Department, but was brought under the A.G. in 1888.—Ellison, xv, p. 8.
[2] Ellison, xi, p. 11.
[3] The R.A.M.C., R.A.S.C., R.A.O.C., and R.A.V.C. all took their present form after 1886.
[4] Hartington Commission (Further Reports) (Command Paper 5979 of 1904), p. 98. Ardagh had been appointed assistant to Brackenbury at the Intelligence Department in 1887.

Already, however, the deliberations of another Committee had produced a report which, for the time being, rendered nugatory General Brackenbury's work upon an overseas force. In 1887 Mr. Stanhope's Committee on Fortifications and Armaments of Military and Mercantile Ports concluded its work.[1]

The Government was experiencing a cold fit. Confidence in the ability of the Navy was weakened by extensive building programmes in France and Russia, and a general overhaul of naval and military machinery was carried out. The naval side of this development took the form of the Naval Defence Act of 1889 and the building of the 'Resolution' class of battleships.[2] The military side took the form of the Imperial Defence Loan of 1888 and the building of an elaborate system of fortifications for the defence of London.

'The whole plan was the apotheosis of the "Blue Funk School" as opposed to the "Blue Water School" which later was to gain the day and give such outrageous follies their quietus.'[3]

Nevertheless, the effect of this period of concentration upon Home Defence was so important upon all portions of the Army that it must be referred to, however briefly. It was in 1886 that General Brackenbury had produced plans for the mobilization of two Army Corps for service 'outside Great Britain and Ireland'. Within two years he was producing another Memorandum upon 'French Invasion'.

As a result of these forebodings, detailed plans were worked out for the defence of London against attacks from the South and South-East. In March 1889, Mr. Stanhope announced in the House of Commons the construction of a series of fortifications to cover London. 'There are certain strategical positions round London commanding roads and railways which are essential to its defence.' The general line of defence

[1] Confidential Paper A 96 of 1887. See 'Chronology', p. 46.
[2] 'In March (1889) the First Lord of the Admiralty announced a Naval Defence Act involving an expenditure distributed over a term of years amounting to £21,500,000.'—Brassey, 1890, p. 98.
[3] Ellison, xii, p. 7.

ran on the North-West from Tilbury through Warley to Epping, while on the South side, sites were selected along the line of the North Downs. To man these defensive positions, volunteer Artillery Corps and volunteer brigades were to be told off to a total of 120,000 men and 233 guns. The forts themselves were to be 'mobilization centres', the connecting works, every trench and gun of which had been planned on large-scale maps, would be constructed when the emergency arose.[1]

Most of these fortifications are now grass-grown and derelict; many are not even marked on the newer Ordnance maps. It may, therefore, be of interest to give the names of these defensive positions which, at the latter end of the nineteenth century, bulked so large in the mind of the military leaders of the country. The full list was given in the House of Commons in 1906 by Mr. Haldane in reply to a question by Mr. Brodie. The forts were constructed at Henley Grove, Denbies, Merstham, Farningham, Pewley Hill, Box Hill, Westerham, Betchworth, Reigate Down, Foster Down, Oxted (Woldingham), Halstead, North Weald, Caterham, Warley and Tilbury. The cost of these works was divided as follows:

Vote 10	£60,499
Imperial Defence Loan, (last three only)	15,048
Military Works Loan	85,124
	£160,671[2]

While the volunteers manned the forts, as troops of position, the role of the Regular Army was by manœuvring in the field to bring the invading army to battle.[3] For that purpose,

[1] 'National Review', March 1897—'The Defence of London', Spencer Wilkinson.
[2] A.D., 1906, p. 1358.
[3] Sir Edward Hamley wrote a book, 'National Defence', on this subject in 1889. He suggested basing the Regular Army on Portsmouth so as to strike the invader on the flank.—'Journal R.U.S.I.', 1901, p. 922.

however, it had first to be concentrated on London. Cavalry and Infantry units had, at their peace-time stations, only their S.A.A. carts. All their 'second Regimental equipment', as their heavier transport vehicles were called, were stored at Croydon, Caterham, or Chatham, or other places connected with the London Defence scheme.[1] It was at these centres that horses would be delivered to units. What was true for the Cavalry and Infantry was true in varying degree for the Artillery and for the Services.

The policy which underlay this conception of the use of the Army found expression in the famous document known as the Stanhope Memorandum. This Memorandum, which took its final shape on June 1, 1891, remained confidential till it was published as Command Paper 607 of 1901. It is printed in full as an appendix to this work.[2] For the present, attention will be concentrated upon Paragraph d: '... To be able to mobilize rapidly for Home Defence two Army Corps of Regular troops, and one partly composed of Regulars and partly of Militia, and to organize the Auxiliary Forces not allotted to Army Corps for garrisons for the defence of London and for the defensible positions in advance, and for the defence of mercantile ports.'

This Memorandum, it is to be noted, was issued within eight years of the outbreak of the South African War, and it is fair comment to point out that, had the mental outlook displayed therein persisted unchecked, the mobilization of the Army Corps for service in South Africa would have been a very lengthy affair.[3]

That any improvement was effected was due to the initiative

[1] Ellison, xii, p. 6.   [2] Appendix A.
[3] The Royal Commission on the South African War in its Report (E.C., pp. 32-3) placed on record the opinion that 'The principles laid down in Mr. Stanhope's Memorandum had, since 1882, governed the whole of the preparations in this country for a possible war. Upon them was built up the whole scheme of mobilization in all its branches'. It is suggested that this view, though true in general, does require certain modification in the light of the work done by Lord Wolseley.

of Lord Wolseley. He succeeded the Duke of Cambridge as Commander-in-Chief in 1895, and at once his mind returned to the scheme of 1886, the possession of an overseas force.

It was perfectly clear that mobilization arrangements which might have been suitable for the defence of London would not be suitable for troops proceeding abroad direct from Aldershot via Southampton. Already the possibility of the dispatch of small overseas expeditions had caused uncertainties in the minds of both Ordnance and Medical authorities. In 1895 the Mobilization Department had become a part of the Directorate of Military Intelligence with, at its head, an 'Assistant A.G. (officer in charge of Mobilization Services)'. The Staff Captain to the A.A.G. was a Captain G. F. Ellison. Together with Colonel John Steevens of the Army Ordnance Department, a plan was worked out which would allow for the mobilization of units at the same place whether they were being mobilized for home service or for service overseas. This place was normally to be the peace-time station of the unit. For formations which did not normally exist in peace, the supply columns and the like, the London mobilization centres such as Croydon or Caterham, would continue to be used. The scheme was submitted to Lord Wolseley. He at once saw its advantages and ordered full preparations to be made along such lines. Lord Wolseley's approval was gained in 1895; it was in November of that year that the work of completely reorganizing this part of the mobilization arrangements was taken in hand. Within two months the Jameson Raid had confronted the country with the possibility of mobilization, and the two reformers might have been caught in the process of swapping horses. However, that danger passed away, and the new arrangements for mobilization were completed before the next period of tension arose in South African affairs. General Ellison, whose recollections of these distant days are of such supreme importance, has placed on record this opinion, 'But nothing is more certain than that it was Lord Wolseley, and Lord Wolseley alone, who conceived the idea of an

Expeditionary Force, and, when he became C-in-C he gave effect to the idea after lesser men had done all in their power to obscure the vital point at issue.'[1]

This is a very noble testimony to a great work. At the same time, it would be quite incorrect to assume that the Field Force of 1899 was in fact comparable with the Expeditionary Force of 1914, either in size, completeness[2] or training.

To quote once again from the War Office Reconstitution Committee of 1904, what had happened was that 'the War Office had been subjected to successive tinkering processes, by which improvements in minor matters might occasionally have been accomplished but which left great principles entirely out of sight'.[3]

Wolseley did his best, but there were serious gaps in the structure.

It will be remembered that the Stanhope Memorandum had spoken of Army Corps. This was the basic formation in 1899.[4] It was proposed that the Home Regular Army would provide two Army Corps if the need was for a force overseas, or three Army Corps for Home Defence, but in this latter case the third Army Corps would contain a substantial Militia element.

In so far as they were composed of professional soldiers the first two Corps should of course have contained good fighting material. That aspect of the case was quite fairly put by Mr. St. John Brodrick, when speaking on the Army Estimates in the House of Commons in February 1898. Dealing first with the Home Defence aspect he said: 'Our organization for Home Defence is familiar to the House. We

---

[1] Ellison, xii, p. 7.
[2] The question of Reserves of equipment will be dealt with in Chapter 5, The Mowatt Commission. It will suffice to say at this stage that though the necessary equipment existed to put three Army Corps in the field, there were no reserves to replace wastage. Industrial organization was of course unknown.
[3] War Office (Reconstitution) Committee, p. 8, para. 6.
[4] The Composition of the Army Corps of 1899 is given in Appendix B.

ORGANIZATION FOR WAR

put in the field three Army Corps, over 112,000 men; we have 120,000 men in garrison; and we have reserve and Auxiliary forces at stated points to the number (after making every reasonable deduction) of over 200,000 men.'[1]

Later in the same speech he turned to the question of sending troops overseas, and, comparing the British troops with those of continental nations, he said: 'The point on which we must concentrate our attention is that, if you do mobilize two Army Corps for foreign service, you will mobilize them, I presume, with a view to encountering European troops, and you will not find any army in Europe which will have in its ranks for the same number of men, the same number of troops actually serving with the colours, and so small a proportion of reservists. This force of 75,000 infantry contains less reservists and a larger proportion of men with the colours than any similar force of any foreign army when mobilized for war.'

It was later in the same debate that Sir Charles Dilke made a comment very much in the sense of General Brackenbury's earlier report: 'Out of the men we have, if cavalry and artillery were provided, 20 corps instead of two corps might be made.'

In truth two Army Corps, just over 70,000 men, was not a very large contribution considering the total number of men carried on the Army Estimates. Nor were even the two Army Corps of Mr. Brodrick's speech very much more than paper concepts. Even the first Corps, based upon Aldershot, did not exist complete as such in peace time. There were, it is true, certain battalions and batteries told off to belong to the Army Corps, but they did not necessarily train together, nor were they, in peace time, under the commander and staff who would lead them in war. When, as a result of the South African War, the Field Force went into battle, the only Brigade which went into action in its peace-time composition was the 2nd Brigade from Aldershot commanded by General Hildyard. Incidentally 'Army Corps' was itself a continental phrase,

[1] A.D., February 25, 1898.

borrowed from the histories of the Franco-German War, and was new to British phraseology.

Taking the Stanhope Memorandum as modified by Lord Wolseley's work on the Field Force, it might be said that the general conception of the employment of the British Army at this date was along the following lines:

(1) The Regular Army—with or without the Reserves—would fight small wars against, generally speaking, savage foemen, armed with inferior weapons.
(2) The Regular Army, with the Reserves, might fight a continental war with or without Allies. It might, also, have to face a major operation in the event of a Russian invasion of India. In the case of this alternative, some Militia battalions would probably be employed to set free Regular battalions from Mediterranean garrisons.
(3) The whole Army, the Regular Army with the Auxiliary Forces, might be called upon to resist an invasion of England.

To meet these various needs there were, provided for in the Army Estimates, a total of over half a million men. Many of these, however, were subject to conditions which limited their employment. The military system of the country had grown up in a haphazard way, and the Army could be divided into at least eight different categories.

The ladder of preparedness was therefore complicated. It included:

	Strength in Round Figures
(*A*) The Regular Army Overseas	124,000
(*B*) The Regular Army at Home	131,000
(*C*) The Army Reserve Section 'A'	5,000
(*D*) The Remainder of the Army Reserve	73,000
(*E*) The Militia Reserve	30,000
(*F*) The Militia Effectives	65,000
(*G*) The Yeomanry Effectives	10,000
(*H*) The Volunteer Effectives	230,000

Two of these stages require comment here. Section 'A' of the Army Reserve was introduced for the first time in the Estimates for 1898.

It was intended to produce a reserve of a maximum of 5,000 men who would be prepared to rejoin the colours without waiting for the proclamation calling out the reserve. Men had to be in their first year of reserve service, and were paid 1s. per day reserve pay instead of 6d. a day.

The Militia Reserve was nominally 30,000 strong. It consisted of men of the Militia who, in return for an extra bounty of £1 per annum, engaged to serve outside the country if called upon to do so. It will be considered further in relation to the Militia as a whole.

The weakness of the arrangement was, clearly, that, unless Militia Battalions volunteered for service overseas, none of the echelons C–H provided any complete units for duty outside the United Kingdom. They provided in greater or less degree reservoirs of drafts for existing regular units, but no method of expansion.

THE HARTINGTON COMMISSION AND THE COMMAND OF THE ARMY

In the year 1888 a Royal Commission had been appointed 'to enquire into the Civil and Professional Administration of the Naval and Military Departments'. From the name of its Chairman, the Marquis of Hartington, it is generally known as the Hartington Commission. Other important members were Lord Randolph Spencer Churchill, Mr. Campbell-Bannerman, and Lieutenant-General Brackenbury. The Secretary to the Commission was an engineer officer, George Sydenham Clarke, who, as Sir George Clarke, and later as Lord Sydenham, was to play an important part in Army Reorganization.

The Commissioners published their Report on July 10, 1889.[1]

---
[1] Command Paper 5979 of 1890.

They had decided to divide the subject matter of their report under four heads.

A. The measures required to secure full and sufficient administrative harmony between the two departments.
B. The internal administration of the Admiralty.
C. The internal administration of the War Office.
D. The relation of the Treasury to both Departments of State and matters of financial control generally.[1]

It will not, in this connection, be necessary to consider more than sub-heading C. In paragraph 42 of their report the Commissioners noted that 'the general tendency of the changes has been to increase the authority of the Parliamentary Chief, but the process has been slow, and the responsibility of the Secretary of State appears to be still, in some respects, less real than that of the First Lord'.

In fact, in these late Victorian days there existed in the War Office a distinct survival of the Stuart struggle between Crown and Parliament for the control of the Army. The Secretary of State represented the Parliament and the control of the Cabinet, the Commander-in-Chief represented the authority of the Crown as the head of the Army. In his journal, at the time of Brodrick's accession to office, Lord Esher wrote: 'The Navy is a constitutional force. Every Commission is signed by the Board. The Army is a royal force and, while the Queen never interferes with the Navy, she interferes very much with the Army.'[2] The members of the Hartington Commission made the same distinction when they pointed out that, unlike any admiral, the Commander-in-Chief had the right of direct approach to the Crown on certain matters affecting the Army.[3]

There had been recent alterations in the organization of the War Office carried out by the Order in Council of December 27, 1887, and its amendment the Order in Council

---

[1] Command Paper 5979 of 1890, p. v.
[2] 'Esher Journals', vol. i, p. 269. November 15, 1900.
[3] Report, p. xxiv, para. 83.

of February 21, 1888,[1] but the effect had been to create an ever greater concentration of power and responsibility in the hands of the Commander-in-Chief. For the Commander-in-Chief was now the sole Adviser of the Secretary of State in military matters, he was the administrative head of the Ordnance Supply, and Works Departments, he was the Commander of the whole British Army at home and abroad, as concerned the issue of orders to secure uniformity of discipline, training and instruction, and to crown all he was the executive commander—in the field if need arose—of the Army in England.[2] Moreover, under the Commander-in-Chief, the Adjutant-General was charged, as chief Staff Officer, with 'exercising general control over the duties of the military departments' and was also made responsible for 'the efficiency of the military forces of the Crown, for their distribution and mobilization, for the technical education of officers and men, and for the efficiency of army schools'.

It is small wonder that the Commissioners felt bound to place on record their view that this system 'appears to us to involve excessive centralization of responsibility in the person of the Commander-in-Chief on whom the whole executive command, administration and supply of the Army now devolve. He is, in fact, the only officer who has any direct responsibility to the Secretary of State'.[3]

At the time of the Commission the Commander-in-Chief was H.R.H. the Duke of Cambridge, and his Adjutant-General was General Viscount Wolseley. It was with full appreciation of the special position of the Royal Commander-in-Chief that the Commissioners made the reservation that

[1] Command Paper 5304 of 1888. The office of Surveyor-General of the Ordnance was abolished.
[2] Report, p. xxv, paras. 88 and 89.
The Adjutant-General was also the executive Second in Command to the Commander-in-Chief and replaced his Chief if the latter became a casualty. 'The A.G. is the principal officer of the Commander-in-Chief and in his absence would command the Army.'—Evidence of Lord Wolseley, Appendix to Report, p. 62. [3] Ibid., para. 60.

the changes they suggested should be made on the appointment of his successor.

They recommended that at the War Office a system should be introduced similar to that of the Board of Admiralty. The office of Commander-in-Chief should be abolished. Outside the War Office the executive duties of command and inspection of the troops in this country should be exercised by a 'General Officer Commanding the Forces in Great Britain'.[1]

In the War Office there should be a Chief of Staff. This officer should be the senior of the five principal military officers and with the Adjutant-General, the Quartermaster-General, the Director of Artillery, and the Inspector-General of Fortifications, should be responsible direct to the Secretary of State for the 'efficient administration of the departments severally entrusted to them, and each (subject to audit) should have full control of his own votes'.[2]

The Report of the Hartington Commission, had it been adopted, would have gone a very long way to reduce to some order the chaotic and top-heavy administration of the War Office. Unfortunately, the very presence of H.R.H. the Duke of Cambridge was a delay to progress of this order. As will be seen later, when, in 1895, he was succeeded by Wolseley, the full opportunity given by the report was not taken. Wolseley received the title and function of Commander-in-Chief, and although there was some reference to the Hartington Report, there was a dangerous lack of clarity. As was well-nigh inevitable the relations between the Secretary of State and the Commander-in-Chief suffered from the anomalous position in which both were placed.

It was not until 1904 that the War Office Reconstitution Committee, with Clarke again at work, picked up the threads of the Hartington Report, and carried the Army Council scheme through. The lack of precision, and unnecessary complication which characterized the organization of the higher command, also extended to certain of the staff arrangements.

[1] Report, para. 92.   [2] Ibid., 96.

The General Staff in the modern sense of an operations staff did not exist.[1] The Staff College had been instituted in 1858 upon the foundations of the old Senior Department of the Royal Military College.[2] In 1871 under a General Order No. 25 of that year, all officers on the staff were consolidated under the designation 'Officers of the Adjutant-General's and Quarter-Master-General's Departments'. This arrangement endured until 1888 when a further alteration was made. The whole staff was now to be styled as of the Adjutant-General's Branch, but it assumed the duties not only of the old Adjutant-General's office, but also of all those departments of the commissariat and transport which had formerly been under the specialized control of the Surveyor-General of the Ordnance and now came under the control of the Quartermaster-General.[3]

Under Queen's Regulations Section V the duties of the staff were classified under three heads, briefly described thus: 'A', Discipline and Training; 'B', Equipment, supply, movement, quartering, etc.; 'C', Engineer Services.[4]

It may be fair comment to say that the result of these changes had been rather in the direction of formalism and centralization. The fact that, for the first time, staff officers were expected to know about supply and commissariat arrangements was all to the good. But, in practice, there was a serious danger of over-estimating the relative importance of these matters, and officers were judged rather by their capacity for rendering barrack returns than by their leadership of troops. Similarly, the very fact that it was the Adjutant-General's Section 'A' which was responsible for Discipline, Drill, and Training, led to a certain formalism in battle tactics.

There existed at the War Office as has been seen, an Intelligence department, but, apart from this, there did not exist

[1] It is to be noted that in the '80's the phrase 'General Staff' was used in the sense of 'Staff officers'.—'Chronology', p. 20.
[2] 'Army Book of the British Empire', p. 44.
[3] Cf. Hartington Commission, p. xx, para. 61.
[4] 'Army Book of the British Empire', p. 340.

in the British Army in 1899 any organization similar to that of the Generalstab at Berlin, which trained officers to study the problems of strategy and tactics. The lack of this was appreciated by some observers. As matters stood, staff officers were administrators pure and simple.

It is, further, to be noted that none of the General Officers in high command in 1899 were trained staff officers. Nor had they had experience in the field of complicated staff organization.

The difficulties were in fact very much the result of the recent history of the Army. While a total force of over half a million men had to be administered or controlled, the total forces that had ever been assembled in one campaign were not more than a few thousand.[1]

The armies commanded by General Roberts at Peiwar Kotal, or Lord Chelmsford at Ulundi had been small enough to be completely under the control of the General, and staff officers were in the nature of personal assistants. Operation orders were the affair of the General Officer Commanding and they were issued to lower formations or to units through the Adjutant-General's branch.[2] At home the situation was much the same. The lack of training ground outside Europe stood in the way of large-scale grouping of units and there had been a 'complete lack of manœuvres on a large scale between 1875 and 1898'.[3]

It was, perhaps, one feature of the absence of an operations branch that the provision of signal communications was on a very modest scale.

[1] The largest British force in the period was that employed in Egypt in 1882. Sir Garnet Wolseley had seven regiments of cavalry, sixteen batteries of artillery, and twenty-five battalions of infantry. About two-thirds of this force were present at Tel-el-Kebir.

At Omdurman the Sirdar had had two British Brigades and four Egyptian and Sudanese Brigades.

[2] It is perhaps a matter of interest to note that, under the same influence of small frontier wars, a similar lack of operations staff, and the issue of orders through the 'Divisional Adjutant' existed in the Army of the United States till 1917.   [3] Ellison, xv, p. 7.

CHAPTER 3

THE REGULAR ARMY

In June 1899 the Regular Army consisted, in the more important arms, of the following units:

Cavalry

Household Cavalry	3 Regiments[1]
Cavalry of the Line	28 Regiments[2]
Total Cavalry	31 Regiments

Artillery

Royal Horse Artillery	21 Batteries[3]
Royal Field Artillery	94 Batteries[4]
Mountain Artillery	10 Batteries
Royal Garrison Artillery	99 Companies[5]

Infantry

Foot Guards	9 Battalions[6]
Infantry of the Line	148 Battalions[7]
Total Infantry	157 Battalions[8]

[1] 1st and 2nd Life Guards and Royal Horse Guards.

[2] Seven Regiments of Dragoon Guards, twenty-one Regiments of Dragoons, Lancers and Hussars.

[3] A to U plus one depot battery.

[4] Plus two depot batteries.

[5] Plus six depot companies.

[6] Grenadier, Coldstream, and Scots Guards, each with three battalions.

[7] All the line regiments now existing plus the six Irish Regiments disbanded in 1922. Royal Warwick Regiment, Royal Fusiliers, Lancashire Fusiliers, 60th Rifles, and Rifle Brigade each had four battalions.

[8] All the above figures are from the Army List of June 1899.

It was, in a very striking way, an army of the three older arms.

Comparison with the figures of 1936 shows notable changes in the relative strength of corps. The establishment figures in this case are for 1898. By June 1899 there would have been an even greater preponderance of infantry.

	1898[1]	1936[2]
Cavalry	19,267	11,055
Royal Artillery	40,152	34,215
Royal Engineers	8,100	8,713
Royal Corps of Signals	—	7,319
Infantry	150,376	118,322
Military Police	—	500
Royal Tank Corps	—	4,795
Royal Army Chaplains Department	—	135
R.A.S.C.	3,577	6,307
R.A.O.C.	1,424	4,110
R.A.M.C.	3,499	4,501
Army Pay Corps	600	916
R.A.V.C.	—	214
Army Educational Corps	—	438
Army Dental Corps	—	357
Colonial and Indian Corps	6,565	2,647
	233,560	204,554

While the striking increase of relative strength in what are generally known as 'services' may be ascribed to the greater complexity of the modern army, there can be no doubt that, at the end of last century, fighting units suffered a good deal through having to detach men on administration duties.

Sir Evelyn Wood tells how, shortly after the arrival of the

[1] General Annual Returns of the British Army for the year 1898, p. 4. 'Distribution of the Army according to the latest returns received on January 1st, 1899 etc.'

[2] Army Estimates, 1936, Vote A, p. 30, 'Regimental Establishments' (excluding Permanent Staff of T.A., etc.).

90th Light Infantry in South Africa, he had to detach five non-commissioned officers and selected men to form a hospital, and five to form a commissariat department.[1]

Geographically, the distribution of the Army formed a contrast to the days earlier in the century when Mr. Cardwell had withdrawn scattered battalions from the ends of the earth. Nevertheless, there yet remained in 1899 single battalions in Canada, Barbados, Ceylon, and Mauritius. The Rifle Brigade had one battalion on international police duties in Crete, while in South Africa there was a garrison of two cavalry regiments, one mountain battery and three field batteries, and seven battalions of infantry. The detailed distribution is given in an Appendix.[2]

At home the progress of concentration had not been rapid. It is true that at Aldershot there were fourteen battalions. On the other hand, there were still a large number of single-battalion stations, Brighton, Preston, Sheffield, Glasgow, and others, a survival from an earlier conception of the use of the army.[3] Warley was a line battalion's station. Ireland held 20 battalions, Dublin with five battalions being one of the largest stations in the British Isles.[4]

Salisbury Plain, in later years to be one of the most important military centres in England, had only just passed into Government possession. In 1896 the Secretary of State had acquired a block of land on the Plain 15 miles by $5\frac{1}{2}$ miles.[5]

There were two battalions of Guards at Gibraltar, not at all a popular move with the Brigade of Guards, so the total of 73 battalions at home to 75 in India, the Colonies and Egypt, was not too bad. The Cardwell system had broken

[1] From 'Midshipman to Field-Marshal', vol. ii, p. 2.
[2] Appendix C.
[3] 'Barracks in those days were erected in places for the reason that there had been riots and it was desirable to have the Military in the neighbourhood.'—Mr. Arnold Forster in the House of Commons, June 7, 1906. A.D., 1906, p. 812.
[4] Army List, June 1899.
[5] 'From Mishipman to Field-Marshal', vol. ii, p. 234.

down in actual distribution, though not too seriously. What was alarming was the strain thrown on the Home battalions.

It was, of course, the basic plan of the Cardwell system that the foreign battalion should be kept up to full strength and that the battalion at home should depend on the recall of reservists on mobilization to bring it up to war establishment. But, to ensure its economic working, the scheme demanded a steady inflow of fairly mature recruits. The difficulties of the end of the nineteenth century had been that recruiting had been bad, and that a large number of the recruits had been very young and very weedy. The standard of enlistment was low enough in all conscience, but for so-called 'special enlistments' it could be reduced still further.[1]

Something over a year before the period under review, in February 1898, there had been a very important debate on the Army Estimates. These estimates with their proposals for a substantial increase in the strength of the Army will be dealt with later. A good deal of pressure had been placed on the Government from a group of Service members in the House, a group 70 strong, according to Mr. Campbell-Bannerman. It was known that the Government proposals were going to do a good deal to meet criticisms, and the debate contained much of interest.

Two incidents had served to bring out the difficulties. A 'brigade division' of Field Artillery had been sent to South Africa to increase the local garrison. To make up these batteries to full strength, men had to be drafted from other units. 'The three batteries which had to go to the Cape last year certainly reduced a number of other batteries to mere skeletons.'[2] Then, there was the case of the Royal Berkshire Regiment. Sir Charles Dilke, in the same debate, referred to 'the condition in which the Royal Berkshire Regiment sailed in

---

[1] Standard for 1898 was 5 ft. 4 in. for infantry. 'Young men below these standards are "specially enlisted" if expected to develop.'—'Army Book for the British Empire', p. 132.

[2] Colonel C. W. Long, Debate on Army Estimates, February 25, 1898.

the "Avoca" last week. The Under-Secretary told us that there were in that regiment between 400 and 500 men with less than one year's service.'[1] And General J. W. Laurie, possibly somewhat of a die-hard, could say in the same debate 'At the present moment there is not a battalion fit for the service'.[2] The long and comprehensive speech of Mr. Brodrick, Under-Secretary of State for War, in introducing the Estimates in the House of Commons became, therefore, of great interest. In describing some of the difficulties with which the Government was faced, he said, 'Since February last year we have been subjected to an incessant strain. We have 20 battalions on the North-West Frontier calling upon us for increased drafts; we have sent two additional battalions and three batteries to South Africa; we have had to furnish three more for active service up the Nile, and may have to send more; and we have sent one to Crete. To do this, we have not called out a single man from the Reserve.'[3]

But in spite of this quite fair boast, the strain on the home battalions was dangerous. Earlier in his speech Mr. Brodrick had put the case thus:

'It is often said that the organization of our Army is unique. It must be so, because the duties it has to perform are unique. Other nations organize themselves for home defence and for foreign invasion. Our Army, with a prodigious frontier to defend, has to provide a force for possible large wars, and at any time to carry on a minor war in every variety of climate, from the torrid zone to the snows of the Himalayas. Beyond this, whether in peace or war, the conditions of the service are exceptional. No other nation maintains half its army abroad in times of peace, mainly in tropical climates; no other nation attempts to defend its own frontier without compulsory service, still less to protect Colonies and Dependencies covering more than 11,000,000 square miles; no

---

[1] Sir Charles Dilke, Debate on Army Estimates, February 25, 1898.
[2] Debate on Army Estimates, February 25, 1898.
[3] Mr. St. J. Brodrick, Under-Secretary of State, Speech on Army Estimates, February 25, 1898.

other nation draws on its population for half the number of seamen and marines now enrolled by this country, and we, who are essentially a maritime nation, are thus forced to compete in the labour market with an admirable and highly popular service, and have hitherto done so at a rate of pay exactly similar to that which the British man at arms received at the battle of Agincourt.'[1]

In his concluding sentences Mr. Brodrick rightly pointed to one of the difficulties. Having regard to the condition of the country as a whole, Army pay was not attractive. The alteration whereby the soldier's pay would no longer be subject to a 3d. per diem stoppage for rations, was, in fact, to be compensated by the cancellation of deferred pay.[2] On balance, however, the ordinary soldier would be about 1½d. per day better off.

To cope with the drain imposed on the Army by small wars, not in themselves large enough to warrant a proclamation calling out the Reserves, it was proposed to create a special section of the Army Reserve. 'In regard to minor emergencies, we shall meet the difficulty by offering to a number not exceeding 5,000 infantrymen in the first years of service in the Reserve, a special payment of 1/- a day instead of 6d. which they now receive, to take part in these if called up.'[3]

Mr. Labouchere, as so frequently in his career, found his opponent's weak point when he said, a few days later, referring to the increase asked for the previous Estimates[4] 'Why could you not rest satisfied with that 3,000 until you had got them, and then come to this House and ask for more?'

In fact, such increase in strength as had taken place was

---

[1] Mr. St. J. Brodrick, Speech on Army Estimates, February 25, 1898.

[2] Deferred Pay was introduced on April 1, 1876. It was first fixed at 2d. a day and was later calculated at 3d. per year. 'The title to this deferred pay accrues to soldiers as long as they serve with the colours or in the reserve up to 12 years.'—'Army Book of the British Empire', p. 149.

[3] Mr. St. J. Brodrick, Speech on Army Estimates, February 25, 1928. These men formed Section 'A' of the Army Reserve.

[4] Mr. Labouchere, Debate on Supply, February 28, 1928.

in part fictitious. It had been gained by offering men special terms to prolong their engagements, and had thus strengthened the Colours at the expense of the Reserve.

The Army was thus suffering from a tradition of bad pay, and, it must be added, rough conditions. The question of nationalities is of interest. On January 1, 1898, there were in the British Army

>   158,566 English
>   16,485 Scottish
>   26,374 Irish
>   8,275 Born in British India or the Colonies
>   142 Foreigners
>   2,551 Not returned[1]
>
>   212,393

The agricultural labourer of Ireland was thus still, in 1899, providing a large proportion of the recruits for the British Army. This high percentage was reflected in the table of religious faiths, for 177 out of every thousand men were Roman Catholics. Though the standard of Army life had risen very considerably since the beginning of the century it is interesting to note that in 1898, in the Infantry of the Line, one man in every twelve had been crimed for drunkenness at some period or other of his army career.[2] Desertion was still too common, so were crimes of insubordination.[3] Loss of efficiency due to preventable disease was still far too great. Lord Wolseley, the Commander-in-Chief, had issued in 1898 a very notable admonition to the troops under his command wherein he stressed the necessity for physical fitness and the avoidance of excess.[4]

[1] General Annual Return of the British Army for 1897, p. 91.
[2] Ibid., p. 55.
[3] General Annual Return for 1898. Desertion, p. 23. Insubordination, p. 50.
[4] 'R.U.S.I. Journal', vol. xlii, p. 1103.

The truth of the matter was, however, that Army conditions were tending to lag behind the very marked improvements in the standard of living of the civil population, and it was, therefore, drawing its raw material from those levels of society that were not too particular in their manners of living. Sir Evelyn had some grim comments to make on the night lavatory accommodation in barracks.[1]

The tradition of the bad old days and the low level of pay still weighed heavily on Army recruiting. On the other hand, the generally low standard of raw material available had its effect on the standard of training that perforce had to be adopted.

MILITARY THOUGHT, 1899

In the course of a lecture delivered at the Royal United Service Institution on May 20, 1897, Lieutenant-Colonel T. Tully, 4th Volunteer Battalion East Surrey Regiment, opened with the following words,

'To the present generation of students of military history, it may, at first sight, appear strange that the history of the American Civil War has met with (comparatively speaking) little attention from those who devote their energies to historical military studies . . . the extraordinary occurrences in Europe during the years 1866 and 1870–71 directed the minds of Englishmen from the doings of their cousins over sea to the vast campaigns executed by thoroughly drilled and organized troops and carried on, so to speak, next door.'[2]

So far as concerns knowledge of the American Civil War, the situation was soon to be remedied. In the summer of 1898 there appeared 'Stonewall Jackson and the American Civil War' by Colonel Henderson, a work that was to become a classic, and that was to turn the minds of English Officers to the mobility of Jackson's 'Stonewall Brigade'. In June 1898

[1] From 'Midshipman to Field-Marshal', vol. ii, p. 233.
[2] 'R.U.S.I. Journal', vol. xlii, p. 1.

Colonel Henderson, speaking at the R.U.S.I. on 'Strategy and its Teaching', had foreshadowed some of the conclusions shortly to be proclaimed in his book.[1]

But, taken as a comment upon Army training as a whole, Colonel Tully's criticisms appear to be very apt.

It might here be remarked that the British Army of 1899 had, in positions of authority, officers with almost unrivalled knowledge of guerilla warfare. Indeed, they possessed a Homeric record of active service and personal gallantry. At the head of the Army, Lord Wolseley had served in Burma, in the Crimea, the Indian Mutiny, the Red River Rebellion, Ashanti, and Zululand and he was the hero of the very successful Egyptian Campaign of 1882. The Adjutant-General, General Sir Evelyn Wood, held the Victoria Cross and had seen, in his younger days, almost continuous fighting in South Africa. The Quartermaster-General, Sir G. S. White, also held the Victoria Cross. So did the Field-Marshal Commanding the Forces in Ireland, Lord Roberts of Kandahar. Finally the Lieutenant-General in command at Aldershot was Sir Redvers Buller, V.C., a mighty warrior of small wars, the hero of the Red River Expedition in Canada, the skilled and resolute leader of Evelyn Wood's Mounted Infantry in the Zulu War, the companion in battle of Piet Uys and his Boers.

The guidance of the British Army was in the hands of a very notable band of veteran soldiers with a vast knowledge of colonial and frontier wars.

Yet, from this distance of time, it appears as if they almost distrusted their own experiences. They appeared to study the lessons of Plevna or Gravelotte, rather than the lessons of Majuba and the Tirah.[2] It is true that there were some quite reasonable excuses for this view point. The general conception of possible dangers to England envisaged, in the first rank,

[1] 'R.U.S.I. Journal', vol. xlii, p. 767, 'Strategy and its Teaching', by Lieutenant-Colonel G. F. R. Henderson, Professor of Military Art and History, The Staff College.

[2] 'The Infantry Drill Book and Plevna', Lecture at R.U.S.I., by Captain Herbert, March 3, 1899.

a physical invasion of England or, possibly, a Russian invasion of India.[1] There was the alternative possibility of an entanglement in a European war, and a continental campaign alongside Allies. It must be remembered, once again, that Fashoda was, in the summer of 1899, a very recent memory, and that the danger of war with France during six weeks of tension had been great. Therefore, there were natural tendencies to use as a measuring stick for our organization and our tactics the organization and tactics of our continental neighbours.

On the other hand, some of the recent 'small wars' waged by England had been so exceptional in their conditions that no lessons for normal wars could be drawn therefrom. And, indeed, there was again danger that such lessons might be false doctrine.

Within twelve months of June 1899, the battle of Omdurman had been, perhaps, the most complete defeat ever inflicted upon a savage army. The losses to the victors had been trivial. As an example of the terrific stopping power of the modern high velocity low trajectory rifle, Omdurman taught most valuable lessons. From the point of view of tactics its teaching was negligible. The Khalifa himself had, at the end, been the greatest contributor to the English victory. His daylight rush upon the Sirdar's Zareba by the Nile was the most suicidal event in English war history, since that day when mail-clad French knights lurched on foot across the mire to meet English arrows at Agincourt.

But if there had been on the Kerreri Hills but one battery of that mysterious new French field gun, the 75 mm. cannon, whose accuracy and rapidity of fire had revolutionized gunnery, then the Anglo-Egyptian Zareba would have been a death-trap.

Or if on Gebel Surgham there had been but one battery of Gatling guns led by another Captain Parker of Santiago, the stately advance en echelon of the Sirdar's Army might have been very costly.

[1] 'To India, Plan of Future Campaign', from the Russian of B. T. Levedev, 'R.U.S.I. Journal', 1899.

The battle of the Atbara had been a most successful assault by British troops, but it was the apotheosis of old tactics and not the first dawn of anything new. The advance of the Cameron Highlanders—a line of eight companies—halting to fire volleys, then pressing steadily onwards—was successful against such Dervish foes. But its success may have been misleading.[1]

The truth was that, in general, the advantage of superior weapons had been very heavily on the side of the British forces. Even at Isandlwana, till ammunition ran out, small groups of the 24th Foot took fearful toll of the attacking Zulus, inflicting losses that did much to smash the morale of the best Zulu regiments. On the other hand, at Kambula, as Sir Evelyn Wood tells, the only severe losses caused to the British force came from about forty Zulus armed with rifles captured at Isandlwana.[2]

The introduction of smokeless powder and the arrival of the machine-gun had, obviously, created new problems, and men were studying them. A paper, 'Modern Weapons and their Influence on Tactics and Organization', given by Captain James in May 1899, had foreshadowed very fairly what might be the effects of the accurate modern firearm using smokeless powder in the hands of a good shot. He quotes Napoleon's motto, 'Le feu est tout, le reste n'est rien'.[3]

And there were officers content to learn from Majuba and the Tirah. Major Hugh Pearse of the 2nd East Surrey, writing on 'Sharpshooters', pointed the moral of the Ingongo river in 1881 when Sir George Colley's guns were put out of action by Boer marksmen.[4] The British attack at Dargai was practically a frontal attack against well concealed tribesmen who were good shots, and it was a costly affair.

Quickfiring field artillery was quite in its infancy. 'You will shortly hear that the French have got a real quickfiring gun',

[1] The Camerons advanced to within three hundred yards of the Dervish Zareba, then halted, knelt, and fired section volleys. Behind the Camerons the Lincolns, Seaforths and Warwicks advanced in company column.
[2] 'From Midshipman to Field Marshal', vol. ii, p. 61.
[3] R.U.S.I., May 17, 1899.   [4] 'R.U.S.I. Journal.'

said Sir Henry Brackenbury, Chairman at Captain James' lecture quoted above.[1] And, certainly, this French gun sounded, in 1899, most revolutionary. The long recoil disturbed the carriage so little that the firer and gun layer could do their working sitting down on seats attached to the trail. A most unprecedented performance. But it was thought that rapidity of fire would cause ammunition problems.

Von Lobell's annual report on changes and progress in military matters from 1874 to 1898, vol. xxv, was, as usual, a comprehensive authoritative commentary on the state of the armies of all great powers. As far as may be judged from the précis prepared by Lieutenant-Colonel E. Gunter it might be fairly claimed that English Military thought, training, and battle tactics were at least on a par with those of all the other great continental powers, were one to consider only military thought as represented at R.U.S.I. Debates.

The general standard of training did not, however, in all cases reflect the best military thought of the period. There were several contributory causes. A number of small single battalion stations existed, where combined training was impossible. The staff officers were overweighted with administrative detail. Visits from General officers took the form of 'inspections'. It is clear that the tactical training of troops was often far below war-time needs. 'It was the period of the smart, clean, adjutant-drilled battalion, of the cavalry regiment with horses in show ring condition, of the first gun to fire battery.'[2]

There were few training manuals worth the name. 'The Soldier's Pocket Book' was a semi-official publication written by Lord Wolseley.[3]

The new Drill Book of 1896 had been described as 'A

[1] R.U.S.I., May 17, 1899.   [2] Ellison, xi, p. 10.
[3] 'The Soldier's Pocket Book' was a most comprehensive work. The first edition was produced by Wolseley at Montreal in 1869 and bore the following illuminating preface:

'During many campaigns and particularly at the outset of my career as a soldier I felt the great want of a practical and portable book upon the ordinary duties that fall to the lot of a soldier when in the presence of an

THE REGULAR ARMY

double work in one volume, the first containing the Infantry Drill, and the second the Infantry Field Service, the latter interspersed with a great deal of what is really Grand Tactics of all three arms'.[1]

It is worth remembering, moreover, that, in a small work called 'Life in the Ranks of the English Army', published officially in 1883, the following illuminating phrase occurs, 'The two duties already mentioned viz., drilling and guard work, are by far the most important that the private soldier has to do'[2] and that there is not one mention in the pamphlet of shooting or of field work, or any suggestion that the soldier's work might be in the slightest degree interesting.

In this regard, the Army had not improved very much between 1883 and 1899, though some units, particularly, perhaps, 58th Foot (the First Battalion the Northamptonshire Regiment) and the two rifle regiments, the 60th Rifles and the Rifle Brigade, did try to devote a good deal of attention to Musketry.[3] Volley firing was the rule. In a paper at the R.U.S.I. Major Sir R. Congleton speaks of 'the indiscriminate use of volley firing during the greater part of the attack' and suggests that it would be 'a very dangerous system to adopt against skilled riflemen in South Africa and Europe'.[4]

enemy.... Some few years ago, when Sir R. Airy was Q.M.G. of the army, he proposed to have a practical handbook for the staff compiled by experienced officers of his department and published for the use of the army. A little money was required, which the War Office from economical motives would not allow....'

[1] 'R.U.S.I. Journal', vol. xliii, p. 1203.   [2] P. 15.
[3] The 58th Foot had fought in 1881 against the Boers at Laings Nek and Majuba. 'There is a tradition in the Regiment that, after the conclusion of peace, a solemn oath was taken by a group of officers in the 58th that they would not rest until the Regiment had been taught to shoot properly.' In 1887 40 per cent of the Battalion were marksmen, and by 1896 it was the best shooting battalion in the British Army and took the field in 1899 with a musketry standard averaging 'marksman'.—'History of the Northamptonshire Regiment', p. 267, and 'A Short History of the Northamptonshire Regiment', p. 29.
[4] 'R.U.S.I. Journal', vol. xliii, p. 147.

It is of interest to note that at Omdurman the Guards had opened fire, by volleys, at 2,700 yards.—'The River War', by W. S. Churchill.

RECENT INCREASES IN THE REGULAR ARMY

Such a general description of the Army is needed to appreciate the atmosphere in which the Marquis of Lansdowne, Secretary of State for War, introduced his two Army Estimates of 1898–9 and 1899–1900.

The first of these was the most important. It will be referred to hereinafter in some detail, but it provided, in short, for the largest expansion of the Regular Army that had taken place for many years.

In 1897, the Infantry strength had been slightly increased by the raising of a second battalion for the Cameron Highlanders, but this had been offset by some reductions in the strength of depots.

In the Estimates 1897–8 a more ambitious programme had provided for the raising of third battalions for both the Coldstream and Scots Guards, and for additions to the artillery.

In the Estimates for 1898–9 however the 1897–8 programme was added to, to such an extent that the total programme of Army Expansion contemplated an increase of just over 25,000 men.[1]

In the Memorandum which accompanied the Estimates for 1898–9, the Secretary of State for War explained the reasons which led the Government to plan this increase:

'Recent developments in various parts of the world and a further consideration of our requirements for the defence of the Empire at home and abroad have shown that the increases contemplated in the Estimates of last year will not be sufficient for the purpose of placing the various branches of the Service in a position to carry out satisfactorily the duties required of them, and the Estimates for 1898–9 therefore, provide for further additions to the strength of the Army.'[2]

[1] 'My Lords, the experience of the past few years has taught us that we must have more men and more facilities for maintaining them, having regard to the increased demands of the Empire.'—Earl of Albemarle, speaking on the Address to the King's Speech, House of Lords, 1898.

[2] A.E., 1898–9.

THE REGULAR ARMY

In the Cavalry, no new units were formed, but two Regiments in Natal were brought up to a higher establishment and sundry increases of strength were made elsewhere.

The 1897-8 programme had added one new battery to the Royal Artillery, bringing the total at home to 55 batteries. The above-quoted Memorandum says,

'Since that time three batteries of Field Artillery have been sent to South Africa. There is, moreover, reason for believing that the scale adopted has not been sufficiently liberal; it is based upon the proportion of about 4 guns to 1,000 bayonets. This proportion will now be increased to one of about 5 guns to 1,000 bayonets or 20 batteries (Horse and Field) for each Army Corps.[1] If this proportion be accepted, and four batteries be allotted to the four Cavalry Brigades, a total of 64 batteries will be required, involving an increase of 12 batteries or 72 guns. It is, moreover, proposed to maintain three batteries of Howitzers in addition to the full equipment of field guns, and there is, accordingly, included in the Estimates a total increase of 15 batteries or 90 guns. The new batteries will be on a peace establishment of 4 guns.

'The formation of the 15 new batteries will be spread over three years, and provision is made for 5 batteries during 1898-9.'[2]

As far as the Infantry were concerned, the Cardwell system had already broken down. The balance of battalions at home and abroad had been upset by the demands of small wars.

'This had as a result the effect of reducing the force of Infantry at home to a point at which it has ceased to be sufficient, either for the purpose of supporting the battalions abroad or for providing the force which, in the opinion of the military authorities, it is necessary to maintain for home defence.'[3]

It was, therefore, proposed to raise six new battalions of Infantry. There had been some attempt to use the opportunity

---

[1] The Army Corps had 25 Battalions. Compare the 1936 allotment of 16 Field Batteries to a Division of 12 Battalions (Divisional Artillery plus one Army Field Brigade).

[2] A.E., 1898-9. [3] Ibid.

to untie some of the more ill-assorted marriages of 1881, but, in the event, it was decided to add new battalions in pairs to the Royal Fusiliers, Lancashire Fusiliers and Royal Warwickshire Regiment.

It was fair criticism on the part of the opposition in the House of Commons that it was small use increasing establishments while recruiting was still so bad. The intake for the Regular Army in 1897 was 35,015 as compared with 28,522 in 1896. 'But this increase in the number of recruits has been in great measure balanced by the unusual number of discharges and transfers to the Reserve.'

The Army was seriously under strength even allowing for a lag in formation of new units.

The establishments laid down in the Estimates 1898–9 and 1899–1900, are compared with the actual effectives as follows:

Vote 'A' Regular Army
    Regimental Establishment
        excluding India . . 1898–99 . . . 171·394
                                1899–1900 . . 176·309
    Actual Effectives . . 1st January, 1899 . 157·863[1]

It is, however, to be noted that, as customary, the actual effectives in India, 74,467, were slightly in excess of the establishment, 73,157.

Therefore it had become necessary to improve the condition of the private soldier. An allowance of 3d. per diem for rations, was, in effect, an increase of pay by that amount, for previously, out of his 1/–, he only received 9d.

The Estimates for 1899–1900 were, after the substantial increases of the previous year, less spectacular. There was an increase of 4,340 in the total of Vote 'A', and an increase in the establishment of the Army Reserve.

To some extent the additional man power was due to the raising of certain local corps to be borne on the Home Army

[1] A.E., 1899–1900.

THE REGULAR ARMY

Estimates. The West India Regiment had long had a place in the Army List. A third battalion disbanded in 1870 was re-formed in 1897 and formed part of the increase effected by the Estimates of 1897–8. In addition there were now formed the Chinese Regiment, raised in 1899 for service in Wei-Hai-Wei; the British Central African Regiment, raised in 1899 for service in Mauritius, and the West African Regiment which had been first formed in 1898 for service in Sierra Leone.[1]

Increases in number, increases in pay, provision in the Estimates for Grand Manœuvres in the Autumn of 1898,[2] all betokened an interest in the Army.

Before long, events were to show what proportions of that care and thought had been in the right direction.

[1] 'Chronology', p. 62.
[2] The Grand Manœuvres of 1898 were almost Augustan in their character. The troops taking part wore the scarlet, blue, black or green of their corps, the infantry wore forage caps, but from contemporary photographs some at least of the cavalry wore their full dress headdress. The Guards marched to camp in bearskins, though they wore forage caps in the actual manœuvres. The weather was very hot, and the infantry, who carried valises and greatcoats, suffered severely.

CHAPTER 4

THE AUXILIARY FORCES

THE Auxiliary Forces in 1899 consisted of: The Militia (including the Militia Reserve), The Yeomanry, and The Volunteers. The duties and liabilities of these three organizations differed in important particulars; they had varying terms of training and of enlistment. In short, the whole organization of the Auxiliary Forces of the Crown was in a highly confused condition. The state of affairs bore eloquent testimony to the fact, which was indeed self-evident, that these various forces had evolved in a haphazard way and had never been properly coordinated.

THE MILITIA

The Militia was the old 'Constitutional Force' of England. As such it was beloved by historians and by military theorists. The Earl of Wemyss speaking in the House of Lords on February 18, 1898, had said:

'That,' referring to the Regular Army, 'is a voluntary matter. Then you have a totally different Army raised under totally different circumstances for a totally different purpose—namely for home defence. This is commonly called the Militia. It is an old constitutional force, which was rightly raised by compulsion, and which can be recruited compulsorily by Ballot, on the principle that the State has the right to call on every one of her subjects to stand forward, if need be, in defence of the country. Lastly, we have the Volunteer force, which represents those who, unwilling to take their chance of service in the Militia, serve their country voluntarily in another form.' Later the noble Lord speaking of the ballot said: 'In the name of duty, enforce it. I have said the Militia is the basis of our military system.'

Before considering further the discussion as to the need or otherwise of the ballot, it would be well to review the actual composition of the Militia as it existed in 1899.

In the Army Estimates, the Channel Islands Militia, about 3,500 strong, the Malta Militia, just over 2,000 strong, and the Bermuda Militia, under 400 strong, are shown as part of the Militia generally.[1] These overseas units were, in their relative places, important, but they do not enter into the present discussion of the part played by the Militia in the order of battle of the British Army. Therefore, in future, when the Militia is alluded to in any form it is to be understood that the Channel Islands, Malta, and Bermuda Militias are not included in any figures or tables.

The Militia, therefore, comprised, in the British Isles; 32 Militia Brigades of Artillery, 2 Corps of Fortress Engineers and 10 Divisions of Submarine Miners, 123 Battalions of Militia infantry and a Militia Medical Staff Corps.[2]

There was no Militia Cavalry, that part being played by the Yeomanry. There was no Militia Army Service Corps,[3] no Militia Field Engineers; in fact, except for the Militia Medical Staff Corps, about 600 strong, there were no Militia 'services' whatever.

The Militia Artillery was, almost without exception, coast fortress artillery, and was not fit to take the field with the Infantry. The Militia, in short, was a collection of units, and not, as a force, organized to take the field.

The strength of the Militia is shown in the attached appendix.[4] It will suffice to say at the present that it had an establishment of 125,113 all ranks, that the enrolled strength was 103,647, but that at training in 1898 only 93,606 turned out.[5]

[1] A.E., 1899–1900.   [2] Ibid., Vote 3
[3] 'I have heard an interesting suggestion, from a practical soldier, as to the feasibility of forming a branch of the Army Service Corps in connection with the Militia, which I should very much like to hear discussed.'—Major Marshall West, speaking on the Autumn Manœuvres of 1898 at the R.U.S.I. —'R.U.S.I. Journal', vol. xliii, p. 499.
[4] Appendix D.   [5] A.E., 1899–1900, Vote 3, p. 43.

The Militia battalion was based on the regimental depot. Its local connection was, as a rule, very much older than that of the line regiment associated with it. The old numbered regiments of foot were very often territorialized for the first time as a result of Mr. Cardwell's scheme. In certain cases, old Militia barracks had existed, but in many cases the introduction of the depot system had resulted in the building of new depot barracks in the country.

The two features of Militia training that differed so much from modern Territorial Army practice that they are in danger of being forgotten were the large Regular cadre and the long period of annual training. A Militia battalion had a total of 30 regular staff.[1] In addition to the Adjutant and the Quartermaster, the Sergeant-Major and the Quartermaster-Sergeant, there was 1 Sergeant instructor in Musketry and 1 Sergeant drummer for the battalion, and for each of the 8 companies there was 1 Colour-Sergeant, 1 Sergeant, and 1 drummer. Training was very largely in the hands of the Adjutant and his permanent staff, and annual training—at which all weapon training was done—was described as one constant fight between the Adjutant and the Musketry instructor.[2]

The Militia Infantryman engaged for six years. As a recruit, he had to do six weeks' preliminary drill, at the end of which he was given £1 Bounty—in certain circumstances £1 10s. Some units made their recruits do their drill as they joined, attaching them for the purpose to one of the recruit squads at the Regimental depot. Other units called up all their recruits together for six weeks' preliminary drill as a body, just before the Battalion Annual training. The latter system was supposed to be the better, but it involved more organization. During

---

[1] This was the average. Actual estimates varied from 24 to 42.—A.E., 1899–1900, p. 178 et seq.

[2] The Records of the Royal Monmouthshire Militia and other Militia histories contain constant records of 'Companies being formed' under certain officers on arrival at Camp. Apparently in many cases no company organization existed in the period between Camps.

this period of preliminary drill, the recruit was paid ordinary Army rates of pay.

The Regiment as a unit 'came out for training' for twenty-eight days, during which officers and men received full army rates of pay.[1] Training was usually done on a regimental basis, either in the depot barracks, or in a camp not far away from the main centre of the Regiment. In former days, Militia units were sometimes billeted (i.e. in licensed houses) for the period of their training, but there were very obvious objections to this and it was avoided if possible.[2] Concentrations of more than one battalion sometimes took place, and Militia training at a military centre was advocated if possible. Militia Battalions took part in the great Autumn Manœuvres of 1898.

It has been said that the Militia was a historical force. Most of the Battalions had been in existence for many years and not many new units had been raised during the century. As befitted a somewhat feudal force, it was particularly strong in Ireland. In the Artillery, more than a third (12 Brigades out of 32), and in the Infantry, 25 battalions out of 124 were Irish.[3] On the other hand the Militia had not kept pace with the growing industrialization of the country. Thus, for example, the Northumberland Fusiliers had only one Militia Battalion, the Manchester Regiment and the Highland Light Infantry each had only two.[4] The strength of Militia units varied in the strangest way. Nor was this a matter of recruiting difficulties, for the variations were in the actual establishments.

---

[1] Fortress Engineers trained for forty-one days.—'History of The Royal Monmouthshire Engineers', by Captain R. E. Sargeaunt, p. 206 (1895), p. 208 (1897). In 1896 'In consequence of an epidemic of small pox' the regiment did not train. In 1897 'The lack of training the previous year had had a bad effect on the men, and many were sentenced to cells for insubordination'.

[2] In 1888 the Royal Monmouth Militia 'returning to Monmouth two days before the conclusion of training, when the men were quartered in billets, which resulted in much drunkenness and difficulty in paying off. . . . Many people in the town hooted as the men were marched to the train.'—'History of the Royal Monmouthshire Militia', p. 195.

[3] It is to be remembered that there were no Irish Volunteer Units.

[4] A.E., 1899–1900, pp. 179 et seq.

Thus Battalion establishments varied from 677 to 1,347, the latter respectable total belonging to two units, the 3rd Welsh Regiment (so spelled) and the 3rd Queen's Own Royal West Kent.

In fact the Militia, as organized, was somewhat out of touch with the times. Its units had great and historic local connections. Its officers originally owed their rank to property qualifications, and the local nobility and gentry often held Militia commissions. The long period of training, however, which might have been very suitable to an agricultural population or to a casual labourer, was very unsuitable to the growing class of skilled artisans and clerks. A man who had a job, and wished to keep it, was very unlikely to be able to go away for twenty-eight days at a time. The Militia was not popular with employers of labour, and, really, the fact is not to be wondered at.

The figures given in the Annual General Return bear out the high proportion of unskilled trades.

Out of a total of 106,153 enrolled men:

> 9,943 gave their trade as Artisans.
> 19,343 gave their trade as Mechanical Labourers.
> 32,691 gave their trade as Agricultural Labourers.
> 12,700 gave their trade as Miners.
> 3,549 gave their trade as Fishermen.
> 27,927 gave other trades.[1]

In Ireland, three out of every five Militiamen were farm hands. The Militia appear not to have used at all the machinery of evening or week-end training which the Volunteers had found so useful, though it is to be noted in this connection that drill 'after hours' had been the usual rule of the Armed Associations of the Napoleonic Wars.

Generally speaking the Militia did not do any training in the intervals between Annual Camps.[2]

[1] General Annual Return, 1898, p. 119.

[2] 'I have heard of cases of Militiamen going to Aldershot and elsewhere, and having had, almost at once, to go through tremendous hard work without having had a single drill since the year before.'—The Marquis of Granby, House of Lords, February 18, 1898.

THE AUXILIARY FORCES

It will be clear, therefore, that the Militia in 1899 was a force very different in character from anything that exists to-day. Lord Raglan, speaking in the House of Lords, said, 'The Militia consists of three classes of men. Recruits who are going into the Militia to feed up the extra half-inch to make up the standard' (i.e. for the Regular Army) 'old soldiers, and pure Militiamen'. And Lord Raglan went on to lament that the last-named class had almost ceased to exist.[1]

A study of the figures will show that a very great proportion of the strength of the Militia was made up of young lads who were using the Militia as a stepping-stone to the Regular Army. Either they were waiting till they met the extremely low recruiting standards of the time, or they wished to have a look at Army life before they made up their minds.

A young lad who was not sure whether he was going to like being a soldier could experiment very well in the Militia. If, after his preliminary drills and his first Annual training, he disliked the life, he could get off his Militia obligations on payment of a very low fine, or could face with equanimity the risks of desertion.[2] On the other hand, once he was in the Army, the process of purchase out was an expensive one, and desertion was a serious matter.

The figures are, indeed, extremely interesting. Firstly, as regards the ages of recruits.

During the year 1898, 40,127 recruits joined the Militia; of that number over half were under 19 years of age, and nearly one-third were under 18. Actually, in the age-group 17 to 18, 13,416 recruits were enrolled. At the other end of the scale, 1,685 recruits over 25 years of age came in, and it

[1] House of Lords, February 18, 1898.
[2] 'It having been brought to the notice of the Commander-in-Chief that very lenient sentences have, in many instances, been passed by courts martial on absentees from the Militia . . . I have the honour by desire of His Royal Highness to point out that if such sentences as one or two days' imprisonment with hard labour are given . . . the hoped-for result of diminishing this offence cannot possibly be realized.'—Horse Guards Letter, July 14, 1894. Quoted 'History of Royal Monmouthshire Militia', p. 205.

is fair to assume that these were mostly old soldiers, though figures to show how many old soldiers joined the Militia are not readily available.

It has been said that many of these young recruits were bound for the Regular Army. In the year under review 15,167 Militiamen joined the Regulars. In the same period, 8,716 deserted or were struck off the roll as absentees. Other tables show that, in the same period, 19,808 men, or just under half the number of recruits, were discharged. From the figures of 'Ages of the Men Discharged' it is clear that 9,525 were discharged under the age of 22 years, by which time they could hardly have completed their six years' service. They were, therefore, probably discharged as sick or inefficient. In other words (and the calculation is borne out by the figure given on page 121 of the Annual Report, 'Years in which the terms of Service will expire'), of the total 40,000 odd recruits, less than a quarter would be likely to complete their six years in the Militia.

In fact, 1893 had been a very good recruiting year for the Militia, 50,421 recruits were enrolled, yet in the year 1899 six years later, only 9,062, under one-fifth, remained to take their discharge as time-expired.[1]

To try and get a fair picture, figures for five years 1894 to 1898 have been taken together, and it has been found that of every twenty recruits that joined the Militia:

> Seven joined the Regular Army
> Four deserted
> Five were discharged for one reason or another before six years
> Four completed their six years.

Those in the last category, the men who went on to do their full time, were, of course, the men who made up the Militia Reserve, for the number of men who went into the Regular Army from the Militia Reserve was very small.

[1] All the above figures from the General Return for the British Army for 1898.

THE AUXILIARY FORCES

Most of the lads who went into the Regular Army did so in the first two years of their Militia Service; in the same way most of those who were going to desert did so in the first two years.

Out of a total desertion figure of 8,718, 3,948 or 45 per cent was in the first year, 1,899 or 22 per cent in the second year.

It was, perhaps, the fact that the Militia was naturally regarded as the stepping-stone to the Regular Army that allowed a scale of crime and punishment unusual in a Volunteer force. In 1898 there were 846 Courts Martial on Militiamen, and of those cases only fourteen resulted in Acquittals. There were 709 sentences of imprisonment, though, as more than half the cases before the Courts Martial were for Desertion or Absence without leave, it is not clear how many of the awards of imprisonment were, in fact, carried out. In the same period, there were 3,093 men fined for drunkenness, and 21,519 minor awards by Commanding Officers.[1]

Excluding officers, about 90,000 Militiamen actually attended training in 1898, and these may be regarded as the effective strength of the Militia. Over 30,000 were in the Militia Reserve, and, therefore, more or less hypothecated to the needs of the Regular Army. Lads under 19 were not allowed to join the Militia Reserve, but there were in the Militia, in 1899, 29,000 lads under 19.[2] If these two groups are added together it will be seen that there was not much left of the Militia to form a Home Defence force. Still less was the Militia much value as a cadre. The standard of Militia N.C.O. was low, partly because of the low standard of original recruit, partly because the training of the unit was almost entirely in the hands of the permanent staff colour-sergeants and sergeants.

The standard of training of Militia officers varied very greatly. Like the men, a large number were on their way to the Regular Army, entry through the Militia being a valuable and economical way of gaining a regular commission. It has

[1] General Return of the British Army for 1898.   [2] Ibid.

already been suggested that the company officers did not have very much to do with the training of their men.

Annual training consisted very largely of Squad drill and Company parades carried on by the Colour-Sergeants, and of Battalion drills carried on by the Adjutant. Nevertheless, the Militia did contain a number of officers who were very keen on their profession, and did their best to improve their knowledge. Since 1877 all officers of the Militia had been subject at all times to Military Law. Non-commissioned officers and men were only so subject when called up for Annual training.

As an avenue of approach to the Regular Army the Militia was functioning fairly well, but as an Army for Home Defence it was very small and not at all organized.

It was, therefore, small wonder that friends of the Militia were worried about the force. Lord Raglan, earlier in a speech already quoted, said,

'The Militia is very much below its strength, but that is not the only thing. Last year, the Militia was about 24,000 below its strength, and not only that, but that strength has fallen off relatively enormously with regard to the population.'[1]

And Lord Wantage, speaking in the same debate said,

'For one thing, you call out the Militia at the worst possible time of the year for its training—namely in the months of May and June. . . . Young Militiamen cannot be got to come out in May or June, because all the hands are wanted on the land. . . . It would be better if you called them out in January or December. . . . But the great difficulty is to make the Militia popular—because it is not popular, my Lords, very far from it."

It may be added that, within a little while, in the same debate, the Earl of Galway was objecting very strongly to Lord Wantage's suggestion of winter training. Nevertheless, the debate as a whole showed very clearly that all was not well

[1] House of Lords, February 18, 1898.

with the Militia. Lord Wemyss and his friend thought that the ballot should be reimposed, but the Government were very chary about such an action. Lord Lansdowne, winding up the debate, quoted the finding of Colonel Stanley's Committee in 1876, 'That it is not necessary to keep the Militia up to its full establishment in time of peace. . . . Experience proves that men are easily obtainable for the Militia in time of great National excitement or emergency.'

And it was perfectly true that noble lords who wished to return to the days of the ballot had perhaps forgotten the change in population and national industrial conditions since the times of Castlereagh. Major-General J. F. Maurice, C.B., speaking at a debate at the R.U.S.I. on November 17, 1897, had said the final word in one direction, 'No nation on this earth has yet ventured to adopt a system of compulsory service for expatriation'.[1] The most that might have been possible would have been to introduce the ballot for home service. But, having regard to the very large increase in the population, the percentage total man power that the Militia could absorb would be low—even if the establishment were doubled. That would mean that the proportion of blanks in the ballot would be high. At first sight that might seem an advantage. Experience, however, had proved that compulsory service only works well when it is nearly universal in its application; when, in the words of the French code, 'Military service is personal and obligatory'. Anything else leads to the system of paid substitutes, with all its abuses, and eventually to the detriment of recruiting for the Line.

The Militia Reserve was actually over strength, against an establishment of 30,000 the General Annual return for 1898 gives a strength on January 1, 1898, of 31,049. It will be remembered that this Militia Reserve consisted of men of the Militia who, in return for an additional bounty of £1 per annum accepted the liability to serve overseas in case of war if called upon to do so.

[1] 'R.U.S.I. Journal', vol. xlii, p. 27.

In this connection, it is worth noting that the Militia Reserve was the only portion of the Auxiliary Forces which was in the position in which the whole Territorial Army now stands. Lord Wantage thought that the 'Militia Reserve is the pick of your Militia Regiments'. The training was exactly the same as the rest of the Militia. On the other hand, the general feeling in the Service seems to have been that these Militia Reservists thought that they were on a fairly safe thing when they took an extra sovereign per annum for a remote contingency, and their arrival at camps in South Africa was regarded as somewhat of a jest.

On many occasions in the past, Militia Battalions had served overseas, notably in the Crimean war, when they undertook the duties of many of the Mediterranean garrisons. The regulations provided that if 75 per cent of any Militia Battalion volunteered for foreign service the Battalion would go as a unit, but it was made quite clear by a reply of the Under-Secretary of State for War, Mr. George Wyndham, that 'the Army Order based on 61 and 62 Vict. c.9 and 45 and 46 Vict. c.48 gives no powers over the 25 per cent who do not volunteer'.[1]

When all was said and done, however, the Militia was a collection of battalions, and not a Home Army.

THE YEOMANRY CAVALRY

The Yeomanry consisted, in 1899, of 38 Regiments, with a total establishment of 11,891 officers and men, excluding the Permanent Staff of 167 all ranks. The 38 regiments were brigaded in pairs, but the 11th (Scottish) brigade had three regiments and the Pembroke Yeomanry—the heroes of Fishguard—were unbrigaded. There were no regiments north of Lanark, and, except for the Middlesex Yeomanry, no unit for London.[2] Regiments varied in strength—some had two

[1] Mr. George Wyndham, in answer to a Question, House of Commons, May 18, 1899.
[2] War Establishments, 1899–1900, p. 190.

squadrons, others, three or four. Similarly, the establishment varied from 200 to 300. A Regular Adjutant was appointed to each brigade, 148 Permanent Staff Sergeants were distributed among the 38 Regiments. The assistance from the Regular Army was therefore much less than in the case of the Militia.

Actually, the Yeomanry was below strength and only 8,829 (exclusive of permanent staff) were present at Annual Training.

The force was in a rather specialized and privileged position, a position which endures till present days in a rather quaint aloofness from the Territorial Army as a whole. In its earliest days the Yeomanry was very largely what might be called, in the language of to-day, a 'White Guard'. It was an internal security force, which, in the absence of an organized police, was used to put down riots, overawe discontented districts, and represent in the country the power of the Crown.

In 1899, it was liable to be called out in case of any actual invasion, or insurrection arising out of an invasion. For this purpose, it could be assembled in any part of Great Britain—but not Ireland.

The Yeomanry could, also, still be called out as Volunteers for the suppression of riots which did not arise from War. A valued traditional privilege was that of acting as escort to the Sovereign.

But the Yeomanry fitted somewhat clumsily into any scheme of National Defence. Prior to 1888 they had only been liable for local action—a French landing at Dover would have been no official concern of the Lancashire Hussars. In 1888, however, an Act had been passed making every Corps of Yeomanry liable to be called out for Military Service in any part of Great Britain.

Even then, the scattered organization in troops, and the fact that each Regiment was very much an independent command made co-ordination difficult. Hitherto, there had been a very definite tendency on the part of the Yeomanry to exist as a resplendent local corps d'é'lite, a nemphasis on good horsemanship and handsome uniforms, while musketry and tactics had scant attention paid to them. As a result of the conclusion of Lord Brownlow's Committee in 1892, War Office control over the Yeomanry was tightened up. The regiments were organized into squadrons.[1] A minimum strength of 70 efficients for each squadron was demanded. If by 1895 this was not forthcoming, squadrons would be broken up. A musketry standard was introduced and a School of Instruction for Yeomanry Officers was established at Aldershot.

The Yeomanry preserved many of the old features of autonomous local forces. They were governed, like the Volunteers, by a code of rules, which, subject to Royal Approval, were voted on by the Corps.

Yeomen provided their own horses, and though there was a contingent allowance of £2 per efficient man, this was seldom sufficient to pay the cost of uniforms, band, horses for the permanent staff and the like. Therefore, each Yeoman had to face a fairly heavy annual cost in the practice of his hobby, while officers and especially commanding officers, provided very considerable amounts out of their own private purses. The esprit de corps of the Yeomanry was very high, but, like that of mediaeval levies, it tended to centre on the locality and the commanding officer rather than on the Army as a whole or the War Office in particular.

The standard of efficiency was not severe. Recruits had to do twelve drills and a modified musketry course. Before annual training, 'permanent duty', as it was called, each yeoman, after his recruit's training, did six squad drills, mounted or dismounted, and five squadron drills mounted.

Regiments assembled for training each year for periods of eight days. Pay was provided for this at the rate of 7s. a day, this rate being applicable to all other ranks, whether Sergeant-Majors or troopers.

There had been some discussion as to the desirability of training the Yeomanry as mounted rifles, but in 1899 the

[1] Army Order 22 of 1893. 'Chronology', p. 55.

THE AUXILIARY FORCES

Yeomanry was definitely trained as cavalry, and was armed with the sword and the Martini carbine.

From the excellence of its material, the Yeomanry possessed great possibilities, but it was very unorganized. Like the Volunteers, it possessed nothing in the way of transport for mobilization, in fact, a Yeomanry Regiment did not have an official Quartermaster.

Any attempt to mobilize the Yeomanry of the kingdom as a whole for action in any one quarter, against, for example, a foreign invasion, would have necessitated an enormous amount of improvisation, and must have caused great waste of men and horses.

It is to be noted that, like the Militia and unlike the Volunteers, the Yeomanry were subject to Military law when being trained and exercised alone. On the other hand, officers of the Yeomanry were like their men in this regard and were not, like Militia Officers, always under Military law—another instance of the strange gradations of the auxiliary forces of the time.

THE VOLUNTEERS

On November 1, 1898, the effectives of all ranks in the Volunteers numbered 231,624. This compared with an enrolled membership of 264,833.[1] Included in this respectable total were the Honourable Artillery Company, with 1 Horse Artillery Battery, 1 Field Artillery Battery and a Battalion of Infantry; 2 Regiments of Light Horse; 66 corps of Volunteer Artillery; 20 units of Engineers, 7 of submarine miners, the Electrical Engineering Corps, the Engineer and Railway Staff Corps; 213 Rifle Corps, a Volunteer Medical Staff Corps of 14 Companies, and the Bermuda Volunteer Rifle Corps. The establishment of the Volunteer Forces is shown in detail in the Appendix attached.[2] There were no Volunteer Army Service Corps units, and there were no Volunteer units of any kind in Ireland.

[1] A.E., 1899–1900, p. 12.   [2] Appendix E.

Before considering the condition of the Volunteers in 1899, it is necessary to review some aspects of the history of the force, because, more than any other portion of the British Army, the Volunteers in 1899 reflect the circumstances of their origin.

The Army Book of the British Empire written in 1893 says, 'The Volunteer Force now existing in Great Britain owes its origin to a wave of patriotic feeling that swept through the country in the years 1858-9'. That is, in many ways, a true statement of fact, but it is a mistake to regard the Volunteer Movement of 1859 as creating something absolutely 'de novo'. The Honourable Artillery Company had existed as a genuinely volunteer organization since the charter granted by King Henry VIII on August 15, 1537. The Princess Victoria's Rifle Club[1] had been in existence, as the Duke of Cumberland's Sharpshooters, for many years, when it received Royal patronage in 1835, and the Devon Volunteers claim to be as old. Moreover, there were plenty of men alive in 1859 who remembered the stories of the Parade of the Volunteer Corps in Hyde Park on June 4, 1799, or the traditions of the still earlier Armed Associations of 1780. In London at least, the new formations of Volunteer Rifle Corps in 1859-60 definitely felt that they were the successors of the Volunteer Corps of the Revolutionary Wars. And this fact in many ways coloured their traditions. For these 'Armed Associations' have been companies of men of substance, householders and professional men, and formed after the Gordon riots to repress lawlessness, and maintained during the turbulence of the French Revolution as serious upholders of the Constitution.

The Volunteer Movement was, therefore, from the first 'respectable'. It was also essentially 'bourgeois'. A movement from the people themselves, it had definitely forced the hand of the War Office and the Government. In April 1859, the Long Acre Indignation meeting had protested against the insufficiency of National Defence. Men like Captain Hans

[1] Now the Queen Victoria's Rifles, K.R.R.C.

Busk and Captain J. E. Acklom had laboured hard, at meetings and in the Press, to arouse public interest. On May 9, 1859, Mr. Tennyson's poem 'Form, Riflemen, Form', appeared in 'The Times'. 'As well say that the Redan was stormed because someone wrote "Cheer, Boys, Cheer" ' was the comment of one pioneer volunteer who thought Mr. Tennyson's influence had been overrated.

Nevertheless, the poem had its value as a pointer to public opinion. On May 12th the Queen signed a letter to the Lords Lieutenant of Counties sanctioning the formation of organized formed bodies of volunteers.

The War Office were rather dubious about the merits of the Volunteer Movement. Many reasons contributed to their distrust. In 1859, Army opinion was wedded to long service. It was not thought possible that any proficiency in arms could be obtained otherwise than by long periods of drill and training. That Volunteer Corps could meet Regular troops in the field was thought out of the question; the best that might be expected was that the Volunteers, like Andreas Hofer's Tirolese, would, by guerrilla tactics, harass and damage the invading columns. In the first days, therefore, the official view was that only small formations were desirable, units of two or four companies. To this cause is, in part, to be ascribed the multiplicity of small battalions that existed all over London, causing a parochialism that bears ill fruit to the present day.

The Militia Colonels distrusted the Volunteers because, as Lord Wemyss said, they suspected Volunteering to be a device to circumvent Militia service. It was fundamentally a movement of the rapidly rising Victorian professional and middle classes, while at the War Office, the landed gentry, and the military families still had a strong preserve.[1]

[1] The manner in which the Volunteers and their successors the Territorial Army have ousted the Militia presents a very interesting study in social history. The Volunteers, by adopting the principle of evening or week-end drills, and a continuous unit existence throughout the year, centred upon their own drill hall, were able to maintain a corporate individuality which

In sympathy with the War Office it must be pointed out that the very men who now in 1859 joined the Volunteers had been among the severest critics of the Army management of the Crimean campaign a few years earlier.

And the new corps were certainly capable of strange sartorial extravagances, such as Garibaldi shirts and Zouave jackets.

However, by 1860 the Volunteer Movement was definitely 'the thing'. Those who find in the pages of 'Punch' a true mirror of the times will note as very significant the different regard paid to the Militia, shown, for example, in such cartoons as 'A Militia Man in 1854', or, more favourably 'Ready when wanted or Militia Volunteers', of the same year; compared with Mr. Punch's cartoons of the early days of the Volunteer Movement; 'Our Volunteers', in 1860, or even 'One of the Right Sort' of the same year. While the Militia were represented as under-sized, clean-shaven boys of somewhat tough countenance, the Volunteers were always middle-aged, bewhiskered, and obviously the height of Victorian respectability. When men like Millais, Watts, Val Prinsep and Fred Leyton were in the 'Artists', it was quite clear that in London, at least, the new Rifle Corps had a strong claim on public opinion. By 1869 48 corps of Middlesex Rifle Volunteers had been formed in and around London.

It is, therefore, only a fair comment to say that in the early days of the Volunteer Movement there was not very much sympathy between the Rifle Corps and the War Office. The Rifle Corps felt that they were getting very little official support, while the War Office regarded these new organizations as ill-disciplined, given to fancy uniforms and likely to be little use in actual war. In this connection, it is to be

was far stronger than that of a Militia Battalion which only 'came out for training' for a limited period annually, and did little to preserve its continuity of existence for the rest of the year. From the political point of view it might be said that the Militia Colonels were in the House of Lords, and the Militiamen, in the '60's, were without votes, whereas the strength of the Volunteers was in the House of Commons.

remembered that these units all adopted their own constitution. They elected their own officers, and were very largely self-governed by the votes of the members of the corps. It was a time when insurrectionary movements on the Continent of Europe were of recent memory and it is not, perhaps, surprising that there were misgivings in certain quarters concerning the possession of arms by a large number of persons about whom little was known, and upon whom military discipline sat very lightly.

Even the story of the first Brighton Field Day is illuminating. The London Corps decided to hold a great Field Day on Easter Monday of 1861. Some corps favoured Wimbledon Common, others favoured Brighton. The issue was largely determined by an offer from the Brighton Railway to transport Volunteers in uniform from London to Brighton for eighteenpence, and to carry guns and horses free of charge. As a result, in the words of 'The Ancient', the War Office

'had looked very askance at seeing 12,000 men in arms on the south-east coast without a general officer, one of whom was sent down, and had, under absence of the rules governing such occasions, to look on'.[1]

By the following year the position had been regularized.

In two important directions the Volunteers in their very earliest days had made a great contribution to military needs. It has been noted that some of the oldest Volunteer corps had had their origins in shooting-clubs. The Queen Victoria's had for many years possessed a rifle range of 150 yards at Kilburn 'a little beyond the place formerly known as the Gate'.

As early as the autumn of 1859 there had been suggestions for the foundation of a Volunteer Rifle Association. The suggestion arose almost simultaneously among a group of officers of the Volunteer Rifle Corps who had attended the Hythe course, and also among the Council of the London Rifle Brigade.

[1] 'The Ancient', p. 68.

Fortunately divided counsels were avoided. A meeting was held at Spencer House in November 1859. Lord Spencer was in the chair; others present were Lord Grosvenor, Commandant of the Queen's Westminsters, Lord Elcho, Commandant of the London Scottish, Captain Wilbraham Taylor, Captain George Adam Gladstone, Mr. Archibald Boyle, and Mr. George Russell. The meeting agreed to the resolution: 'It is proposed to form a National Association for the encouragement of Volunteer Rifle Corps, and the promotion of rifle shooting throughout Great Britain.'

In this manner the N.A.R.A. was founded. Ground was secured at Wimbledon. Her Majesty Queen Victoria fired the first shot on July 2, 1860. From Wimbledon in due course the N.A.R.A. moved to Bisley where the traditions of the 1859 meeting are still maintained.

A few years later, under the leadership of Captain J. L. Rutley of the 1st Middlesex Artillery, a National Artillery Association was formed, the first meeting being held at Shoeburyness in 1865. Colonel Harcourt of the Cinque Ports Artillery Volunteer Brigade became the first President of the Association.

The Volunteers in 1899

Such was the beginning of the Volunteer Force. By 1899 very considerable progress had been made. The Volunteer Act of 1863 had regulated the organization and discipline of the Volunteer Forces, and successive legislation had brought the Volunteers into the general scheme of Army organization.

Home Defence

The scheme of defence which followed the Stanhope decision to erect fortifications to block the routes to London has already been mentioned. When that scheme of defensive works was inaugurated, the proposal was that Volunteer units should be told off to their own particular areas. Mr. Stanhope actually referred to these intrenched camps as places 'where it will be possible hereafter to exercise some of the defenders in the actual place which they might have to defend".

It does not appear, however, that such practice in the manning of defensive positions was ever carried out to any great extent: nor does it appear that Volunteer units as a whole knew where they were allotted in the defence organization.[1]

A further difficulty about the scheme was that Mr. Stanhope appeared to suggest in his original speech that he did not expect the Volunteers to be in their places in less than about nine days from the Government order to prepare. If the theory of a sudden raid were accepted then such an interval was clearly too long.

The Defence of London Organization was of considerable interest in that it gave the Volunteers a role to play in the general scheme of military preparedness. But it had not been worked out very thoroughly as far as the Volunteers themselves were concerned.

Training

The training of the Volunteers varied very considerably in accordance with the keenness of the unit or the individual. The minimum training required was very little. 'Six Company, three battalion drills, class firing and attendance at inspection are necessary to efficiency.'[2] It will be readily realized that such a very low standard of compulsory attendance would not by itself be sufficient to provide either highly trained individuals or an efficient unit. In the case of very many battalions and batteries many more drills were done, and a great deal of time was spent on the rifle range. In attempting

[1] 'R.U.S.I. Journal', 1901. 'National Defence', p. 922. From the evidence of Colonel Barham it appears that as an example, the Bloomsbury Rifles on two occasions camped at Fort Wallington (Portsdown Hill), but only to gain the advantage of the permanent installation of the fort for cooking, etc. There was no practice in manning the fort.

[2] Orders of the Central London Rangers, 1878, etc.

to gain an opinion of the training of the Volunteers of 1899 as compared with their successors, the Territorial Army of 1936, fair comment would probably be along the following lines. In good Volunteer units there was a high standard of tactical knowledge among the officers, and among a fair proportion of the rank and file. Some keen Volunteers, like Colonel Macdonald of the Queen's Edinburgh Rifle Volunteers, were in many ways ahead of their Regular colleagues in military thought. Colonel Lonsdale-Hale, R.E., the famous authority on the Franco-German war, was accustomed to conduct lectures and war games in London for Volunteer officers, which were well attended.

The standard of shooting was good among the keenest men, but the qualification standard was lower than that which holds good in the Territorial Army.

Partly because training was confined to Saturday afternoons and evenings and there was no summer camp to take men away from their families or their businesses, the Volunteers of 1899 were as a whole older men than the rank and file of the Territorial Army to-day. There were married men, small shopkeepers, skilled artisans or professional men. A great deal of emphasis was laid upon drill which was generally conducted by the Adjutant, and at the Annual Inspection senior officers were called out in turn to drill the battalion before the examining officer. In London there was a 'School of Instruction' staffed by a Commandant, Adjutant, and Instructors from the Brigade of Guards. This school was attended by officers from provincial as well as London units. The course lasted a month, and consisted of thorough drill instruction together with a certain amount of tactical work. At the close of the course there was a passing out examination.

The culminating event of the Volunteer year was the Annual Inspection. On that day every man of the unit had to be on parade, if he were an absentee no capitation grant would be received by the unit that year on his account. The fact that the whole year's training led up to this Inspection and not to an annual training in camp as is the case with the Territorial Army of to-day had the almost inevitable effect of creating a certain formalism and attention to drill which has already been noted.

Officially the training year commenced on November 1st. In most cases, however, very little was done during the winter months beyond the holding of a School of Arms in the Drill Hall and the conduct of numerous social events. Company drills commenced some weeks before Easter, but one of the great weaknesses of the Volunteer system was that owing to the small number of compulsory attendances it was very seldom that sufficient men turned up to allow Companies to train by themselves. It will be remembered in this connection that these were the days of the eight-Company system and that, therefore, in any event Companies were small. The result was that in many units on ordinary evenings' drills, such men as turned up were made into one or more Companies according to numbers, without much regard to their Company organization upon paper, and the drill was taken by the senior officer present under the supervision of the Adjutant. Company Commanders could have very little influence upon the training of their Companies under such a system, and Company organization mostly existed for competition purposes and for social life.

For the London units the Easter Monday Field Day at Brighton remained for some years a traditional event. By 1899, however, it had been dropped for some years, and London Volunteer Corps used to go by brigades for Easter Training to various places on the South coast or to Winchester or Colchester. In some cases, Regular barracks were borrowed,[1] more often, billets were used. On such occasions, Companies that were not strong enough to carry out Training by themselves were joined together to form composite Companies.

[1] 'By permission of the War Office, the Corps will be quartered at Shorncliffe from Thursday, 3rd, to Tuesday, April 8th, returning to town on the latter day by 6 a.m. train from Shorncliffe.'—Special Battalion Orders of 20th Middlesex (Artists) R.V., April 1890.

Units left London on Thursday night and returned on Monday night.

During the summer, Hampstead Heath, Wimbledon Common and similar spaces were used for Volunteer sham fights on Saturday evenings.[1] There was no compulsory summer Camp, but Volunteer Camps were held at Aldershot and, to these, units would send detachments, one or two Companies strong, and these detachments were formed into composite Battalions.[2]

Like the Yeomanry and the Militia, the Volunteers possessed practically no machinery for mobilization or for taking the field. Regimental transport was non-existent. One or two battalions had their own machine-guns, but these had in every case been purchased privately. A large number of Volunteers had cyclist detachments, and one Regiment, the 26th Middlesex, was a complete cyclist corps. Except for the batteries of the Honourable Artillery Company, there was practically no Volunteer Field Artillery. Volunteer Artillery Corps either manned coast defence guns, or were so-called position batteries, armed with the clumsy 40-pounder B.L. gun.[3] Even for the occasional journey into the country, horses to draw these guns had to be hired from neighbouring contractors and were frequently led by their civilian drivers.

It follows that there were no opportunities for Infantry and Artillery to practise together.

Administration

The finances of the unit were kept in being by a Capitation Grant received from the Government. Originally on a basis

---

[1] One old Volunteer described such events as follows: 'We used to march, with the Band playing, from Bloomsbury up to Hampstead Heath, have a sham fight all over the Heath, fall out at the Spaniards and fill ourselves with beer, then march back to Bloomsbury with the Band still playing, have some more beer at the canteen and go home.'

[2] Some units occasionally went to summer camp, as complete battalions; when this took place there was no Easter training.

[3] In some cases the 64-pounder M.L.

of 30s. per efficient soldier it had been increased by 1899 to 38s. 'including allowances'. As efficiency within the meaning of the Capitation Grant only demanded nine annual drills and attendance at Inspection, there was a very grave temptation upon even the best Commanding Officers to enlarge their unit with a number of not very zealous soldiers for the purpose of obtaining a large Capitation Grant. In very few units was the Capitation Grant sufficient to pay for the cost of running the Regiment, and in most cases a subscription was demanded from the Volunteers themselves. In addition to this, large sums of money were obtained from outside subscriptions, and all over the country drill halls were built out of subscribed funds. Uniform and equipment were purchased out of the capitation grant, arms and ammunition were supplied by the Government.

The result of this was to make the Commanding Officer very closely involved in the financial working of his Battalion. Wealthy men who were prepared to make their Regiments their hobby were obviously in demand as Commanding Officers and retained their Command far longer than military efficiency would have justified. The Commanding Officer was, in fact, the executive Commander and theoretically the trainer of his Regiment; he was the Chairman of the Regimental Board of Finance, if such a phrase may be used to explain the situation, and, in many cases, he was also legally the freeholder of the Regimental drill hall.[1] It follows that if ever a Volunteer unit of the 1899 pattern had had to proceed to war as a whole, the financial position of the Commanding Officer might have been very complicated.

In a final review of the state of the Volunteers in 1899, it may be said that, although the various units contained a large amount of valuable raw material which might be avail-

[1] 'For the year 1885 ... Colonel Richards had to advance £174 10s. 10d., making ... a total of £583 16s. 10d. advanced by him since the opening of the new Headquarters. To this date, of the 853 men on the roll, only 397 have paid the Regimental Subscription of 5s. Comment is unnecessary.' —Orders of the Bloomsbury Rifles, XIX Middlesex R.V., June 1886.

able in the case of emergency, there was very little machinery whereby this raw material could be rapidly mobilized in case of war. There was, for example, no arrangement at all whereby complete units could proceed overseas, and, from the facts of the case, it was extremely likely that only a small proportion of the men in any given unit would be fit enough or trained enough to go rapidly on active service. As has been said in an earlier paragraph, the weakness of the whole of the auxiliary force in 1899 was that there was no machinery for mobilizing units as opposed to securing drafts of men.

PART II

THE MOBILIZATION AND EXPANSION OF THE BRITISH ARMY DURING THE SOUTH AFRICAN WAR, 1899–1902

CHAPTER 5

THE MOBILIZATION OF THE REGULAR ARMY

IN the opening paragraph of the Report of the Elgin Commission[1] occurs this phrase: 'The whole military system as it stood at that date was tested by the war in South Africa.'[2] In fact, a succession of tests, imposed by the gradual development of the conflict, passed in review the various echelons of the British military machine.

In broad outline, the military system of the time was that devised by Mr. Cardwell and his successor, Mr. Childers, the system of the Army Reserve so much disliked by H.R.H. the Duke of Cambridge.[3]

When war broke out at the end of 1899, it was assumed in many quarters that the dispatch by this country of the Field Force would be sufficient to bring the campaign to a triumphant conclusion. Therefore the military problems, in the minds of many, were chiefly concerned with the mobilization of the reserves. Would the Reservists obey the summons of recall to the colours; would they fight well and would their numbers suffice to make good the inevitable wastage of war?

It must be remembered that the South African War was the first campaign of major importance to be fought with the 'modern army'. It is true that Sir Garnet Wolseley's Egyptian campaign had been fought in part with 'short term' soldiery and that there had been many Reservists in the army of Tel-

[1] Owing to frequency of reference the Elgin Commission is abbreviated as E.C. in footnotes in this Part.
[2] E.C., p. 4.
[3] 'Do not let us sacrifice the Army, our first line, to the Reserve.'—H.R.H. to Wolseley, 1881. 'Life of Wolseley', F. Maurice.

el-Kebir.¹ This, however, could hardly be called an arduous campaign and the victory over Arabi was scarcely evidence enough, one way or another, of the warlike value of units filled with Reservists.

None of the many other campaigns waged by this country since 1882 had necessitated the calling out of the Army Reserve.²

At this distance of time, and against the background of the experiences of the Great War, it is easy to fasten on the errors of the South African War. To gain the just perspective, it must be remembered that a very important change in our Army organization was going to be tried out. From the days of Charles II to the Crimean War this country had fought its battles—or at any rate had commenced its campaigns—with a professional long service army.

Now it was going into action with a Regular Army whose infantry at least did only five years colour service. There were many—and not all fanatical devotees of the old regime—who watched the experiment with anxiety.

Events, hereafter to be studied in detail, showed that much of the work of Mr. Cardwell, Mr. Childers and Lord Wolseley had been well conceived. The Reservists responded well, and fought well, but their numbers were not sufficient to make good the wastage.

The Details of Mobilization

The machinery of mobilization was the care of the Mobilization Division at the War Office. At one time under the Intelligence Division, and later under the Adjutant-General, this Mobilization Department was in 1899, directly under the Commander-in-Chief.³ On the other hand, this Committee

[1] An Order in Council summoned to the Colours nearly 12,000 men of the 1st Class Army Reserve, whose prompt response testified to the success of the new system.—'Life of Wolseley', F. Maurice, p. 145.
[2] 'No Government could call out the Reserves to fight Zulus.'—Ibid., p. 114.
[3] Evidence of General Stopford, E.C., q. 954.

did not concern itself with the organization or mobilization of the auxiliary forces. The evidence of Colonel P. H. N. Lake, C.B., Assistant Quartermaster-General of the Mobilization Division,[1] before the Elgin Commission, explains very clearly the reasons why this was so. Questions and answers were as follows:

Question 1080, 'And the last Division was the 8th?—Yes.'

Question 1081, 'You had nothing to do with the organizing or mobilization of the Militia and Volunteers?—No., etc.'

Question 1082, 'There is no provision in your general scheme of mobilization for your undertaking anything of that kind?—No. There was no provision in the general scheme of mobilization for service abroad for raising such a body as the Imperial Yeomanry or for sending the Militia abroad in organized bodies; because, of course, the Yeomanry, as it then existed, could not be sent out of England; the Militia could not be sent out of the United Kingdom, even to the Channel Islands, without their volunteering to go, and according to law Volunteers as such cannot proceed for service out of the United Kingdom. Therefore we have never considered that it was necessary to make mobilization regulations for that condition.'

In the light of modern ideas it is not quite so clear why, when the decision was taken to send the Imperial Yeomanry to South Africa, the task of raising this force was not supervised by the Mobilization Sub-Committee.

It is to be remembered that at this time there existed no General Staff at the War Office.

On August 1, 1899, the total garrison of Regular Troops in South Africa was 9,940 strong.[2] Owing, however, to the growing tension, additional troops had been ordered to the Cape, and by October 13th, the date of the outbreak of hostilities, all these reinforcements had arrived except two battalions of infantry and half a regiment of cavalry still afloat.

[1] Colonel Lake succeeded General Stopford in October 1899.

[2] E.C., Appendix 3 A. Two Regiments of Cavalry. Six Batteries or companies of Artillery. Six and a half battalions of Infantry.

Including, in the total, the late arrivals just mentioned, the reinforcements came from the following areas:

Half a battalion of Infantry from Mauritius. Three regiments of cavalry, three batteries of artillery and four battalions from India. Four battalions from various Mediterranean garrisons and two battalions and three batteries from home.[1]

It is interesting to note that, of the first reinforcement, totalling nineteen and a half units (regiments, batteries or battalions), fourteen and a half came from overseas stations. That represented, in other words, a mobile surplus in overseas garrisons possessed by the country in 1898.[2]

These units were, of course, composed of mature soldiers and were at full strength. In fact, there was a slight complication inasmuch as units from India and the Mediterranean were on different establishments, and both these establishments differed from those of the garrison already in South Africa.[3] Unfortunately for critical comparison between the battalion on foreign service and the battalion of the Field Force, most of this first reinforcement got shut up in Ladysmith. Thus far there had been no mobilization problem, the reinforcement had largely consisted of moving units from one foreign station to another.

Before, however, all these reinforcements had landed in South Africa, the Government had decided on the dispatch of the Field Force. This was, in fact, about the equivalent of the First Army Corps of the existing mobilization scheme.[4]

---

[1] E.C., Appendix 3 A.

[2] It is interesting to compare the situation in 1927 when the dispatch of the Shanghai Defence Force of three Infantry Brigades necessitated finding battalions from Home.

[3] E.C., Appendix 5 B.

[4] It is important to note that the 1st Army Corps for Service Overseas was not, even on paper, the same as 1st Army Corps for Home Defence. Thus the Guards joined the Field Force from Gibraltar. It may also be mentioned that 'mobilization' in the strict sense was not completed until South Africa, where, for the first time, units received vehicles and animals.
—E.C., Evidence of General Stopford, qq. 935 et seq.

The dispatch of this force was authorized on September 29th, and, on October 7th, the first-class Army Reserve, to the number of 25,000 men, were called up, with directions to report themselves by October 18th.[1] This part of the mobilization scheme worked splendidly, over 98 per cent of the Reservists rejoined the colours[2] and their numbers were amply sufficient to allow the units of the Field Force to complete up to establishment. But the Reservists had not only to complete units from peace strength to war establishment, they had also, to a greater extent than was anticipated, to replace ineffective soldiers. The British Army at home contained a very large number of immature lads, so that Mr. Arnold-Forster speaking in 1903 had to say,

'The First Class Infantry Reserve is still a substitute for, and not a supplement to, the men serving. In 1899 the proportion of Reservists with battalions was as high as 52 per cent, and these Reservists had, in many cases, replaced ineffective soldiers to the extent of from 370 to 460 per battalion."[3, 4]

In the Field Force a total of 47,081 were embarked, of all arms, whereof 20,589 were Reservists.[5] Mr. Forster later quoted, among others, the case of the 1st Battalion The East Lancashire Regiment when, out of a strength of 947, there were only 370 men available to proceed overseas. This large proportion of young or otherwise ineffective soldiers was to prove to be one of the main reasons why the reserves were used up more rapidly than had been anticipated.

[1] E.C., p. 38.
[2] Wolseley's letter to H.M. The Queen of October 24th. Writing of 14,200 Reservists to whom notices had gone: 'Of this number 14,108 rejoined, and of that number 1,271 were rejected by the Doctors as unfit for active service.'
'In the Royal Scots every single Reservist was accounted for.'—Mr. Wyndham in House of Commons, October 26, 1899.
[3] Command Paper No. 1907 of 1904.
[4] 'The percentage in all arms of rejections for foreign service on account of insufficient training, of being under age, or of being medically unfit is $36\frac{1}{2}$.'—Mr. Wyndham in House of Commons, October 26, 1899.
[5] Command Paper No. 1907 of 1904.

It will be seen later that, by an improvisation, 10,000 of these young soldiers were used on lines of communication.

Before the Field Force had all left the country, news arrived of the disaster at Nicholson's Nek, and one additional battery and three battalions were embarked to replace the units lost on October 30th.

That brought the force dispatched under Sir Redvers Buller to a total of:

> Eight Regiments of Cavalry.
> Four Horse Artillery Batteries.
> Thirteen Batteries of Field Artillery and three of Howitzers.
> Thirty-five battalions of foot.

The troops originally in South Africa being at that time considered the 4th Division, the Field Force contained the 1st, 2nd and 3rd Divisions.

Throughout this period Lord Wolseley had been urging upon the Government the desirability of mobilizing the Second Army Corps immediately the embarkation of the First Corps had been effected.[1] Now his representation received added weight by news direct from the scene of war. On November 4th, General Sir Redvers Buller suggested the preparation of an extra Division. This Division, eventually the 5th, was at once organized under Sir Charles Warren, and the Secretary of State informed General Buller that this would be sent forward with the least possible delay.[2] Sixteen days later, on November 30th, the War Office reported that the 6th Division was being prepared, and on December 14th yet another telegram announced 'A 7th Division is being mobilized'.[3]

[1] 'Lord Wolseley knows the Queen will be glad to hear from him that over two Army Corps could be mobilized quite easily in a fortnight, etc.' —'Life of Wolseley', Maurice, p. 320.

[2] E.C., Appendix J, p. 620. Sir Redvers Buller's telegram No. 10 (cipher), and Secretary of State's telegram No. 18 (cipher).

[3] Secretary of State telegram No. 50 (cipher). The Seventh Division (the sixth to be sent from England) represented the end of the Second Army Corps of the Stanhope Memorandum. There had, however, been no attempt, after the dispatch of the Field Force, to dispatch further troops on an Army Corps basis.

THE MOBILIZATION OF THE REGULAR ARMY 75

This was on December 14th, the war had been waged for two months, and the Regular Army had raised Seven Divisions. On the next day, December 15th, was fought the battle of Colenso, the culminating event of the 'Black Week'.

The war was assuming a new, and a serious phase. It was beginning to look as though the Regular Army might not be large enough for the task of subduing the two South African Republics. The telegrams which passed during that fateful week are so illuminating that much must be quoted in extenso. On December 16th, the morrow of Colenso, Buller cabled[1] to the Secretary of State for War,

'I feel sure from what I saw of the enemy's defences yesterday that we shall want 7th Division ... would it be possible for you to raise 8,000 irregulars, organized not in regiments, but in companies of 100 each.'

That same day, the Secretary of State replied[2]

'Four battalions 6th Division embark to-day and to-morrow and the remaining four will embark next week, the infantry of the 7th Division on the 4th January and the following days. ... A considerable force of militia and of picked yeomanry and volunteers will also be sent.'

On December 18th, the Cabinet decided to send Field-Marshal Lord Roberts to South Africa as Commander-in-Chief. Setting aside for the moment any consideration of the methods adopted at this stage of the war to supplement the Regular Army by raising Militia, Yeomanry or Volunteer units, the final stages of the mobilization of the Regular Army remain to be studied. While Lord Roberts was proceeding as rapidly as possible to South Africa, the 7th Division was being mobilized.

On January 9th, the Secretary of State for War sent to Lord Roberts a telegram which is of extreme importance as

---

[1] E.C., Appendix J, Buller telegram No. 91 (cipher).
[2] Ibid., War Office telegram No. 55 (cipher).

giving a picture of the stage reached in the development of the nation's military power.[1]

'Please let us know what you think about further reinforcements as soon as you have thoroughly examined the situation. We have arranged for the following reinforcements in addition to the 7th Division, viz.:

1. Four Brigade Divisions, Field Artillery embarking as soon after January 20th as possible.
2. One Volunteer company for each Line battalion, amounting in all to about 7,000.
3. The City of London regiment of Volunteers and the battery of the Honourable Artillery Company.
4. One Field Artillery battery of Volunteers from Elswick.
5. Colonial contingents, inclusive of 4 Artillery batteries, mostly mounted, and amounting in all probably to about 3,000.
6. Seven Militia battalions.

Of these some have already started. As to the Imperial Yeomanry it is not yet possible to say what number will be raised, but 4,000 at least will probably be the total, and the material, though raw, is good. We have also mobilized a Cavalry Brigade which could embark at once; if, however, it is sent, only the remainder of the Household Cavalry and 5 Line Regiments will be left at home. Do you wish to have it? We are also mobilizing the 8th Division, which would begin to embark about February 20th, but if it goes there will only be 7 Infantry battalions left, and unless the 8th Division is urgently required this reduction of the Home garrison does not appear desirable in view of the general outlook. It might answer your purpose if we sent for the lines of communication 8 or more Militia battalions instead.'

In fact, it was decided, almost at once, that the 8th Division would have to go overseas[2] and by the

[1] E.C., Appendix J. War Office telegram No. 80 (cipher).
[2] 'HOUSE OF LORDS, *January* 30, 1900.
'There is nothing but worrying war news to-day. Roberts has telegraphed for the VIII Division, and I suppose it will go. That will leave literally no one in this country. About three battalions. . . .'—Esher Journal, vol. i, p. 253.

THE MOBILIZATION OF THE REGULAR ARMY

end of February the embarkation of this Division was complete.[1]

That was the end of the chapter.

'With the dispatch of the 8th Division the last organized and mobilized Regular formation left this country, and the work of the Mobilization Subdivision in connection with the dispatch of reinforcements to South Africa came to an end.

The executive work of organizing, equipping and dispatching drafts, Militia, Volunteers and Imperial Yeomanry was carried out entirely by the Adjutant-General, Quartermaster-General and Director-General of Ordnance.'[2]

In other words, the sailing of the 8th Division marked the end of a planned programme, thereafter it was sheer improvisation.

It might be valuable to compare, at this stage, the strength of the expeditionary force of the South African War with the expeditionary force of the Great War.

In 1899–1900 the Regular Army produced eight Divisions each of eight infantry battalions. In this total the Fourth Division, formed by the reinforced garrison of South Africa, is included. In the Great War the Regular Army found six Infantry Divisions for the Expeditionary Force, and a further five Divisions,[3] as soon as overseas battalions were relieved by Territorials. All Divisions in 1914 were of twelve battalions. There were also six white battalions in the Indian Corps. The 1914 expedient of relieving First Line troops in garrison duty by Second Line troops was not adopted in 1899 as far as India was concerned, although, as will be seen, a few Militia units were sent to the Mediterranean

---

[1] It is to be noted that the battle of Paardeberg had been fought before the 8th Division sailed.

[2] E.C., Statement by Lieutenant-General Sir W. G. Nicholson, K.C.B., R.E., Appendix No. 3, para. 30.

[3] 7th, 8th, 27th, 28th, and 29th.

and Royal Reserve battalions went to various foreign stations.[1]

The strength in England of the Regular Army with the colours consisted on October 1, 1899, of 103,052 Non-Commissioned officers and men. By March 31, 1900, these men had been distributed as follows:

To South Africa	61,593
To India and the Mediterranean	4,126
Still at Home	37,333

Of this large proportion still at home, the majority were immature boys.

Of the Army Reserves amounting at the beginning of the war to about 80,000, 42,957 men had proceeded abroad with units of the first eight Divisions.

To take other figures, by the end of February, a total of:

99,510 Non-Commissioned Officers and men had been embarked from this Country and the Mediterranean stations for South Africa. Of these, 56,553 were with the colours, 42,957 were Reservists posted to units.

In addition to these Reservists who were posted to units, others of course went out as drafts to replace casualties. Before the end of September 1900 a further 18,414 had gone out in this way, leaving some 9,000 still to be accounted for. Of those, some remained in the Reserve, others called up at the beginning of the War were found to be unfit, and were struck off the Reserve.

'Up to April 1900 units were, in all cases, supplied with drafts from the Regimental Reserve but after that Regiments who had suffered unusual casualties were filled up with Reservists from other

---

[1] On the other hand, native Indian Regiments were used to replace Regular regiments in some garrisons. Two native battalions went to Mauritius, one to Ceylon, and one to Singapore. It is to be remembered that no Indian troops were employed in the South African Campaign.

THE MOBILIZATION OF THE REGULAR ARMY 79

corps. Sometimes these transfers were made from the Regular Army Reserve and sometimes from the Militia Reserve. In all cases careful note was taken and lists compiled of such transfers.'

'Drafts continued to be sent from the combined Reserve Formations of the Regular Army Reserves and the Militia Reserve until September 1900 when this reservoir was completely exhausted. By that time a total of 52,535 had been sent as drafts, whereof the Regular Army Reserve, A, B and C had sent 8,845, Section D had sent 9,569 and the Militia Reserve had sent 13,014.'[1]

Naturally, all this time, recruiting in the normal sense was going on, and as the recruits of previous years reached military age they could be sent overseas, thus supplementing the drafts made up of Reservists or Militia Reservists. It is, however, interesting to note that recruiting for the Regular Army was nothing like sufficient to make good war casualties. The Report of the Elgin Commission says on this subject:

'To keep pace with the wastage in the Regular Army the normal influx of recruiting was, of course, available and it was in fact found that during the three years that the war lasted there was a net gain during the war of about 13,500 recruits to the Regular Army. This did not take into account the raising of ex-soldiers for the garrison battalions. Nevertheless, in spite of extra pay and a reduction in the standard demanded, there was a definite falling off in recruits for the Infantry during the years 1900 and 1901. Some of this falling off was no doubt due to the counter attraction of extra pay and better conditions of service in such corps as the Imperial Yeomanry.'[2]

The situation, therefore, in the early spring of 1900 was that the last formed units of regular troops had left these shores. The Reserve and Militia Reserve had been drawn on heavily to make up the Field Force and to supply drafts. In fact, by the end of September 1900 these supplies would also be exhausted.

[1] E.C., Evidence of General Kelly-Kenny, Adjutant-General, War Office, p. 86, Appendix 5.
[2] E.C., p. 65.

At home, there remained the balance of the Household Cavalry and Five Cavalry Regiments of the Line, together with seven infantry Regiments. At the depots were a large number of immature Regular soldiers and, on paper, there was a Regular Army in these islands of 100,000 men. But of these Lord Lansdowne was forced to say, in the House of Lords on May 25, 1900, that they were 'Of course in no sense a Field Army. They include a large number of young soldiers, men who have not yet reached the age of 20 and who are, therefore, not fit to be sent out of the country on foreign service.' There were, besides these youngsters, Reservists who had been called up but found to be unfit or too old, and sick and wounded who had by this time returned from South Africa. The force was, moreover, very short of artillery and services.[1]

If the military effort were compared with what had happened in the past, there were of course many signs of improvement.

On January 30th Lord Wolseley wrote a memorandum, afterwards quoted before the Elgin Commission, in which he claimed, (Para. 24):

'I have no hesitation in saying that no army has ever left our shores composed of finer soldiers than those of which our army now in South Africa consists. All are seasoned men. There are no recruits or youths under 20 years of age amongst them. Had we not possessed the Army Reserve—the outcome of our short-service system—it would have been impossible to have sent to South Africa the Regular Army now serving there. Indeed, I would go further, and say that at no previous period of our history that I am acquainted with could England have sent such an army into the field beyond the seas.'

And again in para. 26,

---

[1] 'The residue is the state of things now existing in this country a perfect military chaos.'—W. Arnold-Forster, House of Commons, March 12, 1900. See also 'Mowatt Reserves'.

THE MOBILIZATION OF THE REGULAR ARMY

'Some weak points have been discovered and they will be at once rectified; but although this is the first time we have ever called out our whole Army Reserve we have every reason to be satisfied with the rapidity and ease with which this mobilization of our army was effected.'[1]

Within certain limits the Commander-in-Chief's satisfaction with the Army system he had sponsored was justified.

There were, however, two features which were very disquieting. The first was a matter of high policy but it reflected very seriously upon the military situation. In almost every major war waged by Great Britain since we had a Regular Army we had fought with allies. Only in the American War of Independence did we face alone a group of powers. The Balance of Power had served us well enough, and in times of difficulty we had usually been able to count on the aid of one or other of the great military nations.

The Boer War revealed to the country in no uncertain manner that, at the close of the nineteenth century, England was not popular on the Continent of Europe. In fact, it is but fair comment to say that in 1900 any hostile combination of European powers would have been very serious for this country. Mr. Arnold-Forster, speaking in the House of Commons on February 1, 1900, said of the situation

'It is not fair to state to the country that we are so well provided with troops that the barracks are full to overflowing. As soon as the troops now under orders to go have departed [2] we shall have left only six battalions of Infantry of the Line, and three battalions of the Guards, all under strength, and as far as the Line battalions are concerned largely composed of men who are not fit to take part in active operations. We shall have nine cavalry regiments some without horses and all under strength. Beyond that we shall have nothing, nothing at all. . . . We have got the whole organized army out of the country, and the War Office is face to face with the problem of how to make an army to take its place.'

[1] E.C., Appendix D, p. 277.   [2] That is, the 8th Division.

Therefore, the Cabinet had to consider, in the spring of 1900, not only the successful prosecution of the war in South Africa but also the necessity for some sort of show before the eyes of the European powers.

Perhaps as they received the cabled offers of aid from the Dominions the Cabinet might comfort themselves that like Canning they had 'called the New World into existence to redress the balance of the Old'. The day had not yet come, however, when Dominion troops were to fight in the Low Countries, and the Home Country had to turn to improvisation to protect her own shores.

Meanwhile so urgent in January 1900 was the need for men, for home defence as well as for South Africa, that for two days Lord Wolseley's resignation hung in the balance. In his anxiety to impress on the Government the seriousness of the situation, he had tendered his resignation unless due provision were made for home defence.[1] On the other hand, Lord Lansdowne was complaining that the papers of the Intelligence Division were never officially communicated to him as the basis of any proposals through the regular channel and that it was the accepted military belief at the end of 1899, that as soon as the Army Corps arrived on the scene the war would soon be over.

'The first phase of the war in South Africa showed that 70,000 men were inadequate to our needs. We had thus exceeded our organized field army and were forced hastily to build up the field army to a total strength of 250,000 men; an army hastily improvised in this way obviously labours under many disadvantages."—Sir William Nicholson.

Before considering the manner in which the Auxiliary forces were employed, mention should be made of the Royal Reserve Battalions.

Between February and June a personal appeal from Her Majesty was addressed to retired officers and other ranks of

[1] 'Life of Lord Wolseley', F. Maurice, p. 323.

the Regular Army.[1] They were asked to re-enter upon Army Service for one year at home to replace the Regular Army who had gone to South Africa. A special bounty of £12 was paid to these men on re-enlistment and a further £10 on discharge; 24,130 officers and men thus re-joined the Army.[2] These men were formed into battalions designated 'Royal Reserve Battalions'. A year later under the provisions of Mr. Brodrick's Six Army Corps scheme the Royal Garrison Regiment was formed.[3] The first four battalions were created in the years 1901–2 and they were chiefly composed of the ex-soldiers who had joined the Royal Reserve Battalions. In 1903 there were five battalions of the Royal Garrison Regiment stationed abroad. Three were in Malta, one in Gibraltar and one in Canada. The Corps was a fairly expensive one for the country, for besides the cost of the bounties paid on re-enlistment and discharge, the annual cost of the battalions was high by reason of the large number of married men.

A parliamentary return for the year 1902[4] showed that the 2nd Battalion Royal Garrison Regiment at Gibraltar, with a total strength of 977, had, either on the Married Establishment, or drawing Separation allowances, 748 women and 1,774 children. The detachment of the 4th Royal Garrison Regiment which served at Malta had the high record of 272 fines for drunkenness in the year, among 487 men.

Generally, evidence seems to show that the standard of efficiency and discipline of the Royal Garrison Regiment was not high. On the other hand, this Corps did fill the gaps in home and overseas defended ports left vacant by the departure to South Africa of the Regular Army.[5]

As a further measure taken to increase the strength of the Regular Army may be mentioned the fact that men reaching

[1] The units were formed by Royal Warrant on February 20, 1900.
[2] E.C., p. 41.   [3] Army Orders 59 and 115 of 1901.
[4] Command Paper 239 of 1903.
[5] The Royal Garrison Regiment was almost completely reduced by March 1906.

the end of their service with the Regular battalions in India were offered a bounty to continue their service for a further period.

The necessity for drafts from the Home Country to the Indian battalions was thus greatly reduced.

SUPPLIES FOR WAR

THE MOWATT COMMITTEE

If the strength of Boer resistance, and the war's repercussion upon European diplomacy came as a shock in one direction, the realization of the lack of sufficient war reserves of material was equally disturbing.

General Sir H. Brackenbury, who, it will be remembered had been in charge of the Intelligence Division in previous years, was appointed in February 1899 as Director-General of the Ordnance.[1] Brackenbury was a capable administrator, and, according to the evidence of both Lord Lansdowne and Lord Wolseley, he was specially placed in his new office in order that he might overhaul the Ordnance branch. There was, however, at that time a very comprehensive scheme for the rearmament of the fortresses with more modern guns, and inasmuch as this subject was particularly the concern of the Director-General of Ordnance, Brackenbury found that he had little available opportunity for studying the needs of the Field Army.

He did, however, find out by degrees that there were indeed no reserves. 'We had sufficient material to arm three Army Corps and sufficient material to equip three Army Corps but nothing for their maintenance once they were armed and equipped.'[2] These were the words which in later years he used to describe the situation to the Elgin Commission, and

---

[1] After his work in the Intelligence Division, Brackenbury went out to serve in India. He returned in 1896, and became President of the Ordnance Committee.

[2] E.C., q. 1748.

THE MOBILIZATION OF THE REGULAR ARMY 85

he emphasized them again in answer to the next question. 'We had no reserves, except the trifling quantities which have been already mentioned.'

Three Army Corps were nine Divisions of those days. From the Home Regular Army something over seven Divisions went to South Africa, for the Fourth Division was nominally formed in South Africa from the troops sent there before the outbreak of war and on the other hand extra battalions had been dispatched to take the place of those lost at Nicholson's Nek. It would, even under the Stanhope memorandum have required Militia Units to fill up the Third Army Corps, and, therefore, it might have been expected that mobilization supplies would have allowed a slight margin for reserves if matters had stopped short at seven Divisions. Naturally any expansion beyond the Three Army Corps, beyond the 112,000 men of Mr. Brodrick's 1898 speech could not possibly be supplied from the mobilization stores of the time.

The problem, however, was far more urgent than the equipping of new formations, it was the unexpected, or disregarded claims of war wastage that produced the alarming deficiencies. Mr. Harris, in his evidence said 'the whole of the equipment of harness for the first three Army Corps was in store, but the waste of the war was so rapid and unforeseen that in a very short time what small reserve there was behind the mobilization equipment ran out'.[1] In regard to some items the time was short indeed, for Lord Wolseley told, that on October 11th, the day of the declaration of war, 'I find that a demand for 250 sets of saddlery could not be complied with as early as that'.[2]

Wolseley pointed out forcibly the difficulty he had experienced in securing financial consent for any accumulation of reserves,[3] at the same time it is not possible to exonerate entirely the War Office of the day. There appears to have

---

[1] E.C., q. 7899. Mr. Harris was at this time Principal, Accounting-General's Department.
[2] E.C., q. 8810.   [3] Ibid., q. 8828.

been a failure to consider the problem beforehand. 'Everybody at the War Office, I think,' said Brackenbury, 'was under the impression, and Sir Ralph Knox has stated in his evidence before the Mowatt Committee, that there was no reserve kept up for War upkeep of the Army, because it was supposed that the Ordnance factories and the trade would supply what we wanted from week to week. The earlier stages of this war burst that bubble.'[1]

By the middle of December the situation was evidently serious, Brackenbury could only see one spare battery of field guns after equipping the three batteries ordered to sail before the end of the year. The Army was borrowing gun ammunition from India and from the Navy. Already the trade was forced to go to Germany for the bodies of shrapnel shell although the war had only lasted two months. Moreover behind the shortage of supplies for the forces in South Africa loomed the more remote but terribly serious spectre of complete absence of war equipment for Home Defence. Lansdowne had admitted in Parliament that the 100,000 men in barracks in the United Kingdom were 'in no sense of the word a Field Army'. There is little record that any man at that time said in public how absolutely bare of resources in material was the state of the troops at home. Later, before the Royal Commission Wolseley said 'the Army at home was in a helpless and hopeless position'[2] and he had explained such a statement as follows

'The whole of our Volunteers and Militia and Yeomanry remaining at home would have had guns of such an obsolete pattern that it would have been almost dangerous and criminal to ask men to stand up to them in the face of modern artillery.'

There was one additional complication to add to General Brackenbury's troubles. The entire army as it prepared for service in South Africa had to be reclothed. For the uniform of the serving soldier, as well as the uniform held for the

[1] E.C., q. 1732. [2] Ibid., q. 8814.

Reservist, was red, or blue or black or green, according to the pattern that had been laid down in the Adjutant-General's department. Even his boots would not serve him overseas for the home boot was a big heavy boot with a clump sole; the soldier of those days paid for the repair of his own boots and he wanted something cheap and simple to cobble. The service boot had a sewn sole, so each man had to have a new pair. A helmet also had to be provided. The great-coat of his peace-time uniform, it was proposed, should be taken overseas, but even this did not prove satisfactory. The upshot was that the entire clothing of the British Forces in South Africa, dated, speaking in general terms, from after the period of tension.[1]

On December 15th Brackenbury wrote a Memorandum which he sent to the Secretary of State for War, with the request that it be laid before the Cabinet.[2] It was as strong as it was necessary. The course of the war, he said, 'had disclosed a situation as regards armaments and reserves of guns, ammunition, stores and clothing, and as regards the power of output of material of war in an emergency, which is, in my opinion, full of peril to the Empire'. This was an important document and the Cabinet took it seriously. An inter-departmental Committee was formed with Sir Francis Mowatt, the Permanent Under-Secretary of the Treasury as Chairman. There were only two other members, Mr. Wyndham the Permanent Under-Secretary of State for War, and Mr. Burls, the Director-General of Stores in the India Office. The Committee was a secret one and no report of its recommendations was issued at the time. Later, before the Royal Commission Lord Lansdowne gave a fairly full account of the proposals made by this important body, and of the action that had been taken by the Government.

[1] E.C., qq. 1619 et seq. In April 1899 provision had been made for 40,000 suits of khaki drill. That was all the clothing available before mobilization was ordered. Even so, the khaki drill was later changed to khaki serge.
[2] Apparently this was not sent through the Commander-in-Chief (Wolseley's evidence, E.C., qq. 8815 et seq.). Brackenbury had been on Lansdowne's staff in India, and Lansdowne had a high opinion of him.

Finally in 1904, in the days of Mr. Arnold-Forster a Command Paper[1] showed what had been the recommendations of the Mowatt Committee, and what measures had been taken to carry out these recommendations. The Mowatt Committee itself made recommendations which amounted to a total cost of £6,482,567. In addition an expert Committee dealing specifically with armaments recommended an expenditure of £1,586,338 on movable artillery, and of £3,552,965 on the completion of certain coast defences. This amounted to a total budget of £11,621,870. The Government actually sanctioned an expenditure of £10,500,000. This was found in the Army Estimates of 1901–2, 1902–3, and 1903–4. To this must be added certain smaller sums which were in time to be included in the estimates for 1900–1.

The more important requirements of the Mowatt Committee were: The maintenance of a Reserve of one gun per every ten in fortress armaments. The completion of a siege train. Maintenance of a Reserve of mobile artillery and also machine-guns on the basis of 25 per cent of complete batteries: Reserves of General Stores to equip a force of three Army Corps, one Cavalry Division and lines of Communication troops and to keep that in the field for six months: Reserves of clothing for the whole field force plus a six months reserve stock. There were also recommendations concerning the creation of additional magazines, store buildings and the like.

To anticipate it may be said that by the time the Command Paper of 1904 was issued, most of the recommendations had been carried into effect. A somewhat important exception was that the siege train was not yet ready.

It was made a special recommendation of the Committee that any guns, ammunition, or equipment withdrawn from these reserves for use on service should be automatically replaced.[2]

---

[1] No. 1908 of 1904. See also E.C., qq. 1616 et seq. It appeared also from the evidence of Lord Wolseley that this important report was not, as a matter of fact, ever submitted to him.   [2] E.C., q. 1616.

CHAPTER 6

THE EMPLOYMENT OF THE AUXILIARY FORCES—THE MILITIA—THE VOLUNTEERS—THE SERVICE COMPANIES—THE IMPERIAL YEOMANRY

'We should have come to the end of our tether if we had not had extraneous aid.'—SIR T. KELLY-KENNY, E.C., p. 34 and q. 4837

THE MILITIA

IN an earlier portion of this work it has been pointed out that the ladder of preparedness of the British military forces ran as follows:

(A) The Regular Army overseas
(B) The Regular Army at home
(C) The Regular Army Reserve, Section 'A'
(D) The remainder of the Army Reserve
(E) The Militia Reserve
(F) The Militia
(G) The Yeomanry
(H) The Volunteers

and the comment was then made that the weakness of the system was that unless Militia battalions volunteered for service overseas none of the echelons ever could definitely provide any complete units for duty outside the United Kingdom.

Faced with the emergency which arose at the close of 1899, the Government had to make the best use possible of the echelons available. The first action was clearly to call out the Militia. A Royal Proclamation having been issued on October 26th ordering the Secretary of State for War to give the necessary directions for embodying all, or any part, of the

Militia, a special order dated November 3, 1899, ordered the embodiment of 35 Militia battalions.[1,2] The embodiment of a further 3 battalions was ordered on November 4th, a further 8 battalions on November 23rd, and other battalions later.

It is to be remembered that no Militia unit could be sent abroad unless the men agreed to go. The principle upon which units were selected for embodiment was left to the discretion of the Inspector-General of the Auxiliary Forces. These battalions, as they were called up, were asked to volunteer for overseas service, and on the evidence of Major-General H. C. Borrett, C.B.,[3] care was taken to see that this volunteering was quite honest and compulsion was not brought to bear on the men. In fact, 3 Irish battalions and 1 Scottish battalion (composed chiefly of fishermen) did not volunteer to go overseas. The remainder did go, and 68 Militia battalions left the United Kingdom during the course of the war. Most of these went to South Africa, but in a few cases they were sent to Malta or other stations.[4] Counting officers and men, 45,566 of the Militia went to South Africa. It has been pointed out earlier that one of the great weaknesses of the Militia was, that apart from the Militia Reserve, men in the ranks of the Militia were either very young or very old. That was immediately found out by General Borrett. The regulation for the Line said that no man was allowed to go and fight until he was 20. It was proposed, in the first instance, to have for the Militia an age limit of 19. General Borrett was compelled to tell Lord Lansdowne[5] that if this limit was adhered to the Militia would lose one-third of their men and, therefore, in fact, the Militia went overseas taking boys of 18. Such a percentage of young and immature soldiers

[1] E.C., p. 63.
[2] Mr. Wyndham, speaking for the Government in the House of Commons on the Supplementary Estimates, October 20, 1899, emphasized that the mobilization was for home defence.
[3] E.C., q. 5255.
[4] Five to Malta, three to St. Helena, one to Egypt.—Appendix to E.C., p. 161.   [5] E.C., q. 5259.

was obviously a severe handicap to the Militia. A very much greater handicap, however, was the deficiency in officers; In October 1899 there was a shortage of some 600 officers in the whole of the Militia. General Borrett quotes a case of the Royal Lancasters, who had only 8 subaltern officers when they should have had 24. That deficiency he proceeded to make up and, in fact, all battalions were eventually up to strength in officers, but the procedure was an improvisation of the highest degree. They were 'all ordinary educated young gentlemen',[1] and to quote once again from General Borrett, 'I said I could not train them, I had nothing to do with training. My business was to find the men and the officers. I thought they were better than nothing.'

The Militia battalions were intended, from the first, for employment upon the lines of communication and it is very clear, from the evidence of both Lord Roberts and other officers, that they were regarded as second line troops of inferior quality. Having regard to the lack of training of their officers and the youth of the personnel, it is difficult to see what other conclusion could have been reached.[2]

MILITIA RESERVE

It will be remembered that the Militia Reserve had been formed to provide out of the Militia an immediate supply of

[1] E.C., para. 5259.
[2] Lieutenant-General Sir W. Nicholson (Norfolk Commission, q. 295): 'I found that I had eight battalions of Militia under me during the war, and when they first came out they were practically useless from an absolute want of officers. There were a very few old officers and a good many young ones. . . . Eventually, after a time we got wounded officers and officers from other sources.'

Field-Marshal Earl Roberts (Norfolk Commission, q. 888): 'I think the men would have been better for more training too, but the officers were the weak point.'

Up to the occupation of Pretoria the Militia battalions were used solely on the lines of communication. Afterwards, during the period of guerrilla warfare, Militia units were sometimes used in mobile columns, but even in these later days they were usually employed as garrison troops.

reinforcements by way of draft to the Regular Army. The disadvantages of this proceeding had been pointed out in earlier debates in the House of Lords and the fact had already been realized in many quarters that the best part of the Militia was contained in this Reserve and that if these men were taken away very little would be left.

Experience was to prove the truth of these criticisms. The rapid drain upon the Regular Army Reserve made it clear that the Militia Reserve would have to be used for reinforcement. Some units of the Militia had, by this time, been embodied, some were not so embodied. Some Line Regiments were exhausting their Reserves rapidly, some still had Section D Reservists to call upon. The result was that the drain on the Militia became unequal. When the Militia unit had not been embodied, Reserve calling-up notices were sent direct to the Militia Reservists. When the Militia unit had been embodied, draft notices were sent to the Commanding Officer and the Militia Reservists were taken away from the Regiment. In some cases, however, the Militia Regiment had already gone overseas before its quota of Militia Reservists had been called upon. General Kelly-Kenny in his evidence before the Elgin Commission gave as his view that:[1]

'probably about 10,000 of the Infantry Militia Reserve proceeded to South Africa with their Militia battalions and so were not available for Line drafts and the Artillery Militia Reserve was also left intact'.

In order to set free this Militia Reserve the decision was arrived at in May 1900 to send out a number of 18-year-old soldiers to the Militia battalions on lines of communication and release the Militia Reservists for Regular units.[2]

Taking the pre-war strength of the Militia Reserve as just over its establishment of 30,000 it appears that few, if any, were used to make up to war strength the battalions of the first eight Divisions on their first procedure overseas, that

[1] E.C., Appendix 5, p. 86.   [2] Ibid., p. 84.

just over 13,000 were subsequently sent to South Africa as drafts to these Regular battalions and that about 10,000 went to South Africa with Militia units. Of these last 10,000 some men, while in South Africa, were transferred to Line Units.

As a final comment on the Militia, the following may be quoted from the evidence of Sir Ian Hamilton before the Norfolk Commission:

'First of all the men from the Militia Reserve who were in regular battalions were quite excellent. I had experience, mind, of many of the Militia Reserve with the regular battalions. Every Commanding Officer I asked about them said they were first class men. The Militia battalions that had come out, had lost many of their officers, who had gone to regular battalions to replace losses in the earlier part of the war. They had also been somewhat short of officers to start with. The vacancies these caused were filled up with a number of inexperienced boys . . . there were one or two regiments that took part in engagements that I know of, but as a general rule these regiments were used as L. of C. troops and that, in my opinion, is what they were best suited for under the circumstances.'[1]

THE VOLUNTEERS

The employment of the Militia in South Africa had a certain precedent, for Militia Battalions, if not used on active service, had at least been used for garrisons in the Mediterranean during the Crimean War. There were, however, no precedents for the employment of volunteers from the United Kingdom in overseas campaigns. On the other hand, the general officers in high places at the War Office had, in the course of their fighting experience, often employed colonial forces of a volunteer nature. These local forces were, in those days, frequently called 'irregulars' and it will be noted that this somewhat significant word was to be employed in one of the important cables sent home by General Sir Redvers Buller.

[1] Lieutenant-General Sir Ian Hamilton, K.C.B., Norfolk Commission, q. 1141.

The first move in the employment of volunteers appears to have been made by Colonel Sir Howard Vincent, an officer of very great experience, who had commanded the Central London Rangers before assuming the office of Commissioner of the Metropolitan Police, and had, later, proceeded to the command of the Queen's Westminster Rifles. He was a Member of Parliament and a very strong advocate of the volunteer system. In August 1899, Colonel Vincent wrote to the Under-Secretary of State for War offering, in the event of hostilities in South Africa, to raise a battalion of selected volunteers for active service overseas and at the same time to raise a battalion for home service. In response to this offer the only reply received was an intimation from the War Office to Colonel Vincent that the letter had been dispatched 'through the wrong channel'.[1]

Colonel Vincent's idea was that this battalion should be raised from all the volunteer units in the country, that, in fact, it should be a battalion representative of the whole volunteer force. It is possible that this aspect of the suggestion was not appreciated by the War Office who thought that Colonel Vincent was suggesting the employment of his own battalion only. In fact, as will be seen, the scheme of a selected battalion bore fruit in the establishment of the City Imperial Volunteers. Almost at the same time as this suggestion for a composite battalion, Colonel Balfour of the London Scottish offered to raise a service company of the Gordon Highlanders, to which corps the London Scottish were affiliated. It will be seen that, in the event, both these suggestions were followed.

On October 16th, war having broken out on the 11th, Colonel Vincent renewed his offer, this time through the General Officer Commanding home district, but again no answer was received and on October 26, 1899, in the House of Commons, Colonel Vincent made a final effort in the following words:[2]

[1] E.C., q. 5449. [2] A.D., 1900.

THE EMPLOYMENT OF THE AUXILIARY FORCES 95

'I beg to ask the Under-Secretary of State for War, if, having regard to the acceptance of the services of Volunteer Corps offered for active service in South Africa by the Colonies, and to the raising of Volunteers Corps in Cape Colony, Natal and Rhodesia, some of which have already done good work, the Secretary of State and Commander-in-Chief will, should circumstances demand the dispatch of further reinforcements, bear in mind the offers of service they have received from members of the Volunteer forces in Great Britain, always provided that only the best marksmen and best trained men are accepted and that this can be done without taking such a number from any one regiment as might interfere with its efficiency in the general scheme for home defence.'

To this question the Under-Secretary of State for War, Mr. Wyndham, made the following reply:

'The law does not allow us to employ Volunteers as such outside the United Kingdom. Any Volunteers employed would have to enlist in the Regular Army. Subject to this reservation the patriotic offers from members of the Volunteer force will certainly be borne in mind, though there does not appear to be any immediate prospect that their services will be required.'

Mr. Duncombe then asked:

'May I ask under what law the War Office are not allowed to accept the services of Volunteers?'

and Mr. Wyndham again replied:

'We cannot avail ourselves of the patriotic offers unless the Volunteers enlist for a short term in the Regular Army. As Volunteers they cannot go out.'[1]

This short discussion took place as has been said, on October 26th. The next day Parliament adjourned and did not reassemble until January 30, 1900. During that recess a very profound change had come over the complacency of the Cabinet.

[1] A.D., 1900.

While Parliament was in recess, Colonel Vincent, through ill-health, had to go to the South of France and his scheme for the collection of a composite battalion was not followed up. As a result, when the City Imperial Volunteers were formed action was taken 'very rapidly, very hastily, extravagantly, and to some extent badly'[1] because lack of official appreciation of the possibility of the idea had failed to make the necessary provision.

The next moves were, therefore, taken extremely rapidly, and under the pressure of events. At the risk of reiteration, it is important to emphasize the psychological effect, both on the nation and the War Office, of the Black Week of Stormberg, Magersfontein and Colenso. Up to December 15th, the nation had been assured that the Field Force would be sufficient. Suddenly that assurance was shattered.

Groups of men of good will all over the country at once commenced suggesting methods whereby additional troops might be raised. The War Office, itself suffering from surprise, delegated responsibility rather freely to these various bodies. The result was that at least three separate approaches to the problem were made, along uncoordinated lines. The City Imperial Volunteers, the Service Companies, and the Imperial Yeomanry were raised and administered by separate organizations, and, as will be seen, competed with each other in various ways.

Moreover, both in South Africa and in Canada, Australia and New Zealand, Colonial forces were being raised. The conditions of service and rates of pay of these colonial contingents had their effect on the raising of volunteers at home and these factors will also have to be studied later.

First in chronological order came the City Imperial Volunteers. On December 15th 'the Lord Mayor drove down to the War Office and saw the Commander-in-Chief who gave verbal sanction to the Regiment being raised'.[2] In that typically

[1] E.C., q. 5453.
[2] Evidence of Major-General Mackinnon, E.C., q. 7366.

English way the Regiment was launched. The next day the Lord Mayor received a semi-official letter from Lord Wolseley beginning, 'My dear Lord Mayor—It gives Lord Lansdowne great satisfaction to hear that the City of London proposes to send out a large contingent of Volunteers'.[1] On that somewhat meagre authority the Lord Mayor's Committee got to work, and it was not, in fact, until January 6th that an Army Order gave official sanction to the City Imperial Volunteers and laid down the conditions of service.

The Commanding Officers of all Volunteer battalions in the Home District were summoned to a meeting at the Mansion House and were asked to raise 40 men per battalion for the C.I.V.s. The men were to be unmarried, within severe limits of age and efficiency. Although some battalions were not able to find their quota of 40—it must be remembered that a large proportion of the members of the Volunteer Rifle Corps of 1899 were married men—taking London as a whole there was no shortage of recruits.[2]

To the original battalion there was added a battery of Artillery and two companies of mounted infantry.

A few days after the Mansion House Meeting Earl Denbigh and Desmond, Colonel Commandant of the Honourable Artillery Company read that the War Office had accepted an offer of a battery of Artillery, from the Elswick Works. Previously an offer of a battery from the Honourable Company had been turned down. Lord Denbigh, like the Lord Mayor a few days previously, went off to see Lord Wolseley, who greeted him with the laughing remark, 'We progress here', and accepted a four-gun battery from the H.A.C. The next day Lord Lansdowne handed to Lord Denbigh a cheque for £17,000 and told him to go ahead with the provision of the battery.[3]

Four $12\frac{1}{2}$-pounders quickfiring guns, the first quickfirers with fixed ammunition to be used by a British force in the field,

---

[1] Evidence of Major-General Mackinnon, E.C., q. 7368.
[2] E.C., q. 7373.
[3] 'The Honourable Artillery Company', by G. Goold Walker.

were purchased from Messrs. Vickers and Maxim. Almost simultaneously came the proposal to incorporate this battery in the C.I.V. Though the bulk of the C.I.V. battery were volunteers from the Honourable Company there was a sprinkling of volunteers from other corps, and a few old regular soldiers. A few experts from Messrs. Vickers' works were also specially enlisted to look after the guns.

These latter were, as far as can be ascertained, the only members of the C.I.V. who were not members of volunteer corps before the formation of the overseas contingent.[1]

The City Imperial Volunteers were, therefore, a unique force and entitled to special reference in the study of the various means adopted to reinforce the Regular Army.

Though the press and the public combined in a somewhat ludicrous way to idolize the C.I.V.s, the experiment was truthfully enough an exceedingly interesting one.

The visit of the Lord Mayor to the War Office was, as has been said, on December 15th. On January 13th the first portion of the force embarked to be followed on January 20th and January 31st by the two remaining shiploads.[2]

The four weeks had been busily spent in equipping the force. Rifles and ammunition were drawn from the Tower of London, everything else, guns, gun ammunition, uniform, boots, horses, etc., were supplied by the Lord Mayor's Committee. Waist-belts were a difficulty and 1,400 were lent by the Queen's Westminsters.

Six regular officers went with the corps, all the other officers were Volunteers.

The Volunteer Corps of that period had, of course, no service dress; units wore grey, black, red, green or blue according to their various affiliations.

Therefore the very clothing of the men had to be improvised. Much that was done was perhaps extravagant, but on this occasion the whole strength of the City of London was behind the scheme.

[1] E.C., q. 7486. [2] Ibid., q. 7390.

THE EMPLOYMENT OF THE AUXILIARY FORCES 99

In the interval between formation and embarkation a good deal of time was naturally taken up with administrative work, attesting, fitting clothing, etc. However, for the last three weeks of the period there was drill every morning at Wellington Barracks under the Adjutant, who came from the Grenadier Guards. Every recruit had to be a first-class shot, and, of course, all had had some volunteer training. But before departure from England there was no tactical training of any importance.

Fortunately for the battalion, therefore, they were sent on arrival in South Africa to duty on L. of C. at Orange River.[1] There they did six weeks' real training with the result that when they went forward to join Lord Roberts' force they were hardened and had had a certain amount of training in the country.

The battery and the mounted infantry companies went up ahead of the infantry battalion and, in fact, the complete corps never fought together. As far as the fighting abilities of the unit were concerned, it does not seem necessary to rely on the rather fulsome praise of the newspaper reports. Lord Roberts said, 'They were extraordinarily intelligent fellows . . . they were quite excellent,' and Sir Ian Hamilton said of them, 'They got better and better every day and at the end they were quite famous.'[2] The same evidence was given in varying form by several general officers who spoke before the Elgin Commission.

The terms of enlistment had been for twelve months or the duration of the war, the pay was that of the regular soldier, 1s. per day.

After the capture of Pretoria, there was a period when it was felt that the campaign was over. It was proposed to send the Guards battalions home, and the decision was made, perhaps slightly prematurely, to send the C.I.V.s back from South Africa. The Regiment returned from Pretoria to Cape Town on October 4, 1900, and reached England on October 29th.

[1] E.C., q. 7402. [2] Ibid., q. 10,313.

Their passage through London on return is a matter of history. A number of members of the C.I.V., however, transferred to other units, and remained in South Africa, several as commissioned officers.

The regiment had been in South Africa only some ten months, and Dorncop and Diamond Hill were perhaps its only engagements worthy of the name of battle, yet it is on record that the battalion marched 523 miles in 40 marching days.[1] Above everything else the experiment of the C.I.V. proved to be the birth of an idea.

The Service Companies

As has been previously mentioned the idea of the service companies may have originated with the Volunteers themselves. In the summer of 1899, Colonel Eustace Balfour, commanding the London Scottish, verbally offered a service company for the Gordon Highlanders.

Nothing further came of the suggestion till January 2, 1900, when an Army Order provided for the raising of a 'carefully selected company' of 116 all ranks to serve with each line battalion then in South Africa or about to proceed to South Africa.[2] These companies were raised through the agency of the Regimental Districts, that is to say through the Regimental Depot. They were not, on the evidence of Colonel F. S. Robb, M.V.O., the Assistant-Adjutant-General, formed by Volunteer units themselves. The basis was the district. If there were three or four volunteer battalions in the district, each was asked to provide a quota.[3] Thus there was from the first a radical departure from the suggestion of Colonel Eustace Balfour, who had envisaged his company as being, so to speak, an overseas company of the London Scottish. These volunteer companies were, in the field, integral parts of the regular battalions. Each man had to be not less than 20 nor more than 34 years of age, a first-class shot under Volunteer rules,

[1] 'The Honourable Artillery Company,' by G. Goold Walker.
[2] E.C., Report, p. 67.   [3] E.C., q. 4404.

and been returned as efficient during 1898 and 1899. Men had to be medically fit, and preference was given to unmarried.

The first lot of Volunteer service companies was easily raised, and waiting companies were formed.[1] No volunteer battalions was allowed to send less than a section, and as the men were, by the condition of recruitment active volunteers of at least two years' service, they had some experience of soldiering. Although the original Special Army Order spoke of a Volunteer company for each battalion, in fact only 66 such companies were formed, one for each English Regimental District. The Guards had no volunteer companies; and as there were no volunteers in Ireland, the only Irish battalions which received volunteer companies were those to whom were affiliated the London Irish and the Liverpool Irish.[2] In many cases, both linked battalions of a Regular Regiment were serving in South Africa. In such instances only one battalion received a service company.

From the point of view of the Adjutant-General's department at the War Office, the Service Companies were a simple solution. Though, as Colonel Robb admitted, there was no prearranged plan, 'it was a new departure',[3] the machinery was simple, the staffs of the regimental district raised the unit, and the regular battalion in the field administered it.

From the point of view of tactics in the field, there was little difficulty. With the existing eight-company organization, the addition or subtraction of another unit did not greatly affect the battalion battle order. As a matter of fact, before the war had proceeded very far, forces were largely composed of 100 men of this unit, 250 of that, and so on.

As far as can be judged, the first lot of volunteers created a good impression in the field, 'pulled their weight' in the

[1] E.C., General Bossat, q. 5320.
[2] E.C., Appendix No. 14. 5th (Irish) Volunteer Battalion The Liverpool Regiment was affiliated to the Royal Irish Regiment, and 16th Middlesex (London Irish) to the Royal Irish Rifles.   [3] E.C., q. 4409.

battalions and learnt to respect and like their Regular colleagues.

But the system was faced almost at once with certain difficulties. To begin with, there was, of course, practically no chance of promotion. Each company took out with it one captain and two subalterns. Some of these had previous Regular or Militia experience, many of the subalterns were comparatively untrained. But it was obvious that, once attached to its own regular battalion, the efficiency of the volunteer company would, generally speaking, be taken care of by the Regular unit. In the patriotic excitement of the first year, this consideration did not have much weight, but as men saw that promotion to sergeant or to commissioned rank was far more easily obtained in the Imperial Yeomanry or in the Colonial Corps, then the Volunteer Service Companies began to lose their appeal.

Especially, after January 1, 1901, when the pay of the Imperial Yeomanry had been raised to 5s. per day, the position became farcical. Conditions of enrolment in the Volunteer Service Companies continued to be strict—first-class shot, two years' efficiency in the volunteers—while the Imperial Yeomanry were being recruited, as Colonel Vincent remarked, 'from the street'. It is little wonder that a large number of active volunteers went into the Yeomanry and not into the Service Companies.[1] The Queen's Westminsters sent 160 men into Imperial Yeomanry Companies.[2]

Before, however, considering final figures it is necessary to refer to one or two other Volunteer units of interest.

Sections of one officer and 25 other ranks were raised from Volunteer Engineer Corps (fortress) and sent out to South Africa for general engineering duties.[3] Later, detachments of Volunteer Electrical Engineers and Volunteer Medical Staff

[1] For statistics as to proportion of Volunteers in 2nd Contingent of Imperial Yeomanry, see p. 116.
[2] E.C., q. 5564.
[3] Special Army Order of January 13, 1900, republished as Army Order 30A of February 1900.

THE EMPLOYMENT OF THE AUXILIARY FORCES 103

Corps Bearer Companies were sent out while, towards the end of the war, Volunteer Cyclist Corps were formed.[1]

The competition of the Imperial Yeomanry has already been mentioned. During 1900 this was not too severe, for the first contingent of Imperial Yeomanry was paid at ordinary rates. In the year 1901 the second series of Service Companies was called for and the response showed the effect of the decline in war excitement and the competition of the 5s. per day of the Imperial Yeomanry. By 1902, when it was clear that Volunteer Companies' work in the field would solely consist of block-house duties, the response was practically negligible, a call for 10,500 men only produced 2,413.

The final figures for the City Imperial Volunteers and the Volunteer Companies were 589 officers and 19,207 other ranks[2] and of this total 342 officers and 10,787 other ranks, in other words considerably more than half, had landed in South Africa by August 1, 1900. That is to say, by far the largest proportion of this category of volunteers enrolled in the first seven months of the year 1900.

With the exception of the few civilians in the City Imperial Volunteers, who have been previously mentioned, every officer and man in the above total was a genuine product of the pre-war volunteer organization.

Before passing from the volunteer contingents, it is necessary to mention the volunteer camps of 1900 and 1901. Although not primarily concerned with the reinforcement of the army in South Africa, they were the direct outcome of the shortage of troops for home defence. Debates in the House showed very clearly the anxiety of members in respect of the lack of formed troops in England, and efforts were made to meet this emergency by the holding of volunteer training camps. It was explained in Part I of this work that training camps for the volunteers, in the sense that they are now known in

[1] Army Orders Nos. 30B of February 1900, 58 of March 1900, 66 of March 1901, 92 of April 1901.
[2] E.C., p. 65.

the Territorial Army, barely existed before 1900. The Easter field day at Brighton or elsewhere was the sole occasion on which members of the battalion took the field together, and even on these occasions camping was seldom resorted to. The Volunteer Rifle Corps billeted, for the most part, in schools and similar empty buildings. Composite battalions were formed which camped at Aldershot and similar places in the summer, but these were purely provisional and extemporized organizations. In 1900, for the first time, volunteer units were sent to camp as self-contained organizations, and for the first time the men were paid. These war-time camps were a very important landmark in the history of the auxiliary forces. For one thing, tactical training received a very notable stimulus. 'As regards the work done in this war camp, it was as unlike one of our old battalion camps as anything could be. Not on one single day was anything done of the parade type.' Such was the comment of Brigadier-General J. H. A. Macdonald, C.B.,[1] the veteran Volunteer commanding the Fourth Volunteer Infantry Brigade.

The histories of nearly all Volunteer Battalions and their descendants of the Territorial Army bear witness to the revival of interest in training given by these 1900 camps.

THE IMPERIAL YEOMANRY

Like the City Imperial Volunteers, the Imperial Yeomanry developed under the stress of the emergency of the 'Black Week'.[2]

It will be remembered that on the morrow of Colenso General Buller sent his telegram No. 91 (cipher) wherein he asked, 'Would it be possible for you to raise 8,000 irregulars in England, organized not in regiments but in companies of

---

[1] 'Fifty Years of It', p. 488.
[2] 'The thing became intolerable. It was impossible to go on doing the ordinary things of life. Something had to be done, new men and new measures must be devised.'—'Trooper 8008 I.Y.', Hon. Sidney Peel.

100 each. They should be equipped as mounted infantry, be able to shoot as well as possible and ride decently, I would amalgamate them with colonials.'[1]

There were two significant phrases in the cable which were to have an effect on the raising of the Imperial Yeomanry. The first was the use of the word 'irregular', the second was General Buller's suggestion that they should be equipped as mounted infantry. The Yeomanry in 1899 were dressed, trained and equipped as cavalry. They prided themselves on their cavalry characteristics, and in their drill and their training emphasized to an extreme degree the shock tactics which were then supposed to be the characteristics of the mounted arm. Their weapons were sword and carbine, with the addition, in some Yeomanry Regiments, of the lance.

The Elgin Commission, in its official report suggests that the War Office decision to entrust the formation of the Imperial Yeomanry to a separate Committee was partly dictated by the feeling that it was only reasonable that the responsibility for this new experiment should be undertaken by those who had been urging the employment of auxiliary cavalry units. It is more probable, however, that the chief reason for this delegation of duty was the fact that the War Office in December 1899 was thoroughly overworked. Lord Lansdowne's evidence on this subject is of importance. 'I rather jumped at the proposal', he said, 'because in the first place our hands were very full at the time and also because I was being constantly told that the War Office methods were so involved in red tape that nothing could ever be got through.'[2]

Be that as it may, the actual procedure was as follows. On December 24, 1899, War Office instructions were communicated to the press nominating an Imperial Yeomanry Committee consisting of:

Honorary Colonel A. G. Lucas, Loyal Suffolk Hussars.
Honorary Lt.-Col. E. W. Beckett, Yorkshire Hussars.

[1] E.C., p. 624, Appendix J.   [2] E.C., q. 21546.

Honorary Colonel Viscount Valentia, Oxfordshire Yeomanry.
Colonel T. A. St. Quintin, retired pay.
Honorary Colonel The Earl of Lonsdale, Westmorland and Cumberland Yeomanry.
Captain the Hon. W. L. Bagot, Reserve of Officers.
Colonel the Right Hon. Lord Harris, G.C.S.I., G.C.I.E., Royal East Kent Yeomanry.

These officers were authorized to take all the necessary steps for the raising of the first contingent Imperial Yeomanry. The instructions thus issued on Christmas Eve were regularized by a Royal Warrant, Army Order 1, of January 1900.[1]

The Government provided arms and a capitation grant of £25 per head. The Government also paid for the horses at the rate of £40 each. The whole responsibility of expending the capitation grant for the clothing, equipment, and saddlery of the contingent fell on the Imperial Yeomanry Committee. The Government capitation grant was supplemented by special funds which were raised both by the Central Committee and also by various County Associations. 'The first contingent Imperial Yeomanry raised at a time when the War Office were able to give little or no help beyond the grant of money for each man enlisted was, thanks to the large funds subscribed by the public, sent out to South Africa equipped in a far superior manner to the Regular Army.'[2] Many regiments had machine-guns and light carts supplied from these private funds while the jackets, hats and breeches were of superior material. On the other hand, Yeomanry stores of clothing were not replenished from England, and after some months of campaigning most of the Yeomanry were wearing ordinary Government clothing supplied by the Army Clothing Department. This duplicate system of clothing supply led to difficulties, but a much more serious defect was the separate remount department organized by the Imperial Yeomanry.

[1] E.C., Appendix, p. 148.
[2] Evidence of Major Wyndham C. Knight, C.S.I., D.S.O., late Chief Staff Officer, Imperial Yeomanry, E.C., Appendix D, p. 517.

This latter system worked, in fact, so very badly that the separate Yeomanry remount office was abolished early in the campaign.[1]

It will be observed that practically all the officers of the Imperial Yeomanry Committee were themselves members of the Home Yeomanry Force. It is probable that both the War Office and the Committee thought that the larger proportion of the new force would come from the ranks of Yeomanry Regiments. Yet, for reasons already suggested, this was not the case. A very small proportion of the total of the Imperial Yeomanry were recruits from existing county Yeomanry regiments. A larger proportion came from volunteers and much the greater percentage came from the civilian population of these islands. Compared with the volunteer service companies, the conditions of enlistment were not strict. Recruits were supposed to be able to shoot and ride, but no fixed standards were laid down, and, in consequence, the decision as to what 'ability to shoot and ride' meant was usually left to the officers and even to the Sergeant-Majors of the various companies. The mounted infantry character of the new force was emphasized from the first. They were raised as companies and battalions, not as squadrons and regiments. The horsemen were armed with rifle and bayonet and it must be remembered that the Lee-Enfield rifle of the period was a very long weapon not very convenient for a mounted man.

Three contingents of Imperial Yeomanry were sent out to South Africa, and owing to the different methods employed in the raising of these contingents it is important to differentiate. The first contingent was that raised by the Imperial Yeomanry Committee in the early spring of the year 1900.

It was composed, for the most part, of men of good character who came in as volunteers at a critical period of the war. Quite a number of them could ride, though their knowledge of horsemanship and the grooming and care of

[1] Evidence of Major Wyndham C. Knight, C.S.I., D.S.O., late Chief Staff Officer, Imperial Yeomanry, E.C., Appendix D, p. 517.

horses was not good. Quite a number of them, once again, could shoot in the sense understood by the English countryside, that is to say, they could shoot with the ordinary 12-bore shot-gun or with a rook rifle, but their knowledge of a service rifle and service ranges was not good. The officers and N.C.O.s were, to a certain extent recruited from Yeomanry Regiments and were not always very good.[1] Recruiting was carried out through local Committees. Setting aside, however, all the defects necessarily inherent in an improvised force, the first contingent of Imperial Yeomanry consisted, for the most part, of a good type of man who only required training to make him a first-class soldier. The faults as they showed themselves were, first, that insufficient training had been given before the force left England. The result was that a good many companies went into the field in an unprepared state and suffered sickness or casualties which might have been avoided by better preliminary training. Again, owing to the somewhat careless nature of the system of enlistment, companies took all the way to South Africa and, in some cases, up country, men who were obviously unsuitable. A few bad cases of this description had unnecessarily severe reflection upon the force as a whole. Although battalions were raised, it was very seldom that the Imperial Yeomanry were used in larger units than a company and these companies had to develop an esprit de corps of their own.[2]

While recruiting for the first contingent of the Imperial Yeomanry was proceeding extremely satisfactorily and men were coming forward readily, the War Office was urged to continue an enrolment of men even though the required numbers for the first contingent had been attained. Unfortunately this permission was refused and recruiting was shut down.

---

[1] In few cases were squadrons entirely officered by Yeomanry, and in some cases there were under 50 per cent Yeomanry officers.—Lieutenant-Colonel G. Kemp at the R.U.S.I., 'Journal', 1903, p. 865.

[2] Evidence of Colonel Viscount Valentia, E.C., q. 7015.

As late as December 19, 1900, Colonel A. G. Lucas, writing from the Imperial Yeomanry Office to the Under-Secretary of State for War, was requesting permission to raise more men as drafts to the existing Imperial Yeomanry regiments in South Africa. The only reply then received was one dated December 28, 1900, which said, 'As, however, steps are being taken to enrol a large number of men for service in South African Constabulary, Mr. Brodrick is of the opinion that it it not desirable to recommence recruiting for the Imperial Yeomanry.'

Before considering the raising of the second contingent, it is necessary to point out that the men of the first contingent had been enlisted for twelve months, and there is no doubt that for many of them a period of service longer than twelve months would have meant great financial hardship. While some of the Imperial Yeomen were men in search of a living, excitement or contemplating, in any case, emigration, there were a number of men who, from genuine patriotism, had given up civilian occupations or had run the risk of leaving their firms or their businesses for a certain period. After the capture of Pretoria it could no longer be claimed that the existence of the country was at stake and to have demanded the continuance of the services of these Yeomanry volunteers would have meant the infliction of unnecessary and inadvisable hardship.

To recapitulate the history of the first contingent; the initial movement was taken when, on December 19th, the first conference was held at the War Office. The original interim Committee consisted of Lord Chesham, Lord Valentia, Mr. Walter Long and Colonel Lucas, but on January 4th the full Imperial Yeomanry Committee was constituted and took complete charge. Recruiting had already begun and Imperial Yeomanry commenced to go overseas in January. The first transport, s.s. 'Cavour', left on January 27th, the last transport, s.s. 'Canada', sailed on April 14th. With the departure of the 'Canada', a total of 550 officers and 10,571 other ranks had been dispatched overseas to form the first contingent of Imperial Yeomanry.[1]

On May 25, 1900, the Imperial Yeomanry Committee was dissolved. Lord Chesham and Viscount Valentia went to South Africa and Colonel Lucas alone remained at the Headquarters of the Imperial Yeomanry at home. Once again reference must be made to the general impression on the nation's mind caused by the events of the summer and early autumn of 1900. After the disasters of December 1899 came the slow and triumphant advance through the Orange Free State and the Transvaal. On June 5th Pretoria was captured, and this was followed by the flight of President Kruger and the annexation of the Transvaal on September 1, 1900. Mention has already been made of the return to England in the autumn of 1900 of the City Imperial Volunteers.

There is, therefore, reasonable excuse to be made for the failure of the War Office to maintain an adequate supply of drafts to the first contingent of the Imperial Yeomanry. Nevertheless, subsequent events were to show how unfortunate was the failure to maintain a steady flow of new men to the existing units of the first contingent. In his most careful Précis of Evidence before the Elgin Commission, Major Wyndham C. Knight said, 'There should never have been any second and third contingents'.[2] And reading between the lines it is obvious that the method eventually adopted as an emergency measure in January 1901 was expensive and unsatisfactory. With regard to the conditions of service of the first contingent, it is clear that the Elgin Commission themselves were not able to make up their own minds as to why the men of the first contingent came home. Their original engagement was for one year or the duration of the war, should the war last longer than a year.[3]

[1] E.C., Evidence of Colonel Lucas, pp. 272 et seq.
[2] E.C., Appendix, p. 520.
[3] Lieutenant-Colonel G. Kemp, speaking at the R.U.S.I. in 1903, said that the terms of service were understood by the majority of the men to be 'one year, the conclusion of the war, whichever came first'.—'R.U.S.I. Journal', 1903, p. 865.

THE EMPLOYMENT OF THE AUXILIARY FORCES 111

And, therefore, the Government would have been within its strict rights if it had decided to retain the services of these men beyond twelve months. In fact, however, it is clear that this would have involved a great deal of hardship upon men of the true yeoman class who could not stand being away from their business for long. General Brabazon complained, in his evidence, that as early as June or July, that is to say after the capture of Pretoria, some of the Yeomanry officers were applying for leave to go home on private business.[1] There is no doubt that the Yeomanry were influenced by the terms of service of the Colonial and particularly of the South African Corps. Many of these were enrolled for periods as short as six months and these 'Mounted Rifles' and suchlike were continually terminating their service with one Corps, going home to settle private business, and then joining another Corps. The upshot of all this was that in the spring of 1901 the formation of a second contingent was looked upon as providing in some respect a relief force for the first contingent. A number of Imperial Yeomen who went out in 1900 remained on. Even so, the fact that they were in a minority in the reconstituted Imperial Yeomanry proved a disadvantage, and there were certain difficulties because some of this first contingent who were seasoned men with junior non-commissioned or junior commissioned ranks found it difficult to fit in with newcomers from the second contingent who had been promoted in England. A steady system of drafts would have avoided this difficulty.

On April 29th, the first large shipload of returned Yeomen from the first contingent sailed, and in May 1901, a general Army Order in South Africa authorized the return from active service of all Yeomen of the first contingent who wished to take their discharge.[2]

The total casualties of the first contingent were 3,093 (out of 10,000). Of these

[1] E.C., q. 6855.   [2] E.C., p. 526, para. 3.

112   THE DEVELOPMENT OF THE BRITISH ARMY

    1,397 were invalided home
    216 were killed in action
    330 died of disease
    606 were taken prisoner (mostly at Lindley).[1]

The percentage of those killed in action was, it will be noticed, only just over 2 per cent.

It will be remembered that as late as December, Colonel Lucas had been advised by the War Office that no further drafts of Imperial Yeomanry were required. Once again a rapid change of plan was to take place with resultant improvisation and loss of efficiency.

THE SECOND CONTINGENT

With the opening of the New Year, it became clear in South Africa that the war was not over and that the resistance offered by De Wet and Botha would involve the use of considerable forces for some time. In the early days of January, therefore, Lord Kitchener, Lord Roberts' successor as Commander-in-Chief in South Africa, decided to raise a field force of 35,000 mounted men. Some of these were to be raised on the spot, others were to be obtained from home. On January 14, 1901, the War Office called for more Yeomanry and more Volunteers and on the next day, January 15th, the Commander-in-Chief (who was then Lord Roberts) 'decided that Lieutenant-General Sir A. R. Badcock,[2] K.C.B., C.S.I., and Colonel T. Deane, C.B., should be appointed to prepare a scheme with Colonel A. B. Lucas, the Deputy Adjutant-General, and to advise on the measures necessary for carrying out the organization'. So far, it might have been assumed that this small Committee were to perform for the second contingent the same duties as were performed by the original Imperial Yeomanry Committee. One of the recommendations made by this small group of three was that the men they were now called upon to raise should have two to three months' training on this side

[1] E.C., q. 6568.   [2] E.C., Evidence of Colonel Lucas, qq. 6529 et seq.

THE EMPLOYMENT OF THE AUXILIARY FORCES

before they went overseas. On the following day, however, a telegram from Lord Kitchener to the Secretary of State for War altered the complexion of the proposals. Therein he wrote,

'May I suggest that all Yeomanry drafts should be directly after enrolment shipped to Durban so that men should have preliminary training here instead of in England, they should all bring saddlery with equipment complete.'[1]

At that time Lord Chesham was himself in South Africa, and from his statement[2] it does not appear that Lord Kitchener anticipated that men would be sent out to South Africa who were literally unable to maintain their seat upon a horse.

The effect on the Home Committee of Lord Kitchener's cable was, however, that they considered themselves to be turned into a recruiting organization pure and simple.

The means available were, of course, very different; in place of a powerful Committee with a great deal of influence in the country, there was now merely a small departmental Headquarters staff. Recruiting would have to be done in a very much more centralized way and the pressure thrown upon Colonel Lucas particularly was so severe that it is quite obvious why there was a certain breakdown in organization.

One very important alteration had been made, that of the rate of pay. The first contingent of Imperial Yeomanry, as has been said, were raised at Cavalry rates of pay. As they were, for the most part, men who were impelled by patriotic motives or by the love of adventure, rate of pay was not, in the first instance, a very serious question. On arrival in South Africa, however, they found that the Colonial contingents, whom they considered to be their equals as fighting troops, were being paid at the rate of 5s. a day. After the capture of Pretoria had changed the general aspect of the war, such a differentiation began to cause some grumbling. It was represented that it would not be possible to raise a new contingent or to induce men of the first contingent to stay on unless the

[1] E.C., p. 72 footnote.   [2] E.C., q. 6744.

I

rates of pay were raised to the level of those enjoyed by the Colonial forces. Therefore, the Special Army Order dated January 17, 1901, which authorized the formation of the second contingent of Imperial Yeomanry, increased the rate of pay of the private soldier to 5s. per day, and a Second Army Order, dated February 19th, made this applicable to all Imperial Yeomen.

As has been said, the second contingent was not to be based in the same way as the first, upon the county Yeomanry centres. The Special Army Order above quoted—which in the first instance only envisaged a force of 5,000 men—mentioned four special corps which were to be raised as battalions, the Sharpshooters, Paget's Horse, the Roughriders and the Duke of Cambridge's Own. For the rest, a Yeomanry centre was established at Aldershot with another centre at the Curragh, and all recruits attested at local recruiting offices, whether through Yeomanry regiments or special agencies, were sent direct to Aldershot. The result was, therefore, that there shortly began to arrive at Aldershot small parties of men without officers, often without N.C.O.s, enrolled for various county Imperial Yeomanry corps. A large number of small details thus collected at Aldershot. There the men were equipped, and thence they were sent forward, as transport became available, to South Africa. Many witnesses before the Elgin Commission spoke of the unsatisfactory nature of this arrangement. Men went forward knowing little or nothing of the officers under whom they were to serve, small parties of various corps were mixed up in the same troopship, and commanding officers in South Africa had little idea of what drafts they would receive. A large Yeomanry base depot was opened at Elandsfontein where, theoretically, this confusion was to be sorted out.

The Special Army Order authorizing the second contingent laid down the physical standards required, and in paragraph 5(c) stipulated that the recruit was to be 'a good rider and a marksman according to Yeomanry standard'. The method of enlistment adopted, and the haste, makes it quite clear that this riding and shooting test was only perfunctorily carried out in many cases. In fact, 17,245 men were got together in a very short time, and most of them were sent out within six weeks of the original issue of instructions. Included in that number were about 395 officers. For these positions as officers, something over 3,000 persons applied and about 1,500 were actually interviewed.[1]

There was, during 1901 and later, a good deal of newspaper discussion disparaging the second contingent, and certain letters to the papers commented extremely adversely on their capabilities in the field. To view the matter in proper perspective, it is necessary to consider the extreme difficulties under which Colonel Lucas and his small Committee laboured. A very great number of both officers and men proved inefficient in South Africa and had to be weeded out. Witnesses before the Elgin Commission did not appear to agree as to whether the number of such rejections amounted to 100 officers and 1,000 men or 42 officers and 700 men. It is probably perfectly true that a large number of officers were not sent home but were employed on very unimportant duties in South Africa and were not sent up to the field. Particularly, among the officers there were one or two really bad cases which were emphasized in the newspapers and did a great deal of harm. Taking the average of informed criticism, it appears that the stamp of man recruited for the second contingent was on a higher level of physique and intelligence than the general run of recruits for the Regular Army. The glamour of patriotism was not burning as brightly as in 1900, but 5s. a day and some excitement were quite a good attraction for a reasonably high standard of artisan. In fact, it might be said, that on the 5s. basis the army was for the first time competing in the labour market of the country as an attractive proposition. It was the lack of organization and the presence of an undoubted percentage of bad characters which gave an

[1] Evidence of Colonel T. Deane, C.B., E.C., q. 6675.

unfortunate start to the second contingent. One of the London units, the Duke of Cambridge's Own, which raised a large total, 2,737[1] men, came under suspicion of having enlisted very many who had been rejected by the other London Imperial Volunteer corps.

The figures given for the Sharpshooters are extremely interesting. Lieutenant-Colonel A. Weston Jarvis, who commanded the regiment, had served in the early days of the war with General Plumer. On the disbandment of Plumer's force, he returned home for a few weeks in Christmas time, 1900, and was offered the command of one of the new Imperial Yeomanry Regiments. This battalion, the 21st, afterwards known as Sharpshooters, was one of the special corps provided for by the Army Order of January 17th. It was formed by a Committee under the Presidency of Lord Dunraven. There were 3,762 applicants for enlistment, of these 1,205 were selected.

Of the 1,205   13 were old Yeomen,
               607 were volunteers (i.e. members of
                   volunteer Rifle Corps),
               188 were ex-Regulars,
               397 were civilians.

Of the 2,557 applicants who were rejected, Colonel Jarvis estimated that some 2,000 were immediately enlisted in other corps. In spite of the fact that these men had been put through a somewhat severe test and were enlisting in what was obviously intended to be a crack corps, they did not go out as a complete unit. All the men were sent down to Aldershot to be equipped, as soon as 110 men were ready they were shipped overseas, and it is quite obvious that it was only by reason of his privileged position and his very hard struggles that Colonel Jarvis was able to intercept all his own drafts at Elandsfontein and reconstruct his regiment in the field at

[1] E.C., q. 6803.

Standerton. There he did his regimental training—two drills.[1]

Probably the officers were the weakest part of the second contingent. In the first contingent, the officers, whether well or indifferently trained, had been, on the whole, men of good social standing, who had intelligence and education and picked up their work in the field very quickly. In the case of the second contingent, except where officering was done by decentralized Committees like Lord Dunraven's all appointments were made, as has been said, by the central Yeomanry Headquarters. The figures of interviews have already been given. It is difficult to attach any blame to the Committee, having in view the extremely heavy task set them. It appears, however, that there was neither time nor staff available to take up the references of a large number of men who obtained commissions. Some of these were men who had served in the ranks of the first contingent but had been invalided home; they were often very inferior in calibre to the men still serving in the ranks in South Africa.

In fact, the whole lesson of the second contingent is the story of the impossibility of improvisation of officers.

After the second great wave of Yeomanry had been sent out to South Africa, once again the War Office decided that no drafts should be sent. Once again, this decision had to be rescinded.

THE THIRD CONTINGENT

At the end of 1901, a Special Army Order dated December 19th authorized the raising, on and after January 1st, of the third contingent of Imperial Yeomanry. In this case, learning by experience, the War Office decided that special training camps should be instituted, one at Aldershot, one at Edinburgh and one at the Curragh, at which at least two months' training should be given. In fact, in many cases these Yeomanry had as much as three months' training. As a result, undesirable men were quickly eliminated. Moreover, the

[1] E.C., Evidence Lieutenant-Colonel A. Weston Jarvis, C.M.G., M.V.O.

medical standard was raised and was made the same as that which obtained for the Regular Army. Although recruits were apparently indifferent shots and, for the most part, indifferent riders when they came into the depot, they were of good physique and intelligence. A force of 7,221 men was thus raised. As the war was over before any of the third contingent took the field, it is not possible to give any comparative comment upon their fighting capabilities.

In all, a total of 34,124 men of all ranks in the Imperial Yeomanry were dispatched to South Africa between the outbreak of war and May 31, 1902.

PART III

A PERIOD OF ATTEMPTED REFORMS
1900–1905

CHAPTER 7

MR. BRODRICK AS SECRETARY OF STATE FOR WAR

THE preceding chapters have dealt with the actualities of the military development for the campaign. It is now necessary to consider the repercussions in this country, in Parliament, at the War Office, and among the people of the land.

The first reaction of the British public to the War in South Africa might be described as one of astonishment and indignation. Mr. J. A. Spender has said in his 'A Short History of Our Own Times' that 'When the New Year came it was doubtful whether the British Public were angrier with the Boers for having defied the power of Great Britain, or with the Government which had landed itself and the country in such a position'.[1]

The immediate necessities were, obviously, the rapid reinforcement of the army in South Africa and the dispatch of the requisite material and men. At an early date, however, discussion, both in the House of Commons and elsewhere, had in view permanent improvements which would obviate for the future such disagreeable surprises.

On February 15, 1900, shortly after the House of Commons reassembled, Army Supplementary Estimates were introduced. It was proposed to introduce legislation allowing the Volunteers to go to camp for a month. There were not wanting critics who pointed out the great difficulty which such a regulation would impose upon Volunteers who were business men. In this debate, Lieutenant-Colonel Pryce-Jones said:[2] 'It is proposed to invite the Volunteers to go to camp for a month;

[1] 'A Short History of Our Own Times', p. 44.
[2] A.D., 1900, p. 1472.

I do not like that invitation at all, because I am satisfied that the Volunteer Force throughout the country will not be able to agree to it. . . . At the present time, the Volunteers are expected to go to camp for one week in the year.' Later in the Debate, Mr. Broadhurst said: 'If the Government persist in a month's camp for the Volunteers in each year, I rather fancy they will find that they will kill the Volunteer system altogether'. Mr. Wyndham, in reply to these remarks, had to point out that the period of a month was the maximum period suggested, and that it was necessary to put it in the Estimates in order to secure the necessary power to legalize the payment of Volunteers for such a long period. 'Some units', he said, 'had asked for a month.' The next day, speaking on the same debate, Mr. Campbell-Bannerman made the shrewd suggestion that better arrangements for training the Militia and Volunteers were being made in stress of war, but they were also 'a test of what these forces may be prepared to undergo in quieter times'.[1]

Following this debate, there was a meeting at the Royal United Service Institution, held on February 22, 1900, when Colonel T. Sturmy Cave of the 1st Volunteer Battalion of the Hampshire Regiment spoke on the Volunteers.[2] The lecture is interesting because Colonel Sturmy Cave argued in favour of creating a Volunteer Mobile Force. As he rightly said: 'At the present moment we have over 400,000 troops at home, as well as the Field Force in South Africa and the garrisons in India, Egypt, and elsewhere. Yet we have nothing resembling a Field Force for home defence. Regulars, Militia, Yeomanry and Volunteers alike lack the organization which

---

[1] Later in the same debate Mr. Campbell-Bannerman made a notable contribution when he said: 'Conscription with the ballot seems to me to be nothing but a combination of the press-gang and the roulette wheel, neither a very dignified nor effective way of defending the country.'

[2] 'R.U.S.I. Journal', xliv, January-June, p. 395.
Since the above was written, Colonel Sir T. Sturmy Cave, K.C.B., C.B.E., V.D., T.D., has died on April 15, 1936, aged ninety years. 'The Times' of April 20, 1936, contains an appreciation of this zealous and capable Volunteer.

constitutes any proficient army. . . . No military force can be efficient unless it is organized into a Field Army.' The lecturer reminded his audience that in the House of Commons a week previously hopes had been expressed that it might be possible to form an Army Corps of Auxiliary Forces, but that Mr. Wyndham had, in his reply, considered such a proposal not practical at the moment. The pre-war conception was that volunteer battalions would have allotted places in the passive defence of London. Sturmy Cave was arguing in favour of creating volunteer mobile forces which would incorporate newly raised volunteer artillery, Army Service Corps and Bearer Companies. He suggested, for the Annual Training, a fortnight, with a possible minimum of one week. The whole lecture was an interesting prevision of the Haldane Scheme.[1]

On March 12th, Mr. Wyndham introduced in the House of Commons the Army Estimates, and, on that occasion, said: 'We ought to organize in the course of the spring and summer, in addition to the Auxiliary Forces, who, as I have already pointed out, would keep certain positions round London, a trained, organized and mobile force of 3 Army Corps and 3 Cavalry Brigades.'[2] The Estimates provided for permanent additions to the Regular Army,—7 Batteries of Royal Horse Artillery and 36 Batteries of Royal Field Artillery.—'So as to provide the Artillery for 2 more Army Corps and 2 more Cavalry Brigades'. It was also proposed to raise 12 new line battalions and these would become the 3rd and 4th battalions to certain existing Regiments. A further permanent addition to the strength of the Army would be a rearmament of the whole of the volunteer artillery, part with semi-mobile 4·7-inch guns, part with 15-pounder field guns. The Army Estimates also contained certain temporary measures. Four provisional

[1] In the same lecture Colonel H. A. A. Stewart said: 'The pity, I think, is that on the Headquarters Staff of the Army at the War Office, the Militia, Yeomanry and Volunteers, all three, are not represented by a deputy-Adjutant General from their own Forces.'—'R.U.S.I. Journal', 1900, p. 401.
[2] A.D., March 12, 1900.

Cavalry Regiments were to be formed from men of the Reserve Squadrons, and Royal Reserve Battalions were to be raised. The whole of the Militia was to be embodied in the spring, and Yeomanry and Volunteers would receive special training in camp. The Indian Army would be drawn upon to replace certain British battalions, two Indian Infantry Regiments being sent to Mauritius and one each to Ceylon and Singapore. The debate, which was long, was, perhaps, notable for a very strong speech by Arnold-Forster against the system of recruiting for the Regular Army, in which he pointed out that 'more men deserted or were discharged than ever went to the Reserve'.

By the summer of the year 1900, the British public, in Parliament and the press, was beginning to realize that the lessons of the South African War might be grouped into two main divisions. In the first case, there were manifest certain deficiencies in the training and equipment of the British Regular Army. The lack of a trained general staff was becoming obvious. Speaking in general terms, however, it is perhaps fair to say that the criticism in this category was more severe in the early days of 1900 than was entirely justified by the event. As the months went on, fair-minded observers began to realize that the conditions of warfare in South Africa were difficult, and that smokeless powder and high velocity rifle fire had given very great powers to the defensive.

The second realization concerned the general relations of Great Britain with the Continent of Europe. 'The effects of the South African War on Great Britain's relations to her neighbours in Europe proved in the long run to be among the most serious and lasting of its results.'[1] What was alarming to many military students was the fact that the entire Regular Army had been sent to South Africa, and that the country had no Reserve military force in an organized state to deal with any other war which might break out. On July 17th, in the House of Lords, the Duke of Bedford gave notice of

[1] 'A Short History of our Own Times', J. A. Spender, p. 51.

a motion to ask 'Whether Her Majesty's Government intend to inquire into the deficiencies of our military system and to submit the result to Parliament with a view to the reconstruction of the War Office and the reorganization of the Army'.[1] In reply to this, Lord Lansdowne admitted the necessity of some form of enquiry but suggested that there would be great difficulty in getting the necessary evidence while the war was still on.

Meanwhile, as a contribution to the reorganization of the Volunteers, Mr. Wyndham introduced in the House of Commons on July 18th the Volunteer Act, 1900,[2] which would allow Volunteers to go overseas in that capacity should they so desire, and would remove the necessity of their temporary enlistment into the Regular Army.

Though as the summer of 1900 went by the situation in South Africa improved, there were those in the country who were gravely perturbed at the very serious repercussions on the Continent of Europe caused by our embarrassment in the war with the Dutch Republics.[3]

In a debate in the House of Lords on July 27, 1900, Earl Rosebery and Earl Wemyss painted a gloomy picture of our weakness as compared with other continental nations. The former quoted an anonymous military attaché who advised England to be strong in November of that year, and com-

---

[1] A.D., 1900, p. 1. [2] Ibid., p. 173 (63 and 64 Vic., cap. 39).
[3] The situation in the summer of 1900 was further complicated by the necessity of sending a contingent to join the international force destined for the relief of the Pekin legations. The British detachment sent from India was entirely native with the exception of B Battery, R.H.A., and the 12th Battery, R.F.A. In the first case, two Brigades were sent with Divisional troops and line of communication troops. Later, a third Brigade was sent, and, finally, a fourth Brigade of Imperial Service troops. In all, in addition to the artillery above quoted, there were three Regiments of native cavalry, sixteen battalions of native infantry and services.

In this connection it is interesting to note that the German contingent consisted of four specially created East Asiatic infantry regiments which were made up by Volunteers from the ordinary conscripts of the Guard, Fusilier Regiments, or the Foot Guards.—'R.U.S.I. Journal', 1900, pp. 943 and 1079.

mented upon somewhat injudicious remarks made by General Mercier, the French Minister of War. Lord Lansdowne's apologia did not entirely satisfy the House.[1]

The Secretary of State for War's position was not strong and his continuance in office was probably an embarrassment to the Government. Lord Salisbury, the Prime Minister, influenced by a strong sense of loyalty, had for some time resisted suggestions that he should get rid of his War Minister.

The general situation was now, however, changing fast, and political developments were making easier an alteration in the control of the army. On June 5, 1900, Lord Roberts had entered Pretoria, and the disasters of the end of 1899 had to many minds been redeemed by the success of Paardeberg and the advance, first on Bloemfontein, and then on Pretoria. The success had been rapid and spectacular. The two Boer Republics had been annexed. President Kruger was a refugee in Holland. The two capitals were in British hands. The burghers had no War Office, no munition factories or any other means of carrying out an organized resistance. Therefore, with Lord Roberts' departure from South Africa, in the autumn of 1900, it was generally believed that the war was coming to an end.

In the political sphere, the South African War had very serious effects on the fortunes of the Liberal Party. In the debates at the close of 1899 and the spring of 1900, Liberalism had been violently divided into three sections. The Liberal Imperialists, Rosebery, Asquith and Haldane, however critical they may have been of the Government handling of matters up to the Kruger Ultimatum, were prepared, after that date, to support the Government. Violently opposed to this group were the pro-Boer Party led by Mr. Lloyd George. Between these extremes, the leader of the opposition, Mr. Campbell-Bannerman, gathered round him a central party willing to support the Government up to a point but somewhat pro-Boer in its attitude. Profiting by this confusion in the opposition ranks, Government dissolved Parliament on Septem-

[1] A.D., July 27, 1900.

ber 25, 1900, on the grounds that the war was practically over, and that it would require the authority of the country to deal with the problems of post-war reconstruction. The result of the election was favourable to the Conservative Party and accentuated for the time being the difficulties of the opposition. It is essential that these factors should be taken into consideration, because for many years to come army affairs were going to be the concern of Parliament, and the army was going to be influenced by political and by international considerations to a degree unknown in the quieter times of the close of the nineteenth century.

Hitherto, the function of the British Army had been determined by the words of the Stanhope Memorandum, dating from June 1, 1891.[1] This most important document, which has previously been quoted, laid down, it will be remembered, that the primary aim of the army was to find men for India, for garrisons, for fortresses and coaling stations, and for home defence. Subject to the foregoing, the policy of the Government would be 'to aim at being able' to send abroad two complete Army Corps, and the final wording of the Memorandum ran: 'But it will be distinctly understood that the probability of the employment of an Army Corps in the field in any European war is sufficiently improbable to make it the primary duty of the military authorities to organize our forces efficiently for the defence of this country.'

The years 1901–7 were to see the gradual shifting of opinion away from the concluding paragraph of the Stanhope Memorandum to the Haldane conception of an Expeditionary Force, and military opinion was to march step by step with the development of a new conception of British international relationship and the end of the Salisbury doctrine of splendid isolation.

That foreign affairs were going to be increasingly important was obvious to all, and in that importance the Prime Minister

[1] Appendix A. This memorandum was first issued to the public in 1901 as Command Paper No. 607.

found an opportunity for making the necessary change at the War Office in a manner consonant with his own high ideals of cabinet loyalty. Hitherto, Lord Salisbury had himself held the portfolio of Foreign Affairs. He now decided that the double burden had become too onerous in view of the preoccupation of external policy. Lord Lansdowne was, therefore, persuaded to leave Pall Mall for Whitehall and become the Secretary of State for Foreign Affairs.

In the House of Commons, Mr. George Wyndham, as Under-Secretary of State for War, had, from the autumn of 1899 to the summer of 1900, discharged very ably the difficult task of defending, before a critical House, Army policy for which he was not the senior responsible party. The criticisms had come not only from those sections of the opposition who were opponents of the war, the Radical members and the Nationalist members; it had also come very strongly from a group of back bench members on the Government side of the House who were powerful critics of War Office efficiency.

To succeed Lord Lansdowne, another Under-Secretary was chosen to take Ministerial rank. Mr. St. John Brodrick had previously been the Financial Secretary to the War Office from 1886 to 1892 and Under-Secretary for War, from 1895 to 1898. For two years he had served in the House as Under-Secretary for Foreign Affairs, and, therefore, when, in the autumn of 1900, he returned to the War Office as Secretary of State, he brought with him considerable experience of War Office administration.[1]

A not unimportant result of this change was that it made the House of Commons the centre of gravity for War Department debates, since for many years to come the Secretary of State for War was to be a Commoner and not a Peer.

Before the next Army Estimates, however, other important

[1] 'In the evening I had half an hour with Brodrick at the W.O. He is full of vitality, and keen to sweep out his Augean Stable. All his life his desire has been to occupy the Secretary of State's room at the W.O. It comes to very few men—in the early forties—to realize their political heart's desire.'—'Esher Journals', vol. i, p. 269. November 25, 1900.

MR. BRODRICK AS SECRETARY OF STATE FOR WAR

changes had taken place. Lord Wolseley's tour of office as Commander-in-Chief drew to its end. The Queen pressed Lord Salisbury to appoint as Wolseley's successor her son, the Duke of Connaught. She had already recommended him for the post on the retirement of the Duke of Cambridge in 1895.

Lord Salisbury demurred, holding that Lord Roberts' eminent services in South Africa entitled him to the post. The Queen gave way, and Lord Roberts was called back from South Africa to become Commander-in-Chief of the Army. He landed on January 2, 1901, was received by Her Majesty, and the next day assumed his new office. But the Queen was failing, the very emotion of the meetings with Lord Roberts —for there was a second meeting on January 12th—accentuated her weakness, and on January 22nd the Great Queen passed away.[1]

With her, men felt, passed the end of an epoch.

When, therefore, Mr. St. John Brodrick approached the problems to be considered in his Army Estimates of February 28, 1901, the world had progressed very far from the conditions under which his predecessors' estimates had been framed in the early spring of 1899. There had been given at the Military Club in Vienna, on November 30, 1900, an important lecture by Lieutenant-Field-Marshal Gustavus Ritzenhofen of the Imperial Austro-Hungarian Army, the President of the Military Supreme Court. Over 600 officers, many of them of high rank, attended. The lecture was on the South African War. Its comments were, in many cases, fair and justified, but the author did not fail to point out some of the lessons of the South African War as they appeared to the great powers of Europe.[2] 'When we speak, therefore, of the critical military condition of England, we do not refer to that of the army engaged in South Africa, but to the fact that, by this employment, England was all but denuded of troops.' His final remarks were couched in even stronger

[1] Lee, vol. i.
[2] 'R.U.S.I. Journal' vol.xlv, January–June, pp. 39 et seq.

language. 'When we contemplate the perturbations of the political world brought about, seemingly, by the imperialism of the Anglo-Saxon race; when we note that the War in South Africa revealed, as a sudden flash of lightning illuminates a dark night, the hatred of Great Britain by all but the Anglo-Saxon people, then England as a world power, supported solely by its fleet, stands out in its proper perspective.'

Nothing, during the critical autumn of 1900, stood between Britain and a hostile European combination but the British fleet and the unappeasable feud between France and Germany. 'Angry as Frenchmen might be with England nothing would induce them to join Germany in any adventure.'[1] A new actor in the drama had entered upon the stage in the year 1900, when the German Navy League utilized the anti-British feeling in Germany to support the new Navy Bill of June 12, 1900, a Bill which was regarded in Great Britain as a definite challenge to British sea power.[2]

So, in this critical year, was seen the first shadow of that naval rivalry which was to prove the great obstacle to good relations between Britain and Germany.

ARMY ESTIMATES FEBRUARY 28, 1901

THE SIX ARMY CORPS

Mr. St. John Brodrick came to the leadership of the military machine at a time when reforms were looked for. The new

[1] 'A Short History of Our Own Times', J. A. Spender, p. 53; also Fritz Hoenig, 'Die Woche', No. 1, 1901.

'So long as England has a great naval superiority the Mother Country is best protected by her fleet. This superiority diminished yearly with the French and German plans of 1900 and Russian exertions. Moreover, England is no longer able to man her fleet properly.'—Quoted in 'R.U.S.I. Journal', 1901, p. 289.

[2] This, Admiral von Tirpitz's second Navy Bill, practically doubled the naval programme of 1898.

The German sentiment in favour of a stronger navy had been stirred by the seizure by a British cruiser of the steamers 'Bundesrath', 'Herzog' and 'Marrie' on suspicion of carrying contraband of war to Delagoa Bay.—Lee, p. 757.

minister had both energy and self-confidence. Moreover, he knew that the Cabinet expected him to produce some solution of the military problem which would stave off the criticism of public and professional impatience.[1]

Yet the customary Memorandum of the Secretary of State relating to the Army Estimates 1901–2 contained little warning of changes. The Memorandum, mentioning in brief the new measures affecting army reorganization, spoke of them as being 'fully dealt with on the introduction of the Army Estimates'. Perhaps the most significant paragraph in the Memorandum was that relating to war service, where the provision of some £58,000,000 was based on the assumption that 'for the first four months of the new financial year the Field Force in South Africa will be maintained at full strength and that a gradual diminution will subsequently take place'.[2]

It was, therefore, amid considerable interest that Mr. Brodrick opened the Debate on the Army Estimates on March 8, 1901.

At an early stage in his speech he said:

'I think that the events of the last fifteen months have proved, first of all, that we must be prepared to send more than two Army Corps abroad, secondly that these Army Corps must be better organized, and thirdly that when you have provided for the forces which it is necessary to send out of the Kingdom you must have a sufficient organization at home for our own protection.'

[1] Paul Kluke, in 'Heeresaufbau und Heerespolitik Englands', says that Brodrick had 'praktisch Blankovollmacht', 'to all intents and purposes a free hand', from the Cabinet.

[2] That is that the South African war would end before August 1901. It actually ended in May 1902.

Before his departure from South Africa Lord Roberts had made a speech in Durban wherein he had confidently prophesied an early ending to the war. This speech, having regard to the importance of the speaker, added not a little to the difficulties of the Secretary of State, who had within a few days of Lord Roberts' speech to ask for another large grant for the war, and had to raise 25,000 more mounted troops without delay. In fact these troops were dispatched to South Africa within six weeks of Lord Roberts' arrival in England.—Verbal evidence, Earl of Midleton.

Such a statement represented a step forward in policy, it was a stage along the road towards an Expeditionary Force, and a later sentence in the speech elaborated the theme:

'Therefore my proposition is that besides Home Defence we ought to be ready at any moment to send abroad three Army Corps with the proper Cavalry Division, in fact a force of 120,000 men.

The proposals I have to make to the House are as follows: I propose to reorganize the Army on a new system of which the bedrock will be that the whole country will be divided into six Army Corps by districts, that each district in times of peace will have the same relative proportions to the various arms that are necessary to make up the corps, and that they will be under the commanders who will lead them in time of war.'

Mr. Brodrick then elaborated his scheme. The First Army Corps, entirely composed of Regular troops, would be stationed at Aldershot.[1] The Second Corps, would be centred on Salisbury Plain, where the War Office was 'building large barracks'. The Third Army Corps, 'almost entirely Regular', was to be in Ireland, the Fourth Corps at Colchester. With the Fourth Corps began the most important part of the new arrangement. 'We propose to employ, altogether in the last three Army Corps, sixty battalions of Volunteers and Militia which have been carefully selected . . . the Volunteer battalions will have special training, they will be invited on special terms to undertake special training liability each year.' If the Volunteer units selected for these special conditions failed to come up to the required standard, then they would lose their select status and other units would take their place.

The Fourth Army Corps would only have about half its units on a Regular basis; the Fifth Corps, with its headquarters at York, and the Sixth (Scottish) Corps, with its headquarters at Edinburgh, were to be composed almost entirely of the Auxiliary forces.

It was obvious that the full complement of the artillery

[1] It would contain one Brigade of four battalions of Guards.

of the Six Army Corps could not be found from the Regular Army. The Secretary admitted this and explained:

'We go further, we propose for the first time, to give the Militia and Volunteers, within limits, a certain number of field guns.'

The Regular Battalions allocated to the Six Army Corps could, of course, not be found while the campaign waged in South Africa. Moreover, they could not even be found from the 1899 distribution of the Regular Army. Mr. Brodrick, allowing for a post-war garrison in South Africa, had to set free from overseas garrison duty over a dozen battalions of the line in order to provide the Regular Infantry for the Six Army Corps.

Three steps were proposed. First, the wartime expedient of garrison battalions was to be continued. Eight were to be used to take the place of line battalions at certain overseas stations. These battalions, as has been explained, were composed of old soldiers. Mr. Campbell-Bannerman pertinently asked whether these men were all to have completed their reserve service before they were allowed to enlist in the garrison battalions. The reply was: 'Certainly, we do not mean to infringe on the Reserve in any way.'[1]

Five Indian battalions were to be taken into the pay of the War Office, and used to replace British battalions at certain stations.

Finally, Royal Marines were to replace Infantry of the Line as the garrisons of coaling stations. This last part of the programme, Mr. Brodrick somewhat naïvely confessed, had not yet been approved by the Admiralty. Very soon it was apparent that the Navy group in the House of Commons was certainly

[1] A.D., March 14, 1901.
'This proposal has the merit of employing old soldiers who have completed their Reserve service and assuring them attention: but, since the complete Battalions will not be relieved, their officers will practically be condemned to pass all their service in the monotony and stagnation of a fortress abroad.'—'Army and Navy Gazette,' March 16, 1901, p. 253.

not going to approve of this use of Marines.[1] However, by taking, for the moment, Admiralty approval for granted, then, said the Minister, he would be able to arrange that the distribution of the Infantry of the Line (excluding the garrison battalions) would be:

>   At Home   79
>   Abroad   77

With regard to the Militia, the proposal was to abolish the Militia Reserve. This, it will be remembered, consisted of a portion of the men of the Militia who, for the sake of an extra £1 a year, undertook the liability of General Service. These men had, in most cases, been called up in the winter of 1899 or spring of 1900, had been taken from their Militia Battalions and sent to join the Line Regiments in South Africa. 'I doubt', said Mr. Brodrick, 'whether there are many of these who will take £1 a year for such a liability again.'[2]

Instead of this, a Reserve for the Militia was to be established.[3]

The Yeomanry was to undergo considerable expansion. A Commission under the presidency of Lord Harris had recently been sitting; Colonel Lucas and six other prominent Yeomanry Officers composed it, and their decisions were by no means unanimous.[4] Based in part, however, on the Harris Committee's report, Mr. Brodrick's plans were that the force should be increased to 35,000 men. They should be dressed

---

[1] 'No reference was made to the use of Marines in coaling stations in Lord Selborne's statement on the Navy Estimates.'—Letter to 'Army and Navy Gazette' by Mr. Carlyon Bellairs, March 23, 1901, p. 285.

[2] An interesting warning in 1938 to those who tried to impose similar heavy obligations on the Territorial Army.

[3] A Committee with Lord Raglan as Chairman was appointed to consider this new reserve, but actually no steps were taken to create the force till Army Order 36 of 1903, and shortly after that it was decided to suspend enlistment except for men leaving the Royal Garrison Regiment.—'Chronology', p. 76.

[4] The composition and précis of the report of this Commission will be found in Appendix F.

in khaki, armed with rifle and bayonet, instead of the sword, should receive higher pay than in the past, but should do a longer period of training. The force was to be known as Imperial Yeomanry. Any man who brought his own horse to annual training would receive £5.

The twenty-five Volunteer battalions who were to be selected for service within the Army Corps were to go to camp for thirteen days each year and were to receive a grant of 5s. per day per man in camp.

A further change foreshadowed by the Estimates was that the British Army would have in peace-time a working dress, which would be the dress it would wear on active service.

So the speech closed with the peroration, claiming for the Cabinet that they had 'unflinchingly set their hands to the great national work of the reform of the Army, and thereby gained both for the Government and for Parliament the abiding gratitude of their followers'.

Thus was launched the scheme for Army reform which Mr. Brodrick, within four months of his appointment, and with the responsibilities of a major war still upon him, had produced for the consideration of Parliament.[1] The first reaction was not too unfavourable. The Estimates were introduced as has been said, on March 8th. The Army Debate on March 12th, disregarding the future, was almost entirely occupied with the discussion of the case of Major-General Colville. When the Debate was resumed on March 14th, Mr. Campbell-Bannerman sounded a note of warning with regard to recent history. 'But I think that if we are to be guided by what we call the lessons of the War, great caution must be used.' He pointed out the most unusual circumstances of the struggle and doubted whether similar geographical conditions

---

[1] 'He had to try to reform the administration of the Army, and primarily of the War Office, and at the same time to conduct a great war. That could not be done.'—A speech by Mr. Ritchie, quoted by Dilke, February 23, 1903, in the Estimates Debate.

would be found anywhere else in the world.[1] Other criticisms of the scheme were already forthcoming. Captain Norton, speaking in the House, said: 'These Army Corps with the exception of the one at Aldershot, will be patched-up Army Corps.' Sir William Harcourt doubted if 120,000 men would be forthcoming. Sir Charles Dilke, an advocate of the importance of sea power, pointed out the traditional role of the British Army in small expeditions and said: 'I attach more importance to the smaller portion of our Army, which is organized for the purpose of offence, than to that enormous host of men which remains at home.'

In spite, however, of these criticisms, the House of Commons received very favourably the general tenor of the proposals.

The first public reaction, also, was cordial enough. The 'Army and Navy Gazette', the next day, said:

'The long statement made by Mr. Brodrick in the House of Commons last night, will, we believe, be read with satisfaction by everyone who has the interest of the British Army at heart.'[2]

But it is to be noted that, within six weeks, the same journal had decreased its enthusiasm to the extent of writing:

'As a first instalment of reform on the part of a new ministerial hand the scheme may pass muster, but on no other ground, its defects being too obvious.'[3]

---

[1] He spoke of 'Panic schemes', and two years later explained his meaning: 'The right hon. Gentleman's hands were then presumably full with the war, and he ought to have waited until the lessons of the war, of which we have heard so much, were more fully mastered and seen in their proper perspective. That was the reason why I spoke of the scheme as having been a panic scheme.'—Mr. H. Campbell-Bannerman, House of Commons, February 24, 1903. A.D., 1903, p. 174.

He disliked the 'Army Corps'. 'Sir, the expression "Army Corps" is like the great word "Mesopotamia"—it is a blessed word. It deludes the convert and imposes on the simple.'

[2] 'Army and Navy Gazette', March 9, 1901, p. 230. Also, 'Short of conscription, Mr. Brodrick's proposals seem the most comprehensive and businesslike scheme for a working Army that has yet been offered to the Empire.'—Press criticism quoted in 'Army and Navy Gazette', March 16, 1901, p. 253.   [3] 'Army and Navy Gazette', April 13, 1901, p. 358.

MR. BRODRICK AS SECRETARY OF STATE FOR WAR

The speech of the Secretary of State had not given the detailed establishment of his Six Army Corps, and, as a matter of fact, this can best be seen from a Command Paper published in 1903.[1]

There, the establishment of the Six Army Corps were given as follows:

First Army Corps (Aldershot) and First Cavalry Brigade,
Headquarters, Aldershot

Cavalry	5 Regiments	Regular
Artillery	27 Batteries	Regular
Infantry	25 Battalions	Regular

Second Army Corps (Southern) and Second Cavalry Brigade,
Headquarters, Tidworth

Cavalry	5 Regiments	Regular
Artillery	27 Batteries	Regular
Infantry	25 Battalions	Regular

Third Army Corps (Irish) and Third Cavalry Brigade

Cavalry	5 Regiments	Regular		
Artillery	27 Batteries	24 Regular	3 Militia	
Infantry	25 Battalions	22 Regular	3 Militia	

Fourth Army Corps (Eastern) and Household Cavalry
Brigade, Headquarters, London

Cavalry	5 Regiments	4 Regular	1 Imperial Yeomanry	
Artillery	27 Batteries	18 Regular	6 Militia	3 Volunteer
Infantry	25 Battalions	8 Regular	8 Militia	9 Volunteer

Fifth Army Corps (Northern) and Fourth Cavalry Brigade,
Headquarters, York

Cavalry	5 Regiments	1 Regular	4 Imperial Yeomanry	
Artillery	27 Batteries	18 Regular	6 Militia	3 Volunteer
Infantry	25 Battalions	4 Regular	13 Militia	8 Volunteer

[1] The State of the Six Army Corps Commands, Command Paper 1413. 1903.

Sixth Army Corps (Scottish), Headquarters, Edinburgh

Cavalry	5 Regiments	Imperial Yeomanry				
Artillery	26 Batteries	17 Regular	6 Militia		3 Volunteer	
Infantry	25 Battalions	2 Regular	13 Militia		10 Volunteer	

Thus for the Six Army Corps there were required from the Regular Army:

> Cavalry   20 Regiments
> Artillery   131 Batteries
>   (17 Horse, 105 Field, 9 Heavy)
> Infantry   86 Battalions.

It is interesting to compare these figures with the establishment of the Regular Army in England at the period before the South African War. In June 1899, there were 80 Infantry Battalions stationed in England (7 Guards, 73 Line). The Brodrick scheme claimed 86 battalions. In Artillery, the increase in strength was much more marked. The 1897–8 Estimates started with a strength of 55 field batteries and planned an increase of 15 batteries over a period of years. But the total strength demanded by the completion of the 1897–8 programme was far short of the large artillery programme demanded for the Six Army Corps.

In fact, the Brodrick scheme foreshadowed a substantial and, as men shortly saw, an expensive increase in the permanent strength of that portion of the Regular Army which was maintained at home.

As concerns the Auxiliary forces, it will be seen that the total needed by the Six Army Corps was only a small proportion of the full strength of both the Militia and the Volunteers. An appendix[1] shows the distribution of the entire British Army, Regular and Auxiliary, in the Six Army Corps commands. It will be observed that there was a very great discrepancy between what was demanded of the Auxiliary Forces for the Army Corps organization and what existed over and

[1] Appendix G.

above the Army Corps. For example, in the area of the Fourth Army Corps, whose headquarters was London,[1] there existed 56 infantry battalions and 15 Imperial Yeomanry Regiments. Yet, of this large force, only 1 Imperial Yeomanry Regiment and 9 Volunteer Battalions were brought into the Field Army organization. Similarly, in the Scottish Command there were 125½ Volunteer Artillery units, either Heavy Batteries or Garrison Companies, yet only 3 Batteries of Volunteers were included in the Scottish Army Corps. It was a further weakness of the scheme that, as far as could be gathered from the Secretary's speech, no provision was made for the organization of those Auxiliary units which were not being called upon to take their place in the Army Corps. While to select 9 battalions out of 56 might suggest such a wide field of selection that those eventually chosen would be good, yet for the 47 who were not so chosen there remained very little prospect of employment or of organized training. It is true that the General Officer in Command of the Army Corps was also the General Officer of the Area, and was thus charged with the supervision of all units geographically situated within his Army Corps Area. It should, however, have been fairly obvious that the training of this Field organization, the Army Corps, would have prior claim on his time, and that, in default of any special organization for the unselected units of the Auxiliary Corps, they would fare very badly, and might, indeed, fade out of the picture.

In spite of the Secretary's reference to the use of Volunteer units as Field Artillery, in the actual scheme the only Artillery found from the Volunteers were nine Heavy Batteries armed with 4·7 guns. Even in the Eastern Command, with its headquarters in London, six Militia Field Batteries were to be raised, and the experience of the Honourable Artillery Company's Batteries in the South African War was to be no guidance for the future. It is interesting in this connection, however, to find that Volunteer officers themselves were not

[1] Colchester in the original plan.

over-sanguine of their ability to teach mounted Artillery drivers. The essence of the Heavy 4·7 Battery was, of course, that the teams were led by dismounted drivers after the fashion of a heavy Sussex timber wain, though one Volunteer Officer put forward the plea that it might be possible to drive the teams for the 4·7 guns with long reins from a box seat.[1] Some years were still to pass before Haldane boldly took the decision that Volunteers could be Field Gunners as well as Field Infantrymen.[2]

The Continuance of Guerrilla Warfare in South Africa

It was on March 8, 1901, that Mr. Brodrick launched his scheme in Parliament. Just over a week before, Lord Kitchener had met General Botha to confer upon possible terms for the termination of hostilities. On March 16th, however, these negotiations were broken off.[3]

Mr. Brodrick's reforms were indeed fated by the realities of the situation. Even had the South African War ended within the four months assumed by his memorandum, his scheme, apart from its weaknesses, might have been judged premature. As it was, the continued tension of hostilities, the locking up of the largest part of the British Army in South Africa, and the financial strain therein involved, combined to make progress along the lines of the Six Corps Scheme wellnigh impossible.[4]

There were very urgent problems connected with recruiting, and the supply of drafts to India was complicating an already

[1] 'R.U.S.I. Journal',—'Volunteer Artillery', 1902, p. 788.

[2] Brodrick, speaking in 1903 on the Estimates, said of the Volunteers, 'We believe also that it is impossible to ask of them the time for being trained to serve mobile artillery.'—A.D., March 10, 1903.

[3] 'Chronology', p. 79.

[4] It had been from the first the view of the Secretary of State that the Six Army Corps Scheme could not take its full shape until the necessary reservists were available. Unfortunately for the success of the plan, the continuance of hostilities in South Africa delayed the normal passage of men to the Reserve and made it impossible for the full numbers to be realized until three years later.—Verbal evidence, Earl of Midleton.

difficult situation. It had been nearly two years since drafting had maintained the strength of units in India. It had been necessary to ask men in India to re-engage with the Colours, and the Government of India was offering bounties of from £5 to £15 to time-expired men of British units in India to extend their term of engagement with the Colours. Some battalions had as many as 500 N.C.O.s and men who had completed their Colour service.[1] It was, however, impossible to ship from 15,000 to 20,000 seasoned soldiers home from India while the garrison was already some 10,000 below its nominal strength owing to the absence of troops from India in South Africa.

Apart from the specific need of supplying Indian drafts as soon as possible, there was the further problem that the end of the war would probably see a falling off in normal recruiting, and an increase in the number of men who would wish to take their discharge. There would, also, be a great number of men who would be coming to the end of their Reserve service. As one means of increasing the immediate attractiveness of the Army and of supplying a reservoir of Reservists for the future, the terms of service were made three years for the Colours, and nine years with the Reserve.[2]

The Government also promised substantial improvements in the amenities of military life. Barracks were to be improved and, it was suggested, private soldiers were to have separate cubicles. Many who knew the Army well, suggested that such improvements in amenities, valuable as they might be, were indifferent substitutes for the one real solution, an increase in the pay of the private soldier. The Secretary's task was not

[1] 'Army and Navy Gazette', April 20, 1901, p. 376.
[2] Lord Roberts insisted strongly upon the three year scheme; the Secretary of State was dubious as to its results, and refused to sanction it without an increase of pay to be granted to each man immediately on his undertaking to complete seven years in all after two years' service. Sixpence a day was given to all men so re-enlisting, but none the less, as the Secretary of State had feared, the requisite numbers were not obtained.—Verbal evidence, Earl of Midleton.

rendered easier by the dispute between Lord Lansdowne and Lord Wolseley, brought to a head in the House of Lords on March 4th,[1] nor, later in the year, by an imbroglio involving General Buller.

The appointment of General Buller to the Aldershot Command, on January 10th, had followed his return from South Africa. Critics of Mr. Brodrick were able to point out that, in the autumn of 1901, the first three Army Corps of his scheme were commanded by General Sir Redvers Buller, Sir Evelyn Wood and H.R.H. the Duke of Connaught. These, certainly, were not going to be the generals who should lead the troops of the Army Corps into the field, and it was not hard to deride a reformer who so early in his campaign abandoned one of his main theses.

It was, however, a spirited but injudicious speech at the Queen's Westminsters Drill Hall which led to Buller's enforced retirement.

A number of Army Orders had for their aim the better training of the Volunteers. It will be remembered that, before the South African war, the amount of drill required to qualify for the bounty was very small. Camp was entirely voluntary and seldom attended by more than a portion of the unit.

In 1900, the Volunteers had been called out for training as a measure of war-time precaution. It was now attempted to make such training in camp a permanent feature. The original scheme of March 8th provided that those Volunteer units who formed part of the Army Corps should do special training each year in camp. The 'London Gazette' of November 5th contained an Order in Council of the previous day laying down new, and in many ways important, conditions for the training of the Volunteers. The most important of these new provisions made it quite clear that henceforward annual unit camps were to be regarded as essential parts of training. A regiment could, if necessary, be excused for one year, but, the next year, every officer and man must go to camp for six days.

[1] See post, Chapter 10, 'The Formation of the Army Council'.

MR. BRODRICK AS SECRETARY OF STATE FOR WAR

If men were absent from such a camp, then the unit would not draw the capitation grant for such men.

The Order, no doubt, caused some heartburning. There were units who claimed that they could secure all the efficiency that was required by attendance at drills. It was with a view to clarifying the situation that a Special Army Order was issued of December 24, 1901. Copies of this order were to be posted in the order books of all Volunteer units. After reviewing the Order in Council previously referred to, this Special Army Order emphasizes the vital changes made by modern arms and equipment and urges the importance of securing for the volunteers a higher standard of training than had been previously attained. Finally, a very important paragraph 8 reads as follows:

'The State requires that a suitable standard of military training shall be secured in return for the outlay of public money, and consequently the enrolment in future of Volunteers who are unable to afford adequate time for any military training beyond elementary barrack square drill cannot be permitted.'[1]

All through the year 1901, the struggle against the guerrilla leaders in South Africa dragged on. There were periods of difficulty when Lord Kitchener, in South Africa, felt that he was not being sufficiently supported by Mr. Brodrick. The King himself thought that it was essential that the Government should take definite steps to make the Commander in the field feel that he had every support and in a note to the Secretary of State on September 29th urged this view.[2]

In November, in fact, Kitchener, in a fit of depression, announced his resolve to retire. Brodrick,[3] spurred perhaps

[1] 'Army and Navy Gazette', 1901, p. 1621.
[2] Lee, vol. ii, p. 80.
[3] Ibid., p. 82. It was about this time that the King wrote to Lord Salisbury concerning the war, that there was 'apparently no hope of its coming to an end. The strain on the resources of the country is becoming very great. Additional taxation must ensue, and the amount of troops now in South Africa is becoming most serious, should they, at any time, be required elsewhere.'

by these representations, made a strong speech at the City Carlton Club on Wednesday, November 13th, wherein he reviewed achievements, and, also, pointed out what ought to be done, and what the Government intended to do with regard to exchanging troops loaned two years by India, and Militia battalions stale in South Africa.[1]

The blockhouse system and the mobile columns demanded a large number of men. Imperial Yeomanry Regiments who had gone out in the early days of the War were demanding release. Moreover, it was felt essential that those Militia Battalions who had gone out in the Spring of 1900 should be relieved by other Militia Battalions who had been embodied but had remained in the United Kingdom. During the winter of 1901–2, therefore, eighteen Militia Battalions proceeded to South Africa to relieve the first contingent. The diary for January 1902 shows five such arrivals in one month.[2] On January 1, 1902, recruiting for the third contingent of Imperial Yeomanry was opened and 7,221 men were enlisted. On January 9th the War Office asked for 10,000 more Infantry Volunteers but in this case, owing largely to the competition of the more highly paid Imperial Yeomanry, the response was poor. When the time came for the Estimates for 1902–3 to be put before the House, there was no longer an easy assumption that the War would be over in four months' time. The Memorandum said:[3]

'As regards South Africa the provision made is sufficient to maintain the Field Army at its present strength for between eight and nine months of the new financial year and in the case of China provision has been made for the retention of a reduced force for half the financial year and also for the cost of transport back to India. . . . In the case of the Militia a net decrease of £1,391,000 is explained by the fact that a certain number of battalions recently disembodied after considerable service will not be called up for training this year, while reduced provision has been made for the

---

[1] 'Army and Navy Gazette', 1901, p. 1160.
[2] 'R.U.S.I. Journal', 1902, p. 271.　　　　　　　　[3] A.E., 1902–3.

new Militia Reserve which is not expected to reach more than 25,000 men in 1902–3.'

Other troubles complicated the Minister's task during 1901. There had been the 'Remount Scandal'. Grave dissatisfaction had been expressed with the methods sanctioned by the War Office for the purchase of horses, chiefly in the United States and the Argentine, for shipment to South Africa.

A Committee of the House of Commons reported on January 30, 1902, and recommended very drastic alterations in the Remount Department.

One of the unfortunate features of the early part of the South African War had been a breakdown in the medical arrangements, notably in the case of the epidemic which raged after the arrival of the Army at Bloemfontein. A Royal Commission of Enquiry had been appointed in July 1900, and made its report on the day of the Queen's death, January 27, 1901. As soon as Parliament met after the King's accession, Mr. Brodrick announced his intention to reorganize the medical services. The chief problem was, as so often the case in the Army's difficulties, one of finance. The rates of pay offered in the medical services had not been sufficient to attract suitable men. The Estimates for 1901–2 provided £183,600 additional on the Vote for Medical Services. Some of this was of course for war services, but about £125,000 represented a permanent addition to the amount available for the Army Medical Corps.[1] The reorganization of the work of the Medical Services owed a very great deal to the efforts of Sir Frederick Treves and M. Veagh.

[1] A.E., 1901–2, Vote 2.

CHAPTER 8

THE END OF THE WAR—REFORMS AND COMMISSIONS

THE Army Estimates for 1902–3 signed by Mr. Brodrick from the War Office on February 6, 1902, contained, as has been seen, no promise of any early termination of the War. Moreover, the capture of Lord Methuen and 1,200 men on March 7th by Delarey was an ominous commencement to the new year.

Nevertheless, the burgher resistance was becoming exhausted and eventually the long-drawn-out hostilities ended, on May 31, 1902.

In the United States 'Army and Navy Journal' about this time one, Joubert Reitz, 'late of the Boer Army', wrote a long and interesting article which ended as follows:

'If the British take advantage of the lessons they learned in this War, and I am afraid they are the only ones who will do so, they can in five years' time put an army in the field that will be able to fight almost any army in the world, for, notwithstanding all that has been said about them, the British soldier is a brave man and a good fighter and, were he armed with the latest and best arms would be a dangerous foe to even the mighty armies of Germany and Russia.'[1]

Mr. Reitz' period of time was a little optimistic. It was to take seven or eight years from the date of his article till the British Army did indeed stand forward reorganized and re-equipped.

Fortescue, reviewing briefly the period at the end of the South African War, uses the following phrase: 'For four years there was unprofitable discussion; and then the task of setting the nation's military house in order was taken in hand by

[1] Quoted in 'R.U.S.I. Journal', 1902, p. 1359.

Richard Burdon Haldane.'[1] It is possible that this hasty dismissal of the work of the years 1902 to 1905 reflects a fairly common opinion. Yet, while every regard is paid to the extreme value of Mr. Haldane's reforms, to the clarity of vision and completeness of plan which lay behind them, it is barely justice to dismiss as unprofitable the work of Mr. Brodrick and Mr. Arnold-Forster. Still less, perhaps, is it fair to dismiss the many valuable reforms which were set in motion by the less senior officers in the Army, as a result of the lessons of the South African War. It may well be said that Mr. Haldane's task would have been much harder yet if he had not had to guide him the experiments of his forerunners in office. Even by the somewhat crude methods of trial and error, Mr. Brodrick and Mr. Arnold-Forster had gained much useful experience. The existence of the Army Council before Mr. Haldane took over was of great advantage to him.

Perhaps the greatest of all Mr. Haldane's achievements was the creation of the Territorial Force. But the essence of the Territorial Force was, it is suggested, the introduction of Annual Training. In this direction the way had been partially cleared by the provisions of Mr. Brodrick's time.

It is, in particular, only right that attention should be drawn to those features of Mr. Brodrick's reforms which remain to-day permanent additions to the organization of the British Army. His creation of Salisbury Plain as our second military station, the building of the barracks at Tidworth, remain a monument to his work. His basic plan of decentralization into six Army Corps districts is in the main the model of the system of command as we have it to-day. The policy of linking the Auxiliary Forces into the same general organization as that of the Regular Army has a sound basis, though his Army Corps were, in fact, difficult to train in peace and exceedingly awkward to organize in war.

[1] Fortescue, vol. xiii, p. 570.

The Elgin Commission[1]

As early as the summer of 1900, it had been admitted by the Government that there would have to be some form of general enquiry into Army matters, though Lord Salisbury had steadfastly refused to have any sort of general inquest until the war was over. In 1901 King Edward had urged an enquiry 'searching into the many blunders we made in South Africa'.[2] On the other hand, when Lord Salisbury informed His Majesty of the decision, taken at a Cabinet meeting, to hold a Royal Commission of investigation, the proceedings whereof would be published, the King saw objections to 'washing one's dirty linen in public'. On June 13th he wrote:

'The King has received your Cabinet Note of yesterday, and he greatly deprecates the conclusion arrived at that a general inquiry into the conduct of the war should be conducted by a Royal Commission. The King saw Lord Salisbury last week and urged him not to consent to such an inquiry which Queen Victoria had also desired should not take place.'[3]

Lord Salisbury was bound to reply that he could not override the definite decision of the Cabinet, and the King, with constitutional correctness, accepted the position. He was, however, keenly interested in the personnel of the Royal Commission. Lord Spencer and Mr. Asquith had both been offered the post of Chairman. Finally, Lord Elgin was prevailed upon to be the Chairman of the Commission. Lord Esher, whose qualifications for membership were strongly

[1] The official title was 'The Royal Commission on the War in South Africa'. It is often incorrectly referred to as the 'Esher Commission', and such a title creates a confusion with the 'Esher Committee' properly so called (The War Office Reconstitution Committee of 1903-4). Lord Esher, who was a prominent member of the Royal Commission, used the style 'Elgin Commission' from the name of its Chairman (Letter to Balfour, 'Esher Journal', ii, p. 108), and this example is followed by the German historian Paul Kluke. (See also note in Bibliography.)
[2] Lee, vol. ii, p. 91.
[3] Ibid., vol. ii, p. 91.

THE END OF THE WAR—REFORMS AND COMMISSIONS 149

urged by the King, became one of the most important members of the Commission. The first meeting was held in August 1902, and it was not till after a year of most arduous work that the Commission issued its report.[1]

While the Elgin Commission was painstakingly collecting evidence for its monumental report, while Mr. Brodrick was slowly drawing back from South Africa the Regular Army which he so badly required for his Six Army Corps scheme, while new barracks were arising slowly at Tidworth, events outside the orbit of the British Army were one by one taking place, events which were to have a very great effect on that Army's role. It has been said earlier that any study of the history of the development of the Army during these years must take into account the influence both of political and of international happenings. The Army, keenly alive to its own shortcomings as far as they were made manifest by the South African war, was also to be subject to the influences of these outside factors impinging now from this side, now from that, upon the course of Army development.

The End of Splendid Isolation

A few days before Brodrick presented his first estimates, those for the years 1901–2, Lord Salisbury had written a memorandum in which he had set down what he conceived to be the cardinal principles of British Foreign Policy. The

[1] The report of the Elgin Commission is dealt with in Chapter 9.
The members of the Commission were:
    The Earl of Elgin, K.G., G.C.S.I.
    Viscount Esher, K.C.B., K.C.V.O.
    Sir George Dashwood Taubman-Goldie, K.C.M.G.
    Field-Marshal Sir Henry W. Norman, G.C.B., G.C.M.G.
    Admiral Sir John O. Hopkins, G.C.B.
    Sir John Edge.
    Sir John Jackson.
To whom were added:
    Lord Strathcona, G.C.M.G.
    Sir Frederick Darley, G.C.M.G.
The Secretary was Mr. Bernard Holland.

memorandum reads almost as the dying declaration of the policy of Splendid Isolation. 'It would not be wise', wrote Lord Salisbury, 'to undertake novel and most onerous obligations in order to guard against a danger in whose existence we have no historical reason for believing.' 'The British Government,' he said, 'cannot undertake to declare war, for any purpose, unless it is a purpose of which the electors of this country would approve. If the Government promised to declare for an object which did not commend itself to public opinion, the promise would be repudiated and the Government would be turned out. I do not see how, in common honesty, we could invite other nations to rely on our aid in a struggle which must be formidable and probably supreme, when we have no means whatever of knowing what may be the humour of our people in circumstances which cannot be foreseen. . . .'[1]

Thus Lord Salisbury, in the Spring of 1901. Yet within twelve months, on January 30, 1902, the Anglo-Japanese Alliance was signed in London.[2] So far, Lord Salisbury, at least, was prepared to go. The next, and greater step, that of an entente with France was already being mentioned, but before plans for this had gone very far there was a new Prime Minister in charge of England's destinies. Lord Salisbury's health had for some time been failing. On July 11, 1902, he withdrew from office, and was succeeded by 'his nephew and political heir', Mr. A. J. Balfour.[3]

It is not necessary, in a work of this nature, to pass in review all the stages of negotiation with France. It is, however, essential to realize the influence upon military thought played by this orientation of a foreign policy, an orientation which may be said to have its beginning in the early months of 1902.

On May 1, 1903, King Edward VII visited Paris, and his personal triumph there was the outward and visible token of an alteration in English foreign affairs.

---
[1] Quoted in 'A Short History of Our Own Times', J. A. Spender, p. 56.
[2] Lee, vol. ii, p. 143.   [3] Ibid., p. 159.

THE END OF THE WAR—REFORMS AND COMMISSIONS 151

At home, another event of importance had taken place. On May 15, 1903, Mr. Joseph Chamberlain delivered at Birmingham a speech on Colonial Preference whereby, in the words of Mr. Asquith, 'he launched his new policy on the ocean of public controversy'. 'It became from that moment until the general election of 1906 . . . the paramount and dominating issue in British politics.'[1]

Thus within a few days of one another, in May 1903, King Edward and Mr. Joseph Chamberlain so played their parts that events therefrom led steadily to Mr. Haldane at the War Office and Military conversations with France.

Meanwhile, the Norfolk Commission had been appointed, in April 1903. This Commission was specially concerned with the function of the Auxiliary Forces, but somewhat early in its career became involved in the consideration of the value of compulsory service for Home Defence.[2]

Compulsory Service was, in fact, at this time, being actively canvassed by a number of people. The pages of the reviews and the Service journals of the time were full of articles advocating various remedies for the military problems. Some saw the solution of the problem in a great increase in the Volunteer movement and thought that an invading army could be checked by Volunteer riflemen trained in Volunteer and Cadet Rifle Clubs. Others thought that conscription would alone give England a large enough Home Army to meet invasion. This was the view actively championed by the National Service League, whose President was the Duke of Wellington, and Secretary Mr. George Shee. A debate at the Royal United Service Institution initiated by Mr. George Shee on February 14, 1902, had been adjourned for two successive following dates, so great had been the number of members who wished to speak.[3]

---

[1] Asquith, 'Fifty Years of Parliament', p. 8.
[2] For the composition and report of the Norfolk Commission, see Chapter 9.
[3] 'R.U.S.I. Journal', 1902, pp. 570–656.

On the other hand, Mr. Brodrick was being assailed from another direction by those who thought that his plans locked up too much money in the purely home defence—'sedentary' was the word used—part of the army.

One rather interesting new development in Army political affairs was the tendency to regard Mr. Brodrick's plans as a direct challenge to the doctrine enunciated by the active and propagandist Navy League. The Navy had become aware of some of the lessons of the South African War, and had been acutely interested in the German Navy Law of 1900. It was the view of this school of thought, sparklingly championed by Mr. Winston Churchill, that the British Navy should have first claim on all money available for the defence forces, and that any part of our land forces which was solely concerned with Home Defence should be regarded as of secondary importance until the Navy had reached that strength which the Navy League thought necessary. Mr. Brodrick had, therefore, to deal with critics from his own party who were even more brilliant in debate than the members of the opposition.

To these difficulties might be added criticism from the monarch. King Edward was keenly interested in Army Reform and active in comment and suggestion. Finally, after a long audience on October 13, 1902, the Secretary summarized his various difficulties, which, as he with some justice claimed, were not lightened by the King's comments. The King's autograph reply of October 15th was a genuine appreciation of the minister's very difficult situation.[1]

In one direction, at least, the years of Mr. Brodrick's office were fruitful. The material of the British Army in the South African War was in many respects behind the times. Lord Roberts and the technical officers of the Army were able to take action at an early date to remedy some of those faults, and lead the way to the satisfactory armament of 1914.

[1] Lee, vol. ii, p. 93.

THE END OF THE WAR—REFORMS AND COMMISSIONS

Improvement in Material

The new uniform of the British Army was introduced by the Army Order of February 1, 1902. Henceforward the Army would train at home in the uniform which it would wear when it proceeded overseas to fight.[1]

The headdress provided some difficulty. The helmet of South African days was obviously unsuitable at home. The Imperial Yeomanry slouch hat, adopted by very many Volunteer units of the period, had disadvantages for peace-time wear. Mr. Broderick's invention, the round peakless cap, was unpopular and ugly.[2] It was left to Mr. Arnold-Forster to produce the present pattern of peaked cap, a frank imitation of German wear, in 1904.

In Artillery, the need for new weapons was obvious. The Armstrong gun, which was not quickfiring, which required, in other words, that the shell, powder charge, and primer should each be loaded separately, was obviously antiquated compared with the French 75 mm. gun, and with the latest pattern Krupp gun used by Germany. Ehrhardt guns had been ordered from Germany of a quickfiring pattern. Their telescopic trail was a weakness and made them unpopular. Nevertheless, as a stopgap, and as a means of experiment,

---

[1] This Army Order brought into effect the majority of the proposals recommended by a Committee, under the chairmanship of Major-General Vetch, appointed to consider the question of clothing.—' Chronology', p. 80 (1901).

This was one of the recommendations of the Mowatt Committee. 'A pattern of the universal service dress for home and abroad can be seen in the Museum of the R.U.S.I.'—'R.U.S.I. Journal', 1902, p. 258.

[2] 'It was introduced by a decision of the Clothing Committee in 1901.' —Answer to question in House of Commons, June 17, 1903.

The round, peakless cap associated with Mr. Brodrick's name was ugly and unpopular. As a matter of fact, the maligned Secretary of State had in this particular matter a very small share of responsibility. The pattern was chosen by a War Office Committee, and was submitted to King Edward, who preferred it to others; and the Secretary of State revealed many years afterwards that he himself had never seen it.—Verbal evidence, Earl of Midleton.

they had their uses.¹ For the final period of the South African War, heavy super-elevation Howitzers of 9·45-inch calibre had been obtained from the Austrian firm of Skoda.

In the meantime, however, the period was frankly one of transition. Von Lobell, in his report for the year 1901, spoke of the British Army as having sixteen different kinds of guns, howitzers, and machine guns in South Africa, and the 'R.U.S.I. Journal' adds the comment that nine different Field Guns of British make were to be the subject of experiment in England during the year 1902.²

The decision had to be made between 'barrel recoiling' guns, of the type made famous by the French 75 mm. gun, and by the Krupp pattern, and cradle recoil guns with some form of return spring on the spade. Most of the great powers during the period 1900–4 were carrying out tests of various systems.

It was not until 1903 that England decided on a barrel recoil gun, containing the best points of designs submitted by the firms of Armstrong and Vickers. Large orders were accordingly given to these firms for this new field gun, the Mark I 18-pounder.³

Army Estates 1904–5 reported, however, that the decision had been taken to give the India Government priority in the supply of the new artillery equipment.

'It will not be possible to receive delivery during 1904–5 of more than the number of complete batteries assigned to India; but manufacture will be in full swing in the latter part of the year,

---

¹ '108 quickfiring guns were purchased from Germany.'—Reply by Mr. Arnold-Forster to a question in the House of Commons, February 4, 1904. A.D., 1904, p. 23.

² 'R.U.S.I. Journal', 1902, p. 1327.   ³ Ibid., 1904, p. 431.
The first conditions for the new guns were sent out to makers in 1901. Eight trial guns were ordered in February 1902. They were delivered that summer and were the subject of exhaustive trials during August and September. These were not satisfactory, and a modified design was therefore drawn up in December 1902.—From an answer by Mr. Arnold-Forster in the House of Commons to a question by Captain Norton March 1, 1905.

THE END OF THE WAR—REFORMS AND COMMISSIONS 155

and rapid delivery of batteries for the Home Army will take place throughout the following year.'[1]

A new 13-pounder quickfiring gun was at the same time introduced for the Royal Horse Artillery, replacing the B.L. 12-pounder.[2]

Small Arms

Experience in the South African War showed the importance of accurate and rapid snap-shooting at ranges of 600 yards and under. During the War, Lord Roberts had telegraphed home pressing for the short rifle to be proceeded with. Moreover, the War had proved that the rifle must, in future, be regarded as the principal weapon of cavalry. The carbine carried in pre-War days was neither an accurate nor a long-range weapon, and in South Africa the carbines were taken from the cavalry and rifles were issued to them instead. The Lee-Enfield rifle of the Boer War was, however, too long to be conveniently carried by cavalry, and the War Office determined to bring out a pattern of rifle which should be about five inches shorter than the existing Lee-Enfield, and which should be a universal weapon for cavalry and infantry alike. Preliminary trials showed that such a rifle could be produced, and, in 1902, 1,000 shortened rifles were issued to the Royal Navy, Royal Marines and the first Three Army Corps. A little later, 100 rifles were sent out on test to

---

[1] A.E., 1904–5.
[2] As a temporary expedient a number of 15-pounders had been converted to quickfiring pattern. 'In the year 1901, the Q.F. 15-pounder, of which eighteen batteries had been obtained the previous year, was approved for service. This gun and equipment may be said to have been the first that approximately fulfilled modern field artillery conditions in the British Service.

'In the years 1900–1902 a certain number of Q.F. 4·7-inch guns were adapted for use in travelling carriages and formed the armament of the Regular Field Artillery until the B.L. 60-pounder gun was introduced.'— 'Treatise on Service Ordnance', 1908, p. 390.

It will be remembered that these two pieces, the 15-pounder converted and the 4·7-inch gun, became the armament of the T.F. Artillery and were the weapons with which the T.F. batteries went to France in the Great War.

Somaliland. All these tests were satisfactory, and in the years following 1902 the short Lee-Enfield became the standard rifle of the British Army.[1]

Slow Progress in 1903

Though there might be improvements in some directions, there was little progress in the grand plan for Army reorganization, the Six Army Corps scheme. The long-continued struggle in South Africa had ruined any chance for the great idea of 1901 to move forward as a coherent whole. Though the latter half of 1902 saw the steady return of British troops from South Africa, many still remained abroad. The formation of the Militia Artillery units proceeded but slowly. New barracks had in many cases not yet started.

When Parliament reassembled in the early spring of 1903, the dissatisfaction with Mr. Brodrick s military administration was expressed on February 23rd in an amendment to the Address: "But we humbly regret that the organization of the land forces is unsuited to the needs of the Empire, and that no proportionate gain in strength and efficiency has resulted from the recent increases in military expenditure.' The amendment was moved from the back benches of the Government side of the House. Major Seely, who seconded the motion, made two points. The first was the standard argument of those who looked for a large navy: 'Therefore, as a navy could not be improvised, while an army, to a large extent could be, any scheme which proposed to spend as much on the Army as on the Navy was based on a wrong principle and would have to be abandoned. . . .'

His second thesis was that the Government was endeavouring to create too large a Regular Army. 'It was too large because it was beyond the power of our purse.' The debate on the whole was a very fair representation of the schools of thought of the time. On the second day of the debate

---

[1] 'The Short Lee-Enfield Rifle, Mark I', communicated by the Director of Artillery, 'R.U.S.I. Journal', 1904, p. 669.

Mr. Winston Churchill, in the course of a very clear and clever speech put the dilemma thus: 'As to a stronger Regular Army, either we had the command of the sea or we had not. If we had it, we required fewer soldiers, if we had it not we wanted more ships.' Earlier in the debate he had said: 'They did not want a large Regular Army for Home Defence. They were agreed that they ought to place for home defence greater reliance on the Volunteers, Yeomanry, and Militia forces or forces organized therefrom. . . . For foreign expeditions one Army Corps was quite enough to fight against savages, but three Army Corps were not enough to fight against Europeans.'

The supporters of the Navy, the 'blue water' school were strong advocates of reduced expenditure on the Army. Colonel George Kemp pointed out that Parliament had been asked in that year to spend £29,000,000 on the English Army 'and only £31,000,000 on the Navy which is the first line of Defence'.[1] Sir Edward Grey, speaking a little later added in the cost of the British Army in India and made the figures £50,000,000 for the Army.[2]

The Army Corps system came in for a good deal of banter; Seely besought the Secretary to 'look the facts frankly in the face, and if there are 10,000 men fit for service call them a Division and not an Army Corps'. Winston Churchill made the House laugh with a fanciful sketch of Lord Grenfell, lately appointed to command the Fourth Army Corps, arriving at his Corps Headquarters, being received in state by the Mayor

---

[1] It is interesting to note that the relative figures for the Budget, 1935–6, are:

Army	£35,300,000
Navy	£50,500,000
Air	£19,700,000

'Armaments Year Book', p. 172.

[2] Sir Edward Grey also said this: 'Our Militia and Volunteer Forces have never had a chance. . . . But, if it is once understood that they are clearly separated from the Regular Army, that they constituted a citizen Army for defensive purposes, then I am confident that our Volunteer and Militia forces will develop into a force upon which the country could rely for any purposes of home defence.'

and Corporation of Colchester, while on all roads horse, foot, and guns converged to meet him. The reality, he pointed out was quite different. The Secretary of State had by a stroke of a pen created an Army Corps, but there were still just the same heterogeneous collection of Militia and Volunteer units, scattered about East Africa.

The weight of argument was running against the Government. Brodrick could only point out that recruiting was good, that the Yeomanry was doing well, and that changes were always unpopular. The scheme of decentralization had been started and that took a lot of people away from their jobs and created some discontent. Of course the strongest of Brodrick's replies was that two years ago the same House of Commons said that they wanted a bigger Army, and now the same people stood aghast at the cost.[1] Balfour said that, apparently, according to supporters of the amendment we 'were to have fewer troops and no organization'. The debate lasted for three days. As Mr. Asquith pointed out, a vote on the amendment was a vote of censure on the Government, and was not likely to succeed. The Division was, however, a close one; over a score of Unionists voted with the Liberals[2] and Mr. Balfour could have had few illusions left as to the position of his Secretary of State for War.[3]

In the course of the debate a Command Paper was called for to show the state of the Six Army Corps Commands. From that it was quite clear that, two years after the scheme was launched, there were still grave shortages in the organiza-

---

[1] Sir Edward Grey said of Brodrick's defence: 'The right hon. Gentleman's reply is that the country should give him more time, and then he will establish his scheme, and the country may be sure of having to pay for it.'

[2] 'Twenty-five Unionists voted against the Government.'—Mr. Labouchere's speech, March 12, 1903.

[3] In 1904, speaking in the House on the Army Estimates, Mr. Winston Churchill described as follows the three years of the Brodrick regime: 'He was able to carry all before him the first year. But when the second year came round it was found that the scheme did not provide the men and there was no sign of the men being forthcoming. The House knows perfectly well how they got through the third year.'—A.D., 1904, p. 553.

tion.[1] Thus the Fifth and Sixth Army Corps were both shown as 'not yet formed'. In the Fourth Corps the six batteries of Militia Field Artillery were not yet raised, and three of the Regular field batteries required for the corps were still in South Africa. Even the first three corps were nothing like complete. In the Aldershot Corps, six field batteries were still quartered in other Commands because barracks were not yet ready for them. Four battalions were similarly dispersed. The three heavy batteries for the First Corps were 'now being organized', but the barracks were not available. In the Third Corps the heavy batteries were 'not yet organized'. The summary totals for the first three Army Corps gave:—

	Required	Available
Cavalry Regiments	15	11
Artillery Batteries	78	75
Infantry Battalions	72	63

In the case of the Cavalry and Infantry the deficiencies were due to units still being in South Africa. But, as has been seen, though units were sometimes available, they were not always in the right place. Nor were they always completely organized. The King wrote to Lord Roberts on this subject:

'For instance, the King understands that at Aldershot, where the First Army Corps is supposed to be trained with a view to being ready at any moment to be sent on active service nearly all the Brigades have no Brigadiers and will only receive one on mobilization. This seems contrary to the fundamental principle of the Army Corps system. The appointment of the senior Battalion Commander the King considers a great mistake, for not only would this officer not command in time of war, but he is temporarily relinquishing the Command of his Battalion just when its own training comes under his special direction, and, moreover, the fact of his being senior Battalion Commander in no way implies he is a suitable Brigadier. . . . The King would urge on

[1] 'The State of the Six Army Corps Commands', Command Paper 1413 of 1903.

you the necessity of having at least the First Army Corps in a satisfactory condition thoroughly prepared for mobilization. . . .'[1]

Numbers also were short. But most serious of all was the threatening breakdown of the three-year system. A table was published on August 11, 1905, showing what happened to the recruits taken in for the year ending December 31, 1903.[2]

During the year, 2,040 were enlisted for long service.
38,299 were enlisted for short service.

40,339

But of that number there were still with the colours on July 1, 1905:

On original long service engagement . . 1,749
On original short service engagement . 23,500
Extended 5,370

30,619

The Secretary of State's fears as to the working of the three-year service were proving all too well founded.

Thus, in the first place there was a wastage, from various causes of about 10,000 men in two years, and in the second place, of the 38,299 who in the first instance signed on for the three years' short service, only about one-sixth had decided to extend their service. This calculation agrees with the other, which, for the whole army, gives the percentage of extensions as, in 1902, 16·6 per cent, and in 1903, 17·8 per cent.[3] Such figures of extensions were, of course, hopelessly below what was required to make up the drafts for battalions on foreign stations. Men could not be sent abroad till they were twenty,

[1] Lee, p. 194.
[2] Return to an address in the House of Lords. No. 179 of August 11, 1905.
[3] Paul Kluke, p. 46.

THE END OF THE WAR—REFORMS AND COMMISSIONS

but to send out men to India within a year of the expiry of their service was very expensive in transport, and not satisfactory to the overseas battalion.

A return compiled in July 1904, and published as Command Paper No. 1905 of 1904, gave the figures of men extending service in the 69 infantry battalions at home, with their depots. The figures covered, apparently, the three months from April 1, 1904. They varied considerably. Scottish regiments did well, Royal Scots with 56, and Gordon Highlanders with 47 were the best. Irish regiments, on the other hand, had few extensions: Royal Irish Fusiliers and Leinster Regiment had none, Royal Munster Fusiliers and Royal Dublin Fusiliers had 8 each. The figures for all the regiments were 711, an average of just over 10 per regiment.

Mr. Arnold-Forster, after he took office, devoted a good deal of his explanation of the difficult position of the Army to this very question of the failure to secure the necessary number of extensions of service.

'The whole of the Army is now enlisted, primarily, for 3 years service. In view of the fact that, if drafts are to be provided, from 75 to 80 per cent of the men in all branches must extend, and that, in some branches, notably the Garrison Artillery, the extensions must reach 100 per cent, it is not easy to see how this system can be successfully maintained. It does not appear that, at the time of its adoption, sufficiently exact calculations were made with a view to demonstrating that the system would work satisfactorily, and closer calculations which have since been made, joined with the evidence of the actual extensions hitherto, indicate that the working of the scheme may easily become disastrous.

The average extensions among the Infantry ought to be at least 75 per cent. At present, it is about 12 per cent in several battalions; in several battalions it is as low as 3 per cent or 4 per cent; and in at least one battalion not a single man has extended during the last month.'[1]

---

[1] From summary of the speech of the Secretary of State for War, Command Paper 1907, 1904, p. 5.

The Militia also was dwindling away and on January 1, 1903, the force was 20,596 below strength.[1]

Therefore, it was no question of enlarging an army to grandiose schemes of six Army Corps. The great problem of 1903 was to keep the Army functioning at all.[2]

Cabinet Changes

The repercussions of Mr. Chamberlain's fiscal policy were, however, soon to affect the Army. After an uneasy summer of Cabinet vacillations, on September 16, 1903, Mr. Joseph Chamberlain tendered his resignation. He was followed by Lord George Hamilton, Secretary of State for India, and Mr. Ritchie, Chancellor of the Exchequer. Lord Balfour of Burleigh and Mr. Arthur Elliott also retired at this time. The Duke of Devonshire, though he promised to reconsider his resignation in mid-September, did, in fact, leave the Cabinet after three weeks' further deliberation.

'It looks as if the opportunity might be taken to get rid of Brodrick and I fervently hope this may be the case', wrote Lord Esher on September 18th. 'Perhaps he will go to the India Office and then Douglas or A. Chamberlain might go to the War Office. I hope the King will use all his influence to bring this about.'[3] Indeed, Mr. Balfour, with little hesitation, took the opportunity of transferring Mr. Brodrick to the India Office.[4] The first choice for the War Office, however, fell on Lord Esher himself.[5]

---

[1] Memorandum of the Secretary of State.

[2] 'All sorts of wild schemes are on. Indian drafts can't be found and general hell is expected. The whole situation is gradually becoming impossible and we are nearing universal service.'—Diary of General Grierson, May 11, 1903. Macdiarmid, p. 202.

[3] Esher Journals, vol. ii, p. 13. Mr. St. John Brodrick had previously been Under-Secretary of State for India.

[4] 'And that fertile imagination which used to call forth Armies so easily was now condemned to exile in the frozen deserts of Thibet.'—Winston Churchill in the House of Commons, February 23, 1905. A.D., 1905, p. 276.

[5] Lee, vol. ii, p. 177, says that the Prime Minister's first choice for the War Office was Mr. Akers-Douglas, but it seems fairly evident from the

THE END OF THE WAR—REFORMS AND COMMISSIONS 163

Lord Esher had, of course, created a very great impression by his work on the Elgin Commission. The Report of the Commission had been signed on July 9th, and was being widely studied and quoted.[1] In particular, Lord Esher's own proposal for a Board for the War Office on the lines of the Board of Admiralty had attracted a good deal of attention.[2] The King and Prime Minister, both anxious for Army Reform, wished Esher to continue his work, in the capacity of Secretary of State for War. Esher protested, and at length with success, that he did not wish for public office.[3] He was, however, prepared to continue with the task of Army reform by acting as the chairman of a small committee of three charged with the task of carrying out a reorganization of the War Office. He wished the Committee to be Fisher,[4] Brackenbury,[5] and himself. 'If this plan is adopted,' he wrote to Knollys, 'and I am chairman of such a body, I shall propose to take the War Office administration right through from top to bottom, and endeavour to make it a first-class business machinery, and do, in fact, for the War Office as a whole, what Treves is doing for the R.A.M.C.'[6] In reference to Lord Esher's refusal to take office, there is one important comment that must be made. In the very early days of Mr. St. John Brodrick's Secretaryship, he was approached by Lord Esher with the

many letters in Esher Journals (which, published in 1934, was not available to Sir Sidney Lee) that from September 21st to 27th considerable pressure was being brought to bear on Lord Esher by the King and Mr. Balfour. Lord Rosebery wrote a note (September 24th) to Lord Esher to 'Hope it is not true', and advising against the War Office post.

[1] It was published as Command Paper No. 1789 of 1903. Public interest led to the issue of a reprint of the findings.—Lee, p. 192.

[2] 'I have a long letter from Knollys in which he says the King has returned from Marienbad strongly in favour of a Board for the Army and has spoken already to Balfour.'—Esher Journals, September 7, p. 10.

[3] 'Political office is abhorrent to me.'—Esher to A. J. Balfour, September 25. Ibid., p. 19.

[4] Admiral Sir John Fisher, then Commander, Portsmouth Dockyard.

[5] General Rt. Hon. Sir Henry Brackenbury, then Director-General of Ordnance at the War Office.

[6] Esher to Knollys. Esher Journals, September 27, p. 23.

suggestion that he, Esher, should become the Permanent Under-Secretary of State.[1]

Akers-Douglas having, in his turn, refused the War Office, Mr. Balfour suggested Arnold-Forster, who had been Secretary to the Admiralty. The King would have preferred Lord Selborne, who was First Lord, but Selborne backed up the candidature of Arnold-Forster, and the King gave way.[2]

So, on October 6, 1903, Mr. Arnold-Forster became the Secretary of State for War, a post which he was to hold for just over two years.

[1] There can be no doubt that Lord Esher did in fact wish to secure for himself a position where he could control War Office developments without the public responsibilities of political life.—Verbal evidence, Earl of Midleton.

[2] Lee, vol. ii, p. 177.

CHAPTER 9

MR. ARNOLD-FORSTER TAKES OFFICE, OCTOBER 6, 1903

THE NORFOLK COMMISSION—THE GENERAL AND HOME SERVICE ARMIES

THE new Secretary of State for War had taken office at a difficult time. The Balfour Cabinet itself was, in the expressive words of John Morley, 'a scratch crew on a raft'.[1] The Government's majority in the House of Commons was highly precarious, and during the latter half of Mr. Arnold-Forster's tour of office, outsiders, at least, were busy speculating as to who his successor might be. 'The Cabinet's gravest preoccupation', writes Mr. Asquith, 'was to avoid any forcing of the crisis of Tariff Reform in the House of Commons.'[2] Internationally, the situation was clouded by the steady expansion of the German Fleet, and was soon to be even more overcast by the Russo-Japanese War.

The Army was costing a great deal of money,[3] and the National financial situation was not too good. There was considerable unemployment and industrial unrest, and there were calls for national economy. In the previous July the Report of the Royal Commission of Inquiry into the South African War, the 'Elgin Commission', had been published. It was realized by all that this Report was a very valuable contribution to the general study of military reform and its conclusions were the subject of considerable discussion.

It is to be remembered, however, that in its essential features,

[1] Quoted in Asquith's 'Fifty Years of Parliament', vol. ii, p. 16.
[2] Ibid., p. 20.
[3] The Estimates for 1903–4 had amounted to a total of £34,245,000, and to this was to be added a Supplementary Estimate on February 11, 1904, for £2,700,000.

the Elgin Commission was a Commission of Record and not a Commission of advice.

Its terms of reference had been: 'To inquire into the Military Preparations for the War in South Africa, and into the supply of Men, Ammunition, Equipment, and Transport by Sea and Land in connection with the Campaign, up to the occupation of Pretoria' and 'to report their opinion upon the matters . . . submitted.'[1]

The members of the Commission therefore, considered their main duty to be the collection of all available evidence bearing on the subject under review, and their researches were very comprehensive.[2] In fact, however, the Report did contain some very important comments for the future guidance of the Government.

Two recommendations stood out, perhaps, above all the others. One was contained on page 83 of the Report, under the heading, 'General Observations with regard to Imperial Forces'. After reviewing the deficiencies with regard to the various 'services', even for the Regular Army Corps, and after commenting on the lack of training of Militia Officers, the Commissioners said this:

'But the true lesson of the War in our opinion is that no military system will be satisfactory which does not contain powers of expansion outside the limit of the Regular Forces of the Crown, whatever that limit may be.

If the war teaches anything it is this, that throughout the Empire, in the United Kingdom, its colonies and dependencies, there is a reserve of military strength which for many reasons we cannot and do not wish to convert into a vast standing army, but which we may be glad to turn to again in an hour of need as we did in 1899.'

[1] Second and seventh paragraphs of the Royal Warrant constituting the Commission.
[2] The Commission sat on fifty-five days to take evidence, heard 115 witnesses, received 22,200 answers to questions. The Report, Minutes of Evidence and Appendices occupy three volumes and a total of 2,015 pages of foolscap.

The second comment of major importance was contained in part in the concluding portion of the Report—a portion headed 'War Office Reform',—and in part in a separate report, submitted by Lord Esher, and supported by Sir George Taubman-Goldie and Sir John Jackson.[1]

This was the suggestion for the reconstitution of War Office control in the hands of a Board on the lines of the Board of Admiralty.

Even before the change of Secretary, Lord Esher had expressed a hope that the matter of War Office reorganization would be followed up, and, as has been mentioned previously, when the question of a new Secretary for War was under discussion, the matter of a special committee to carry out the reorganization was among the principal points debated.

This Committee was in fact constituted very soon after the change of minister. Esher's first suggestion had been that the other two members should be Fisher and Brackenbury. But Brackenbury was in the War Office already, and there were objections about that.[2] Lord Grenfell was then approached. He was a serving soldier, at that time commanding the 4th Army Corps Area, and he risked a good deal of royal displeasure by refusing to serve on the Committee. He pointed out that he, a soldier on full pay, might, on the Committee have to comment on the posts occupied by officers senior to him.[3] Eventually, Sir George Clarke (the Governor of Victoria), whom the King thought 'well fitted to aid War Office reconstruction' was selected to be the third member.[4]

[1] 'It seems to be the fate of any discussion of the War Commission's Report to resolve itself into a discussion of the Report appended by Lord Esher to that Report.'—Mr. Spencer Wilkinson, speaking at the R.U.S.I. Debate, February 29, 1904. 'R.U.S.I. Journal', 1904, p. 231.

[2] And apparently Fisher objected to serving with Brackenbury.—Esher Journals, October 19, 1904, vol. ii, p. 28.

[3] 'Lord Grenfell's Memoirs', pp. 170–1.

[4] Lee, vol. ii, p. 195.

Sir George Clarke in his younger days had been the Secretary of the Hartington Commission and he had served on the Dawkins Committee. He was actually in Australia when this Committee of three was formed.

At the King's express stipulation, the Committee was appointed by the Prime Minister and not by the Secretary of State for War. Moreover, royal approval was to be specifically indicated in the message to the press.

The notice issued on November 7, 1903, therefore ran:

'The Prime Minister, with the King's approval, and after consultation with the Secretary of State for War, has appointed a Committee . . . to advise as to the creation of a board for the administration of the War Office, and as to the consequential changes thereby involved.'[1]

The work of this Committee and the important changes that were to follow its discussion will be dealt with in a following chapter.

In the meantime, the new Secretary had already got to work. Mr. Arnold-Forster might, in all fairness, be described as somewhat of a fanatic. Lord Esher, writing earlier in 1903, before the change of ministers, described him as 'a pale-eyed, determined-looking fellow, with enough earnestness to carry him far'.[2] He had long been interested in Army matters. He had published 'Army Letters' in 1898, a collection of various articles, and throughout the South African War he had been a frequent speaker in the House of Commons debates whenever military matters were under discussion. A severe critic of the existing military system, he specially inveighed against the terrible wastage involved by the prevalent method of recruiting.

[1] Lee, vol. ii, p. 195.

It is, perhaps, desirable to place on record Mr. Campbell-Bannerman's comments upon the method of appointment of this Committee. Speaking in the House of Commons on the Army Estimates after the Report of the Committee had been published, he said: 'I am not discussing the details of the plan itself, but I say that the manner of constitution, the whole procedure is without any precedent, and I believe it to be an infringement in some respects of constitutional practice, and certainly of the decent conduct of public affairs if the House of Commons and Parliament are to keep their rights firmly established.'—A.D., 1904, p. 445.

[2] Esher Journals, vol. ii, p. 9.

MR. ARNOLD-FORSTER TAKES OFFICE

Speaking in general terms, he was inclined to a reversion to pre-Cardwell thought, to an army of long-service soldiers chiefly destined to overseas duty.

Some years before this debate, replying to Mr. Brodrick in the House of Commons, Mr. Arnold-Forster had specially referred to the linked battalion system.

'The Right Honourable Gentleman says that it is absolutely out of the question to get rid of it, and that in order to get rid of it you must substitute depots which would be enormously expensive. . . . I believe that to be a delusive conclusion arrived at by people who do not desire to see a reasonable system put into force. . . . Results which have been obtained in the Guards and Royal Marines can be obtained in the Line Regiments.'[1]

His recent connection with the Admiralty had, perhaps, strengthened certain of the views which he had gained from the analogy of naval recruitment and training.

He was to suffer, like other would-be reformers, from the fact that he took office with a preconceived remedy for the problems with which he was faced.

He became Secretary of State for War in October; before a month was out he was producing memoranda on Army Reform. Esher counselled delay. He wrote to Balfour on November 27th: 'My suggestion to you comes to this, do not let Arnold-Forster be in a hurry. Brodrick created six beautiful Army Corps *on paper*. Let his younger colleague beware.'[2] Esher wanted to get the War Office Reorganization completed, supply the new Secretary of State with a technical Board of Advisers, and then let him get on with the work of Army reorganization.

Arnold-Forster, however, persisted with his scheme and submitted the memorandum to the Prime Minister. Balfour sent it along to Esher, who returned to the argument that what was required above all else was the creation of a Board of Management.

[1] Debate, February 25, 1898.　　[2] Esher Journals, vol. ii, p. 31.

'Evidently, in Arnold-Forster's mind, there is running some scheme which is the reversal of the principles upon which our Army has been based since the days of Cromwell. He may be perfectly right, but does it not prove the necessity for some body or department, containing elements of permanence and continuity whose business should be to deal with these problems?

Brodrick is a very able, hardworking Minister with years of official experience behind him. He deliberately adopted certain principles of "Army Reform". Within a few months we have Arnold-Forster, equally able, with another scheme, based on different principles. Probably in (as nations go) a short time we shall have Asquith or Edward Grey or heaven knows who with a third scheme. If Arnold-Forster is wise, he will bury his memorandum for the present, and will throw all his energy into the creating of a "Department" for the Defence Committee (we will call it a General Staff) and a War Office Council, as an executive authority. To the former you as Prime Minister can then put the following questions:

        What is the minimum regular army we require?
        On what terms can it be enlisted?
        What will it cost?

It is not a question of Home Defence. The Navy can deal with Home Defence. It is a problem of foreign defence.'[1]

In the meantime, Lord Esher was doing everything in his power to hasten forward that part of the work to which he had particularly set his hand. The 'Committee of Three,' as the War Office Reconstitution Committee was also called, issued its first report on February 1st, its second report on February 29th, and its last and final report on March 26th.

The effect of the work of this little group of men was all-important, but in a sense these effects were a side-issue in the scheme on which Arnold-Forster had set his heart, and so it is possible to make these important reports the subject of a special study in a subsequent chapter.[2]

On February 2, 1904, Parliament reassembled, having been

        [1] Esher Journals, December 15, 1903, vol. ii, p. 33.
        [2] Chapter 10, Esher Committee.

prorogued since August 14, 1903. On February 6th, the Russo-Japanese war broke out. The lessons of this campaign were, in fact, to be available to the British Army before reorganization took final shape, though at that time such an advantage from delay did not seem very apparent.

The Army Estimates for the financial year 1904-5 were issued on February 27th. The preliminary Memorandum was not revolutionary. Substantial reductions were made, though these were largely in the nature of general economies and did not, as yet, reflect any great scheme of reorganization. The establishment of a battalion of the Brigade of Guards was reduced by 94 men, the establishment of a battalion of the Line by 50 men. The Royal Garrison Regiment was reduced from eight battalions to five,[1] and three batteries of artillery were transferred to the Indian establishment.

The reduction in the establishment of the Royal Garrison Regiment was important because it indicated a definite break with Mr. Brodrick's scheme. A further emphasis of change of policy was contained in the note that, for the coming year, enlistment into the Militia Reserve would be discontinued.

Provision in the Estimates was made for a permanent garrison in South Africa of 21,500 men, including four regiments of cavalry, ten Line battalions, and four Garrison battalions. The total Effective and Non-Effective services were estimated at £28,830,000. This was a reduction of £5,500,000 on the previous estimates, which, of course, still bore traces of the expenditure on the South African War. The total establishment on Vote A of 227,000 may be compared with the 171,000 of the 1898 estimates, the last estimates unclouded by the threat of hostilities.

The opening debate on the Estimates took place on March 7th. Out of a long speech, three phrases used by Mr. Arnold-Forster may, perhaps, be quoted as showing his views on certain subjects.

[1] This was only a paper reduction; there never had been more than five battalions formed.

Of the general position he said, "I confess that I do not view with equanimity the condition of the Army at the present time'; of the Volunteers: 'At the present moment I am confident the Volunteers are not fulfilling to anything like the extent they ought to fulfil the duties which the country hopes they may fulfil in time of war.'

Finally, one very pregnant sentence when referring to the first allocation of the new guns: 'India is our only possible place of contact with a great European Army.'[1] Mr. Balfour, two days later, emphasized this aspect of the military problem, the influence on political thought of Russia's steady advance in a South-Easterly direction.

'But Sir, though I do not believe that this landing of a great organized force competent to quell this country and reduce it by force is possible, no man can blind himself to the fact that the whole trend of circumstances in the East is to make us a Continental Power conterminous with another Continental Power, and that is the dominating circumstance which we have to take into account in framing our Army Estimates.'[2]

In truth, however, the debate was somewhat unreal, for it was clear to all that the Six Army Corps system was dead. It was not supported by the new Secretary of State, although, so far, his plans were not known. As Mr. McCrae said in the first day's debate, the estimates were based on a scheme of Army Reform 'repudiated and condemned by the Cabinet, by the Secretary of State, and by the Committee of investigation'.[3]

Before the Estimates emerged from the Committee stage—and it was late summer before that took place—substantial changes had been made in the organization of the Army.

Meanwhile, another Commission was bringing its work to an end.

---

[1] Speech on the Army Estimates, March 7, 1904. A.D., 1904, p. 435.
[2] Mr. A. J. Balfour, House of Commons, March 1904. A.D., 1904, p. 888.
[3] A.D., 1904, p. 532.

The Norfolk Commission

The Norfolk Commission had been constituted during the Secretaryship of Mr. Brodrick, and had been pursuing its labours during the period of the change of Ministers. The Royal Warrant of April 23, 1903, had appointed:

The Duke of Norfolk, the Earl of Derby, Baron Grenfell, Sir Coleridge Groves, Sir Ralph Knox, Lieutenant-Colonel O'Callaghan Westrop, (Clare Royal Garrison Artillery), Lieutenant-Colonel E. H. Llewellyn, (4th Battalion Somerset Light Infantry), Lieutenant-Colonel E. Satterthwaite, (2nd Volunteer Battalion Royal West Kent Regiment), Lieutenant-Colonel J. A. Dalmahoy, (1st Midlothian Royal Garrison Artillery.), H. Spencer Wilkinson.

To these, the Earl of March was added on May 15th. The purpose of the Commission was:

'To enquire into the organization numbers and terms of service of our Militia and Volunteer Forces, and to report whether any, and if any, what changes are required in order to secure that these forces shall be maintained in a condition of military efficiency and at an adequate strength.'[1]

The Commission, however, at an early stage in its history, endeavoured to extend its scope of research. On May 30, 1903, the Commission gave an indication of what was in their mind by requesting the attendance of the Director of Naval Intelligence, and advising him that they would require from him evidence on the subject of six questions set out in the letter to him.

The first, fifth, and sixth of these questions were:

(1) To what extent can the Navy be relied upon to protect the country against invasion?
(5) If the country can be invaded what are the limits which the Admiralty puts to the force which could be landed?

[1] Second paragraph of Royal Warrant.

(6) On the assumption that this country is at war with one or two Continental Powers within what time do the Navy expect to have command of the seas?[1]

The Commission received the reply that the Lords of the Admiralty could not permit the Director of Naval Intelligence to attend to answer such questions. The Admiralty suggested that the matter might be referred to the President of the Council, who was the Chairman of the Committee of Imperial Defence. The Duke of Norfolk, therefore, wrote to the Duke of Devonshire, President of the Council,[2] for the following information:

'We gather', he wrote, 'from the nature of the enquiry referred to us, that the possibility of an invasion must be reckoned upon as accepted. So far as Home Defence is concerned, no Auxiliary forces need be maintained if the Navy and Regular Army are capable of making impossible or ineffective the hostile landing of a large force on our shores. Should, however, such a landing be effected, there can be little doubt that the Auxiliary Forces would find themselves opposed to troops as perfectly trained, as scientifically equipped, as ably commanded as any which a great military power can bring into the field.'

The Duke of Devonshire's reply deprecated such an extension of the enquiry. Such matters, he suggested, came properly under the purview of the Committee of Imperial Defence.[3] The purpose of the Commission was to accept the approximate present establishment of the Militia and the Volunteers and to consider what were the steps which might be taken to render these forces more efficient.

On July 22nd a further memorandum from the Committee of Imperial Defence enlarged this argument and

[1] Norfolk Commission, p. 74.
[2] This took place, of course, before the Duke of Devonshire's retirement from the Balfour Ministry in consequence of the fiscal dispute.
[3] 'This question has been for some time, and still is, under the consideration of the Committee of Imperial Defence.'—Duke of Devonshire to Duke of Norfolk, June 22, 1903.

finally, on August 5, 1903, the Committee of Imperial Defence laid down that an effective force of 100,000 Militia and 200,000 Volunteers would meet with requirements of the mobilization scheme for Home Defence.

Nevertheless, the Norfolk Committee had definitely in their minds the menace of the invasion by 'perfectly trained, scientifically equipped' masses of conscript armies.

Before the receipt of the above-quoted memorandum, during the month of June 1903 a great deal of the examination of witnesses like Lord Wolseley, Major-General Turner, Colonel P. H. N. Lake, Admiral Sir J. Ommanney Hopkins,[1] and Major-General Sir J. C. Ardagh, K.C.I.E., C.B., had dealt with this possibility of invasion. Lord Wolseley had been very pessimistic. General Ardagh, on the other hand, had emphasized the very great limitations imposed upon any would-be invader, the difficulty of assembling sufficient tonnage, the impossibility of keeping such an assemblage secret.

Later on, the Commission proceeded to collect some exceedingly valuable evidence on the subject of conditions in the Militia and the Volunteers. The difficulties under which the Militia laboured, the transitory nature of the services of both recruits and young officers—both classes using the Militia merely as a stepping-stone to the Line—were clearly brought out. The recommendations concerning the Volunteer Force, printed as paragraph 58 of the Report, were of extreme importance, and in very many ways acted as a guide to what was to be eventually carried out under the Haldane Scheme.[2]

But the majority of the Commission had already made up their minds on the subject of compulsory service. After having, in paragraph 68 of the Report, laid down the principle

[1] He had previously been Naval Lord of the Admiralty and Controller of the Navy.
[2] Appendix H gives paragraph 58 of the Norfolk Commission's Report and also an extract from the Report on the position of Militia Commanding Officers.

that: 'If the purpose is to produce a force which, without substantial help from the Regular army, can be replied upon to defeat an invader, then improvements in the Militia and Volunteer Forces will not be enough', the Norfolk Commission proceeded to advocate some system of compulsory service.

The various continental systems having been mentioned, and a modification of the Swiss system recommended, the Commission's report closes with the statement:

'But that a Home Defence Army capable, in the absence of the whole or the greater part of the regular forces, of protecting the country against invasion can be raised and maintained only on the principle that it is the duty of every citizen of military age and sound physique to be trained for the national defence, and to take part in it should emergency arise.'

The report was dated May 20, 1904. Such a pronouncement from such a Committee was, of course, not without effect in the Country. The mind of the Secretary of State was, however, made up, and the Prime Minister was, as he made clear in his speech of March 9th previously quoted, in support of the general theory of the difficulties of invasion.

On June 2nd, in the House of Commons, Mr. Arnold-Forster announced that the Government was not prepared to look favourably on any scheme of conscription.[1]

His own scheme for Army Reform was at this time being considered by the Cabinet and being submitted for Royal approval. All was not plain sailing. The King instructed Lord Knollys to write to Mr. Balfour:

[1] 'No, Sir, the Government does not intend to make any proposals to the House in favour of a system of conscription.'—In reply to a question by Mr. Herbert Samuel. A.D., 1904, p. 995.
On June 8th, Mr. Balfour make a similar reply to a question by Sir Frederick Banbury. A.D., 1904, p. 1005.
He followed this up with a printed statement, issued on August 2nd (Command Paper 1909 of 1904), showing that the additional cost of conscription to the country would be £25,900,000, taking as a basis the annual class of 380,000 suggested by the Norfolk Commission.

'I am desired by His Majesty to say that your letter giving an account of Mr. Arnold-Forster's latest scheme affecting the Army which was laid before the Cabinet, and agreed to, gives His Majesty much concern.

The King is strongly of the opinion that what the Army, especially the officers throughout the Army, requires at the present time, is a period free from disturbance and constant change.'[1]

In the Cabinet, the proposals were not unanimously supported. As will be seen, the plan was to involve a Home Service Army. Mr. Arnold-Forster's own scheme was to use some of the Militia Regiments in this Home Service Army. Such a suggestion aroused strong opposition.[2] Eventually, the compromise was effected which would allow the Secretary to make his statement in the House, explain what, in his view, was the best method of using the Militia, but at the same time give a pledge that there should be no alteration in the constitution of this force unless and until the consent of Parliament and the approval of the country had been obtained.[3]

The relevant paragraphs of the Secretary of State's Memorandum would, therefore, read:

'The best way of meeting this deficiency (i.e. of Regular battalions in the Home-Service Army) would probably be to absorb a certain number of selected Militia battalions into the Home-service territorial army, bringing them up, both as regards officers and men, to the standard of the other short-service battalions. . . .

But however desirable on general grounds, there are serious practical objections to such a proposal for the absorption of Militia

---

[1] Lee, p. 205. Sir Sidney Lee gives the date of this letter and Mr. Arnold-Forster's speech on July 14th as 1905. This is clearly an error of one year. The speech was July 14 1904. It appears, therefore, from the context that the letter must be the same year.

[2] 'The Cabinet has been sitting all day to try and work out a compromise on A.F.'s scheme. The Government are so frightened! It appears that the Tory members are all against the abolition of the Militia, of which they got wind through the newspapers.'—Esher Journals, July 12, 1904, vol. ii, p. 58.

[3] 'Memoirs of H. O. Arnold-Forster,' p. 250.

battalions into the Territorial Army,[1] an absorption which, for financial reasons would necessitate the reduction or abolition of the remaining Militia battalions, and any such change can only be made with the full concurrence of Parliament and the support of public opinion.'[2]

In the meantime, pressure on the Government to make some pronouncement on Army Reform was increasing both in the press and in Parliament. One important change had been announced in a somewhat casual manner. While the Army Estimates were dragging their interminable way through the Committee stage, on April 14th, in the course of the consideration of the vote on Warlike Stores, Mr. Arnold-Forster killed the Army Corps. 'Estimates', he said, 'would be prepared in reference to Districts . . . the exact form was under consideration, the Army Corps organization would not be continued and there would be substituted for it another form of divisions not based on the Army Corps or organization.' On June 28th, the Adjournment of the House was moved to call attention to the alarming deficiency in drafts to India and South Africa, and to the confusion and uncertainty caused by the delay in submitting the Government's proposals.[3]

Finally, on July 14, 1904, being the seventeenth allotted day of the Committee stage of the Estimates, the Secretary of

[1] This is, of course, the 'Territorial Army' of Mr. Arnold-Forster's speech and not the Territorial Force later constituted by Mr. Haldane.

[2] Summary of the Speech of the Secretary of State for War (Command Paper 1907 of 1904, pp. 11 and 12). The proposals would involve the incorporation of thirty-five Militia battalions into the Home-service army.

[3] The Adjournment was moved by Mr. Becket 'for the purpose of discussing a definite matter of urgent public importance', viz.: 'The alarming deficiency in the drafts required for India and South Africa, and the confusion and uncertainty now prevailing in the War Office and the Army owing to the prolonged delay in the announcement of a definite scheme of Army reorganization.'

In the course of his speech Mr. Becket said: 'The War Office were sending men out to India who had not ten months to serve, and men to South Africa who had not six months to serve.'—A.D., 1904, p. 1148.

State for War made his long-awaited speech on Army reorganization. It was, at any rate, a drastic condemnation of things as they stood. The speech was reissued as a Summary,[1] and while it is impossible in a work like this to cover all the points, it will be necessary to quote one or two of the most important paragraphs. There was at the outset a definite pronouncement:

'It is absolutely necessary to make a change in the organization, composition, and distribution of the Army.

The late war and the Commission on the War which had recently reported, have made it abundantly clear that the army in its present form is not suited to the requirements of the country or adapted for War.

The annual Estimates show that the cost of the Army is excessive.'[2]

Such an opening was at least definite. Mr. Arnold-Forster then went on to examine, largely in the light of the findings of the Elgin Commission, the present position of the Army. He claimed one great advance: 'The Committee of Defence has been instituted.'[3] 'The whole of the War Office organization has been reconstituted in accordance with the recommendations of the Esher Committee.'[4] For the rest, the Regular Army was in a bad way. The Norfolk Commission had reported, among other things, that 'the Militia in its existing condition is unfit to take the field for the defence of this country', and that the Volunteer Force, 'in view of the unequal military education of the officers, the limited training of the men, and the defects of equipment and organization, is not qualified to take the field against a Regular Army'. And yet, said Mr. Arnold-Forster, the country was spending

[1] The Command Paper quoted above. The Summary was dated July 14.
[2] The first three paragraphs of the Summary.
[3] That is, in its new form. As will be shown in Chapter 10, there had for some years been a Committee of Defence in the Ministry.
[4] The Committee of Three—The War Office Reorganization Committee. Its report is dealt with in Chapter 10.

just on thirty millions that year on the Army. 'In the Navy it is the Shipbuilding Vote that is the principal item of cost. In the Army it is the number of men that governs all other Votes.'

The total number of men maintained in the Army, including India, and the Reserves, was, said Mr. Forster, 539,112.

'Is this enormous number of troops necessary?

If the British fleet be efficient, clearly it is not necessary. The Admiralty are of the opinion that, while they cannot guarantee this country against "raids", they can guarantee it against serious invasion. If the Admiralty are right, then we need not maintain an Army for Home Defence, capable of resisting serious invasion. If the Admiralty are wrong, then no Army we can maintain will be sufficient to protect us from hostile attack. If we have command of the sea, we can prevent any invading Army landing. If we have not command of the sea, it will not be necessary for an enemy to land, it can starve us into submission.

It is evident, therefore, that the Army we want is an Army which will enable us to maintain our Empire across the sea in peace and in war, and which will enable us to resist raids at home attempted in the absence of the fleet. It is to create such an Army that our efforts ought to be directed. Obviously, the Army which we now have is not the one we require, for it includes over 400,000 men who are not down to go abroad, and the majority of whom are not required for defence at home.'

Mr. Arnold-Forster therefore proposed to make a fundamental alteration in the plan of the British Regular Army. He would divide it into two parts: a General Service Army and a Home Service Army.

'The General Service Army will serve both abroad and at home in time of peace and in time of war.

The Home Service Army will serve at home in peace, and abroad, if necessary, in time of important wars.'

The General Service Army was to consist of men engaged for fairly long periods of service. It was proposed that they should enlist for nine years with the Colours and three years in first-class Reserve. The rigid linking of battalions in pairs was to be abandoned. Mr. Forster proposed that, while all the overseas battalions would, naturally, belong to the General Service portion of the Army, only a few battalions of this General Service Army would be maintained in England, and these would be concentrated into the striking force which would be maintained at Aldershot. On the supposition that certain battalions abroad could eventually be withdrawn, the Secretary of State proposed an eventual distribution of Battalions as follows:[1]

	Number of Battalions		All Ranks
	Foot Guards	Line Battalions	
Home	10	—	9,079
	—	26 General Service	21,024
	—	71 Home Service	36,920
Total for Home	10	97	67,023
Total for Colonies and Egypt	—	26 General Service	22,438
Total for India	—	52 General Service	53,924
Total	10	175	143,385

In order to get rid of the necessity of having one battalion at home for every battalion abroad, it was proposed to establish large depots for the General Service battalions, on the principle adopted by the Guards, the Royal Artillery, and the Marine Depots.

The Battalions which were not going to be required for the striking force were to become Home Service battalions. Excluding the Guards there would be some forty of these

[1] Particulars regarding the Proposed Army Organization Scheme, Command Paper 1910, August 1, 1904.

battalions from the existing Regular Army, filled with men recruited on a short-term enlistment, two years with the Colours, followed by six years in the first-class Army Reserve. The peace strength of the battalions would be 500. There would be 20 officers permanently attached to each battalion who would be fully commissioned officers interchangeable with the officers from the General Service battalions, and, in addition, there would be attached to each battalion ten Reserve officers. This Home Service Army was to be completely Territorialized. The Regiments would serve in their own Territorial districts, they would have the same barracks assigned to them. 'And their furthest move in peace will be to the nearest training ground, or to Aldershot or Salisbury Plain, in the case of certain battalions taken in rotation for a period of training.'

Militia

The Militia question was skated over lightly. The Secretary read the agreed paragraphs which have been already quoted, explained, and deplored the existing desperate state of the Militia, and promised consultation with Militia officers, 'in order to discuss any further changes that might, with advantage be introduced'.

Volunteers

In the case of the Volunteers more definite steps were taken: Mr. Arnold-Forster was a somewhat critical observer of the Volunteer Corps. He felt that it absorbed a good deal of money without giving an adequate return. He proposed, therefore, to reduce the strength of the Volunteers and, at the same time, to take steps to increase its efficiency.

'That strength, which on 1st of January, 1904, was 241,000—though 100,000 short of the establishment of 347,075—is actually in excess of the requirements, though nobody can contend that the efficiency of the force is in excess of what is required for war.

MR. ARNOLD-FORSTER TAKES OFFICE

A reduction of the numbers and an increase in the efficiency are obviously indicated.

It is proposed to reduce the establishment of the Volunteers to 200,000 and the present strength to 180,000, in other words, to reduce the force by one-fourth.'

It was proposed, moreover, to divide the Volunteers into two classes: approximately 60,000 would be on the higher formation, would be expected to give a good deal of time to drill and training, and would be organized into the higher field formations in association with Yeomanry, Artillery, and Engineers. They would receive a higher Grant. The remaining 120,000 Volunteers would be on a lower standard of efficiency and would receive a lower Grant.

In the second paragraph of his summary, Mr. Arnold-Forster had used a phrase which had occurred before in his speeches. 'The first-class infantry Reserve is still a substitute for, and not a supplement to, the men serving.' His point was that the Army at home could not send the smallest force abroad without calling up the Reserves, and, moreover, that the Army at home was so youthful that the reservists had not only to fill home battalions up to war strength, but had to take the place of a very large number of men under 20 years of age, or otherwise unfit, in the Home Service battalions. Mr. Arnold-Forster's cure for this was to maintain a small striking force at home composed of units of grown men ready to go overseas at short notice.

It was a fairly comprehensive change in Army organization. That day, the House of Commons had four and three-quarter hours, only, available for the War Office vote, and the Secretary of State's speech had taken up two and a quarter hours of the total time.[1]

So there was not very much time for criticism, destructive or constructive, that day. Before long, however, murmurs were heard. On July 28th, in the House of Lords, the Earl of Wemyss moved, 'That in the opinion of this House any

[1] Mr. Winston Churchill on July 18th.—A.D., p. 1407.

scheme of Army reorganization that does away with the militia force is contrary to sound policy destroying as it does the ancient constitutional foundation of our existing military system.' That was a warning of hostility from one quarter. In the House of Commons the debate was resumed on August 8th. Members were very doubtful of the wisdom of dividing the Regular Army into two. Lord George Hamilton spoke of the Home service battalions who were 'to be kept at the interminable drudgery of drilling recruits'. Mr. Churchill, on the other hand, wondered if the long-service recruits would be obtained:

'Would 6d. a day make the difference to the man who had the choice of shipping himself off to the East for five or six years, when he could serve for two years in his own country, and after that have six years in the Reserve with pay in civil life?'

From the supporters of the Militia came, almost without exception, steady opposition. Mr. Griffith Boscawen said that the 'existing force might be boiled down to thirty-three home service battalions, in that sense its identity would be preserved, but it would not be preserved as Militia'.

The House of Commons adjourned on August 15th, having, on the whole, had little opportunity of considering the very revolutionary proposals that had been made to it by the Secretary of State. Five days before the adjournment, on August 10th, he had refused to give any date on which he would start his new system of recruitment.[1]

That new system of recruitment was destined never to take effective form. The clamant need was to get the long-service soldiers for the overseas portion of the Army. The three-years system, introduced to provide for the needs of the South African War, had blocked the Army with a large number of men serving on contractual terms which could not be altered. The short service was not the only difficulty; uncertainty added its problems, men might or might not re-engage.

[1] A.D., 1904, p. 1738.

MR. ARNOLD-FORSTER TAKES OFFICE

The condition of civil employment, the station of the battalion, and any proposed change of station, all made it very difficult for a Commanding Officer to know what his short-service man would do in the matter of re-engagement.

It has been said that Mr. Arnold-Forster proclaimed his scheme in the closing days of the session of 1904. Even before Parliament reassembled in the early spring of 1905 the great plan had been altered in its most important feature. On October 20th the Army Council decided to suspend all recruitment on the three-year engagement and take men only for nine years' service with the colours and three years with the reserve.[1]

Thus when Parliament reassembled, Mr. Arnold-Forster was in the weak position of having to admit defeat, even if only temporary defeat, on one of his main points. No sooner had the Houses reassembled than attacks were made in both the Lords and the Commons.[2] On February 14th, on the motion on the Address, Earl Spencer said:

'Last year great changes in the Army were foreshadowed. Unfortunately during the last few years we have had many changes in the Army, and schemes have been rushed into one after the other, several of which have been torn to ribbons. We know that there has been enormous expenditure and a great deal of this has been almost entirely thrown away owing to the change in principle on which the expenditure has been made.'[3]

[1] 'Three months ago, in considering the state of the Infantry and framing Estimates for the year, we were naturally anxious to make a start with the system of general and short service; but those who are particularly acquainted with these matters came to us and advised us that owing to the very small number of extensions of three-years men, Indian drafts in the next few years would be in serious jeopardy.'—The Earl of Donoughmore (Under-Secretary of State for War), speaking in the House of Lords in the Debate on Army Reorganization, February 21, 1905. A.D., 1905, pp. 40 et seq.

[2] It is perhaps rather interesting to note that the volume, Army Debates, 1905, is over four times the thickness of the similarly printed volume, Army Debates 1932–3, and that the three volumes 1903, 1904, and 1905 take up more space in the library shelves than all the volumes from 1927 to the present date.

[3] A.D., 1905, p. 5.

In reply, Lord Lansdowne claimed for the Secretary of State some achievements:

'He has completely reorganized the War Office. I am in the recollection of the House, but I think it has always been assumed that reform of the War Office was a matter to be attacked first before the problem of Army organization could be profitably approached.'

Such a defence was, of course, in a measure a condemnation of Arnold-Forster's impetuosity in publishing a full-scale and revolutionary scheme before the War Office reorganization had taken full effect.

Within a few days the Duke of Bedford had moved in the House of Lords a Debate on Army Reorganization. Supporters of the Militia protested against the part they were being called upon to play in Mr. Forster's plan.[1] The short-service system came in for a good deal of criticism. The Duke of Bedford called it 'two years boy service' and wondered whether reservists after this short tour of duty would come forward readily for distant expeditions. He questioned whether these reservists would be so very different from the Militia obtained under the existing arrangement.[2] At the end of the debate, however, an important development took place, for Earl Donoughmore announced that he would at once introduce a Bill, 'authorizing us to enlist the Militia for service abroad in time of war or emergency'. This was of course a very violent alteration in the status of the Militia. Although Militia battalions had in the past served overseas, the volunteer principle was always, at least in theory complied with.[3]

The staunch supporters of the rights of the Constitutional Force were up in arms at once. Earl Wemyss within a few

[1] 'The Militia is in a state of great uncertainty.'—Viscount Hardinge.
[2] 'Your Lordships may depend on this, if the War is a just war both Militia and Home Service Reserve will come forward for foreign service. If not they would not come forward.'—Duke of Bedford, A.D., p. 40.
[3] 'The Militia being made reliable for service abroad will ipso facto become the Reserve of the Regular Army.'—Donoughmore.

days had moved that, 'In the opinion of this House it is contrary to sound policy to tamper with the Militia forces or alter as is intended, its conditions and terms of service'.[1]

While in the House of Lords the supporters of the Militia were perhaps strongest, in the Commons the struggle raged round the question of the Volunteers. There, Sir Howard Vincent, Major Seely, and others conducted a vigorous campaign against the Secretary of State for War. The debates on the subject of the Volunteers take up many pages. Reading them all in the light of later days, judgment would probably say that in many things the Minister was right and the fanatical devotees of the Volunteer system, as it then existed, were wrong. Unfortunately, Mr. Arnold-Forster's method of presenting his case, and the suspicion, or even the knowledge, that his plans had not the wholehearted support of the Government, did give some excuse to his adversaries. The Volunteers were declining in numbers and worried by uncertainty.[2, 3]

On February 23rd, once again, an amendment on military matters was moved to the Address in reply to the Speech from the Throne. This one deplored the 'continuous and continuing' changes in the Army, disordering the system of the Regular Army and discouraging the Militia and Volunteers. The debate went on for two days. A great deal of the discussion was taken up with the question of the Volunteers. That question in turn was affected by the views held by individual speakers on the possibility of invasion. Many held that invasion was possible, and the Volunteer forces could not be too large to meet with that danger. Several speakers

[1] Amendment to the Militia Bill, February 23, 1905.—A.D., 1905, p. 220.
[2] On February 14th Sir Howard Vincent 'appealed to the Rt. Hon. Gentlemen to put an end to the present suspense which was operating so seriously on the efficiency of the Militia and Volunteer Forces'.—A.D., 1905, p. 10.
[3] In answer to a question by Sir Howard Vincent on February 20th, Mr. Arnold-Forster submitted a report covering certain of the London units which showed a rapid decline from 1902 to 1905. Some units were 300 to 400 men down.—A.D., p. 34.

urged quite legitimate grievances, though most of them were local or sectional in their effect.

The main difficulty under which the Secretary laboured was that his premature offensive of the preceding July had left him in a vulnerable position. As Mr. Campbell-Bannerman pointed out: 'The Government we assume by this time have either accepted, or modified, or altered, the scheme of last year.'[1] But the truth was even more serious, modification, and eventual abandonment, was being forced on the Government in successive stages with cumulative effect. An example was to be seen at once. One of the suggestions of the Arnold-Forster scheme of the preceding July was that the Volunteers were to be divided into two categories, 60,000 on a higher standard with higher pay, and 120,000 on a lower standard.[2]

In his reply to the amendment to the Address, he counter-attacked his critics with some effect, but gave way another point. 'I have done my best in the time that has been given me to alter a state of things which I, in common with most of the members of the House do not approve.' He claimed that the whole of the Mowatt programme of reserves had been carried out.[3] He emphasized the difficulty caused by the three-year system of recruitment inherited from his precursor in office. 'One battalion at home had 625 men under two years' service and 42 per cent of the men were under 20 years of age.'

He had once again to tackle the difficult question of the Militia, a question upon which as much as anything else his plans were to founder. He confessed that in regard to the Militia he had his own ideas which he realized did not agree with those of the majority of the House. Finally, he turned to the Volunteers. His plan, it will be remembered was to reduce the establishment of the force to 200,000 and the actual numbers to 180,000. In fact the strength of the force

---

[1] February 23rd.—A.D., 1905, p. 220.
[2] Summary of the Speech of the Secretary of State for War. Command Paper 1907 of 1904, p. 14.   [3] For Mowatt Committee see Chapter 5.

was on January 1, 1904, 241,000, and the establishment 347,075, so there was at least something to be said for the writing off of what had been for some years a paper strength. But during the South African War the strength of the Volunteers had risen to over 300,000 and the supporters of the force claimed that, with better treatment of the Auxiliary forces as a whole, that number could again be reached, and once again spoke of the danger of invasion.

Arnold-Forster wished for a reduction in numbers as an aid to efficiency. 'The Volunteers are not efficient and they ought to be made so.' It was possibly true, but it was not a popular remark. Then came another weakening in the plan. 'I do not desire or propose to press this plan of dividing Volunteers into two classes.' Then followed a portion of the speech which must be quoted in extenso, for it was a fair comment on the situation and a foreshadowing of what might be accomplished by a more prudent man.

'I ask everyone whether I do not correctly interpret their views when I say that the present needs of the Volunteers are more officers, better-trained officers, more ranges, more firing—both rifle and artillery firing—more training of non-commissoned officers, larger contributions towards the expenses of officers in camp, a longer time in camp, greater freedom as to going into camp and stopping out of it, and at any rate the embryo of a transport organization and a divisional organization. . . . We can get all these things, and more, if this reduction—not a large reduction, I speak of a moderate reduction—of the Volunteer Forces be effected.'

He hoped to get a fortnight's camp. Finally he said:

'I believe absolutely in two main principles. We must in the first place have a reduction of expenditure and secondly we must have greater efficiency.'[1]

Much of what he said was absolutely correct, but his opponents had two powerful war-cries: 'No tampering with

[1] A.D., 1905, p. 270.

the Constitutional Force'—'No reduction of the Volunteers.' Winston Churchill towards the end of the debate had plenty of material for a destructive speech. All sorts of experiments had gone on. Garrison battalions had been created with much explanation of their advantages—they had been swept away. The Militia Reserve had been created on a new basis, it had never taken effect. Terms of enlistment had been altered; there had been two complete changes of the War Office staff.

Without intermission the struggle went on. Two supplementary estimates gave further opportunities for debate. On the occasion of the first of these[1] another alteration was wrung out of the Secretary. The July, 1904, plan had contained, as a great measure of economy, the reduction of fourteen Regular battalions of the Line. But they had not been reduced, they were still in existence, and Mr. Arnold-Forster had to point out that until he could get his Militia scheme through, these battalions could not be reduced. Moreover, it had to be disclosed that at the outbreak of the Russo-Japanese War an unusual number of three-year men had been taken on, and that these men, whose terms of engagement obviously could not be cancelled, were costing more than was anticipated.

The second Supplementary Estimate[2] referred to the expenses of the Somaliland Expedition. Once again the occasion produced a change of policy, or rather the admission of a change. Mr. Arnold-Forster said that he hoped within ten or twelve months they would be able to start short-service recruiting. This he confirmed two days later in answer to a question.[3]

The date was March 9th. For some two weeks the Balfour administration had been in very difficult water owing to the Macdonnell incident.[4] Lord Londonderry and Carson had

[1] March 2, 1905.   [2] March 7, 1905.
[3] March 9th. Answer to Captain Norton: 'Short service enlistment is not abandoned, only postponed.'—A.D., 1905, p. 528.
[4] 'The position of the Government has been very insecure from day to day and it is contrary to their anticipations that they are still in office.'—Esher Journals, March 7th, vol. ii, p. 76.

both been prepared to leave the Government. The Unionist members were very uneasy, and nothing but personal appeals by the Whips to the members' loyalty to Mr. Balfour prevented wholesale abstentions from the vital debate. The Government majority fell to 42.

Small wonder then that Arnold-Forster's speech to open the Army Estimates on March 28th was subdued in tone. More than once he referred to 'whoever his successor might be'. The Memorandum which accompanied the estimates referred to the present abandonment of the idea of a short-service army. 'Until the Infantry at Home have a sufficient number of long-service men it is useless to organize a Striking Force.' 'To keep battalions up to a strength of 900 men for the purpose of a foreign expedition is useless and extravagant so long as 800 out of the 900 are boys unfitted by age or length of service for fighting at all.'

Nevertheless, his speech was a very fair-minded exposition of the Naval viewpoint of the use of the Army, and he scored a telling hit at Seely who had earlier chided him with talking about the work of the Navy—exclaiming 'this is an Army Debate'. He replied firmly to those who painted pictures, derived from the phrases of the Norfolk Commission, of masses of continental soldiery landing in these islands. 'If the hostile power were sufficiently strong at sea to land 100,000 men in this country it would not be necessary for it to land the crew of a single barge. The invading Power would command the whole of the avenues of the sea.'[1]

[1] 'We have been adding million after million to our naval expenditure. Are these millions wasted? If it is true, as we are told by representatives of the Admiralty, that the Navy is in a position such as it has never occupied before, that it is now not only our front line of defence but our guarantee for the possession of our own islands, is this to make no difference to a system which has grown up avowedly and confessedly on the basis of defending these islands by an armed land force against invasion? Is that to make no difference? Is this view some invention of my imagination? No, Sir, that is the deliberate conclusion of the Government advised by a body which has been called into, I believe, a useful existence, during the last 18 months, and which I regret was not called into existence much longer

So the struggle between the two schools of thought went on. The Prime Minister himself was firmly on the side of those who did not believe in the possibility of invasion.[1] Having made up his mind on the subject Arnold-Forster could not see the sense of maintaining a large part of the Army purely for Home Defence. He said so on many occasions.[2]

To those who maintained that, quite apart from their value for home defence the Volunteers provided a reserve in the event of a war overseas, he replied that the figures for the Volunteers who served in the South African war were not entirely convincing.[3] He also had a good deal of justification for his complaint that the medical standard of the Volunteers was not high.

'Are these Volunteers,' he asked, 'to be an immense, unlimited force with little training and imperfect equipment, or are they to be a smaller compact force well drilled and

ago, the Committee of Defence. I have seen it stated that, provided our Navy is sufficient, the greatest anticipation we can form in the way of a landing of hostile army would be a force of 5,000. I should be deceiving the House if I thought that represented the extreme Naval view. The extreme Naval view is that the crew of a dinghy could not land in this country in the face of the Navy.'—Another extract from the same speech, House of Commons, March 28, 1905. A.D., 1905, pp. 679 et seq.

[1] 'I have to say that, in the opinion of the Defence Committee, invasion for the conquest of these islands is an impossibility. The question of raids is a less important one and is also a more complicated one. . . .'—Mr. Arthur Balfour, in answer to a question, House of Commons, March 15th. A.D., 1905, p. 546.

[2] '360,000 men tied to the soil of this country in time of war.'—Debate on the Estimates, A.D., p. 694.

'We have, roughly speaking, 600,000 men amongst the forces of the Crown; of that number 360,000, or 60 per cent, are for service at home in the defence of this country.'—Donoughmore, House of Lords, Militia Bill, March 30th. A.D., p. 824.

[3] Sir Howard Vincent claimed that out of 204,000 Volunteers on the strength in 1900, 71,758 volunteeerd for overseas service, and 29,049 actually served, 17,344 with service companies and 11,705 in other ways. Arnold-Forster said that the War Office figures, which only covered the Service Companies and the Imperial Yeomanry, were 19,856 and 6,209. There was no official record of the number who volunteered but did not go.—Debate on Volunteer Vote, July 7th. A.D., 1977.

well equipped?'¹ The Prime Minister and Lord Lansdowne both spoke of the limits of cost.²

One further and quite fair point of view was made by Sir John Colomb, himself a strong advocate of the Naval point of view, when he spoke on the Army Debates. The Volunteers, he said, had been created out of a false conception of military necessity. The difficulty was to know what to do with the force. It was obvious that they could not be wiped out of existence. In the meantime, moreover, some prominent members of the force were vigorously resisting any suggestion of change.

The Secretary of State's lack of tact dogged his movements. On June 20th a circular was issued to the War Office addressed, as confidential, to the Commanders-in-Chief of Districts, seeking information as to the position of Volunteers within their areas. The first paragraph read: 'Sir, I am commanded by the Army Council to invite your attention to the fact that many Volunteer units are reported upon various causes not to be in an efficient state to take the field.' And the last paragraph read: 'I am also to request that you will be good enough to state, for the information of the Council, whether you recommend that any units in your Command which you consider to be inefficient should be disbanded or amalgamated with other and more efficient corps. . . .'³

There was, as might be anticipated, a terrific row. The

¹ Debate of April 5th. A.D. 1078 et seq.
He pointed out that in 1904 21,000 Volunteers had gone into camp for a fortnight and had been paid 5s. a day. Further, that (including this 21,000) about 175,000 Volunteers had gone to camp for a week. This was out of a strength of 245,000. His suggestion obviously was that the proposed reduction to an establishment of 200,000 and a strength of 180,000 roughly corresponded to the existing actual strength of efficient men.

² Notably Mr. Balfour on April 5th, and Lord Lansdowne on March 30th, when, speaking on the Militia Bill, he said: 'The pruning knife cannot be applied to our Naval expenditure.' Fortescue says of the period: 'But the Government was already spending vast sums on the Navy and, rightly attaching most importance to the Fleet, could spare little money for military service.'

³ Command Paper 2437 of 1905.

O

Daily Chronicle' published an article on the subject on July 4th and questions were asked in both Houses. So great was the pressure in the House of Commons that the Prime Minister agreed to bring forward the day for the discussion of the Volunteer Vote in Committee stage and there was a full-dress debate in the House on July 7th.[1]

The result of it all was that on July 11th another circular had to be brought out 'in substitution for that of June 20th', which considerably watered down the offending paragraphs. The first paragraph was now to read;

'Sir, in view of the fact that during the South African War large numbers of the Volunteers offered themselves for service in the field and in view of the many expressions of readiness on the part of the force to take a similar step in the event of the country being again engaged in a serious war, the Army Council consider it necessary to ascertain beforehand what proportion of the Volunteers in your Command are likely to be qualified for active service abroad.'

And the last paragraph was also amended so that it now read:

'I am also to request that you will be good enough to state, for the information of the Army Council, whether there are any Volunteer units in your Command which are inefficient from any cause, and, if so, whether you recommend etc. . . .'[2]

A brief foreword to the memorandum over the signature of the Secretary of State for War said: 'As it appears that the object of the circular issued on June 20, 1905, has been misapprehended in some quarters, the Army Council have thought it desirable to reissue the circular in an amended form, which it is believed, will remove all ambiguity.' The explanation, however, was not calculated to explain away the incident. The truth was that once again the Secretary of State had been forced to climb down.[3]

[1] A.D., p. 1977. [2] Command Paper 2439 of 1905.
[3] Over a year before Esher had written: 'At present a man like Arnold-Forster may have convictions, but he has not the courage of them.'—June 20, 1904. Esher Journals, p. 55.

In any case, the sands of time were running out for the Balfour Government. On July 20th an amendment of Mr. Redmond regarding the Irish Land Act was carried against the Government by two hundred votes to one hundred and ninety-six. On the 24th, following a Cabinet Council, Mr. Balfour announced that he would neither resign nor dissolve. His chief reason, although not stated at the time, was that he wished to get that Anglo-Japanese Treaty signed first.

From July onwards, however, the position of the Government was so patently insecure that no great scheme of Army Reform could possible have been carried through.

In the meantime, abroad, an event of capital importance had taken place. On March 31, 1905, the Kaiser Wilhelm II landed at Tangier, and, mounted upon a white charger, made his way to the German Legation. He was determined, he told the German colony, to uphold 'the interests of the Fatherland in a free country. . . . Commerce can only progress if all the Powers are considered to have equal rights under the sovereignty of the Sultan and respect the independence of the country. My visit is the recognition of this independence.'[1]

This was a clear challenge to the existing French policy in Morocco and it was realized as such by the Sultan who, on June 3rd, invited the Powers to join in a conference to decide the future of his country. On the advice of M. Delcassé, the Foreign Minister of M. Rouvier's Ministry, France refused the Sultan's invitation. On this the German Ambassador in Paris, Prince Radolin, on instructions from Berlin, conveyed to the French Government in very strong terms the information that Germany was behind the Sultan of Morocco. This was a challenge so menacing that M. Rouvier and his colleagues (M. Loubet alone supporting Delcassé) did not feel themselves able to withstand the pressure and M. Delcassé resigned on June 6th. This forced departure of the French

[1] Lee, vol. ii, p. 340. King Edward's comment was: 'The Tangier incident was the most mischievous and uncalled-for event which the German Emperor had ever been engaged in since he came to the throne.'—Ibid.

Foreign Minister who had been responsible for the Anglo-French Entente was regarded in Germany as a triumph for German might and German diplomacy, and in France was regarded as an insult and a threat never to be forgotten or forgiven. Another Government was to be in power in England, and a stronger man in power in France when the next threat arrived.

The long-delayed demise of the Balfour administration took place on December 4, 1904, and Mr. Arnold-Forster's tour of duty at the War Office came to an end.[1]

His task had been great and in many ways his failure was quite complete. Writing the next year to Mr. Campbell-Bannerman, Lord Esher summed up the reason for this lack of success:

'Several reasons contributed to this failure of purpose, but the primary cause was the production of a large scheme for Army organization, by the Secretary of State for War, which that Minister had evolved before he assumed office, and which he determined to press upon his colleagues. Unhappily no resistance was made to this fresh attempt to follow the idiosyncrasy of a minister rather than the lines of a rational and comprehensive plan; and though the particular scheme was ultimately defeated by the resistance of the Cabinet and the House of Commons, the mischief was done and Mr. Balfour's intentions were nullified.'[2]

If considerable space has here been given to the account of the debates in the House of Commons, where Mr. Arnold-Forster faced his critics, it is because the fact must be emphasized that the defeat of his schemes came, not from the soldiers, but in the House of Commons. Whatever might have been their view, Senior Officers did their best to cope with the changes imposed upon them by succeeding Secre-

[1] 'Said good-bye to Arnold-Forster and thanked him for my promotion to Major-General. A.-F. leaves the War Office unlamented, but at least I owe him my step.'—Macdiarmid, p. 213.
[2] Letter from Lord Esher to Sir H. Campbell-Bannerman, March 1, 1906.—Esher Journals, vol. ii, p. 147.

taries of State. As will be shown later, a great deal of valuable work was being put in by men who had been Colonels and equivalent ranks in the South African War, and were in 1914 to be in the places of great responsibility. These men were doing hard, consistent, and in some cases, almost concealed work, for the good of the army.

The three main parties who in combination brought the scheme of 1904 to its doom, were, in the first case, the ordinary private soldiers who did not see why they should extend their service. The second group of adversaries were to be found in the senior Militia officers and particularly those in a powerful position in the House of Lords. The third group, and perhaps the most dangerous, comprised the combination of political and sectional adversaries in the House of Commons. There were to be found the Volunteer group led by Sir Howard Vincent and Major Seely, who, with an intransigence worthy of a better cause, resisted attempts to alter the status of the Volunteers,[1] a younger group led by Mr. Winston Churchill and Mr. Guest, who wanted to economize on the Army by reducing the strength of the Regular Forces for the benefit of the Navy Estimates, and finally, of course, the constant mass of Liberal and Radical members hostile to any Government proposition.

In the days to come, Mr. Haldane was to bring to the problem a clear vision, together with a great degree of prudence and patience. The natural bent of his character made him take time to study the problem and gave him patience to reason with his opponents, but it must never be forgotten that during the most critical years of his scheme he also had the supreme advantage of a strong Government majority in the House of Commons.

[1] 'I find I am dealing with at least six Armies. I am dealing with the Army in India, the Indian Army, the Army at home, the Militia, the Volunteers, and the great Army of those who had left the Colours and are now entrenched in the Clubs of this City.'—Mr. Arnold-Forster, speaking on Army Estimates, March 28, 1905.

CHAPTER 10

THE FORMATION OF THE ARMY COUNCIL

LORD ESHER'S COMMITTEE AND THE COMMITTEE OF IMPERIAL DEFENCE

DURING the Secretaryships of Mr. Brodrick and Mr. Arnold-Forster, most important reforms had been taking place in the central control of the Army. In a rather singular degree these reforms lay aside from the particular theories upon which the two Secretaries of State had set their hearts. Therefore, although the events recorded in this chapter cover a period of several years, it is possible to consider the formation of the Army Council, or the creation of the Committee of Imperial Defence, as matters separated from the main current of the Six Army Corps Scheme, or projects for a Home and General Service Army.[1]

The South African War had been embarked upon by a War Office under divided control. The relationship between the Secretary of State for War and the Commander-in-Chief was laid down by an Order in Council of 1895. The circumstances giving rise to that Order were as follows.

In 1890 a Royal Commission on the Naval and Military Departments, usually called the Hartington Commission from the name of its Chairman,[2] had recommended the abolition of the office of Commander-in-Chief, the distribution of his

---

[1] It is only fair to Brodrick and Arnold-Forster to point out that Esher himself, in a letter to Lord Knollys dated September 27, 1903, gave it as his opinion that 'Ordinary business of the War Office cannot, pending reform, be carried on by a Minister who at the same time is engaged on reconstruction'.—Esher Journals, vol. ii, p. 22.

[2] Lord Hartington, afterwards Duke of Devonshire.

THE FORMATION OF THE ARMY COUNCIL 199

duties among the heads of the military departments, and the appointment of a Chief of Staff.[1]

At that time, in 1890, the Commander-in-Chief of the British Army was H.R.H. the Duke of Cambridge. In virtue of his special position as a member of the Royal House, it was not expected that important changes would be made during his tenure of the office. When, however, the time drew near October 1, 1895, the date of his retirement, it might have been expected that the recommendations of the Hartington Commission would have been followed. This, however, was not done.

Sir Henry Campbell-Bannerman, in the very last days of the Rosebery administration, gave the House of Commons the principles which would be followed in the appointment of the new Commander-in-Chief. He claimed that the 'main principles' of the Hartington Commission were adopted, but actually the arrangements then being made deviated in important respects from the recommendations of the Hartington Commission.

The title Commander-in-Chief was to be retained, and it was laid down in the Order in Council of November 21, 1895, that he should be the 'principal adviser of the Secretary of State on all military questions, and shall be charged with the general supervision of the Military Departments at the War Office'.

But Lord Lansdowne, when he succeeded to the War Office in the Salisbury Administration in 1895 produced a very long, indeed somewhat prolix, memorandum wherein he discussed, for the benefit of the Cabinet, what were the proposed arrangements. He pointed out that the new plan was a compromise between the one school who, following the Hartington Commission, wished to abolish the Commander-in-Chief, and the other school who wished to have a real Commander-in-Chief who was in fact supreme in Army matters. Lord Lansdowne

[1] Memorandum of Lord Lansdowne dated May 8, 1899, quoted in E.C., p. 133. See also Chapter 2.

reviewed the historical, constitutional, and administrative factors bearing on this point and suggested certain advantages in the existing compromise. But the important paragraph, the one which contained the germ of future disputes, was the penultimate: 'With this object in view each head will have free access to the Secretary of State as well as an opportunity of recording his opinion upon the papers concerning his department, and of raising his voice at meetings of the Army Board or the War Office Council.'[1]

This was the gravamen of the complaint by Lord Wolseley:

'As I suppose every one of the Commission is aware, when I was Commander-in-Chief, the War Office was divided into four great departments—the Adjutant-General, the Quartermaster-General, the Inspector-General of Fortifications and the Director-General of Ordnance. Now, of all those four officers not one of them was an officer belonging to the Commander-in-Chief; they were all officers belonging, I might say, to the Secretary of State for War, and went to him, and saw him without any sort of knowledge whatever of the Commander-in-Chief.'[2, 3]

There was almost bound to be friction. This friction was brought to a head by the outbreak of the South African War, and was brought into the open by the full-dress debate in the House of Lords on Monday, March 4, 1901. By the time

[1] Minute by Lord Lansdowne dated October 31, 1895, quoted in E.C., p. 528.
[2] Evidence of Lord Wolseley, E.C., q. 9082.
[3] 'To call a man a Commander-in-Chief who in his relations with his Secretary of State for War was on the same level with his Adjutant-General, Quartermaster-General and Inspectors-General of Fortifications and Ordnance, was in any case a mistake, but it was especially the case when the officer thus placed in a false position was Lord Wolseley. To him the incongruity of the circumstances was especially galling, for he had, himself, served as Adjutant-General and Quartermaster-General under a very different régime, and must for years have been looking forward to the day when, as the real military head of the Army, he would stand between the departmental heads and the Parliamentary Chief as the Duke of Cambridge had done for nearly forty years.'—'The War Office Past and Present', Captain Owen Wheeler, p. 255.

THE FORMATION OF THE ARMY COUNCIL

Lord Wolseley had finished his denunciation of the Order in Council of 1895 and his disapproval of the existing system of War Office administration which he had 'honestly tried for five years and found wanting', the House of Lords realized that the problem was more serious than could be solved merely by Lord Lansdowne's reply that Lord Wolseley had largely brought his troubles on himself.[1]

Changes in one or two directions were indeed made very soon. Shortly after the debate in the Lords an alteration of importance was made in the position of the Adjutant-General. By an order in Council dated November 5, 1901, the Commander-in-Chief was made responsible for the control of the Adjutant-General's Department. In fact Lieutenant-General Sir T. Kelly-Kenny who became Adjutant-General in October, actually took office under the terms of this new Order.[2] By this measure the Commander-in-Chief was made more clearly responsible for the discipline of the forces under his nominal command.

Other changes had been made under the stress of hostilities, and some of these eventually led the way to permanent improvements in organization.

In the days of the Duke of Cambridge, when the Royal Commander-in-Chief was not always inclined to do a great deal of routine work, a good deal of responsibility fell on the Adjutant-General. The practice had grown up of holding from time to time a series of unofficial conferences known as the Adjutant-General's meetings.[3]

When in 1895 Lord Lansdowne became Secretary of State for War—and almost at the same time Lord Wolseley became

---

[1] 'The whole country was electrified by the Debate so unexpectedly raised in the House of Lords on the subject of Army administration. There was nothing to show that behind the mild display made by the Duke of Bedford, the ex-Commander-in-Chief was coming up in force with horse, foot, and guns. So the speech he delivered was all the more convincing.'—'Army and Navy Gazette', March 9, 1901.

[2] E.C., Evidence of General Kelly-Kenny, qq. 4479 et seq.

[3] E.C., q. 21471.

Commander-in-Chief—this somewhat irregular organization, the Adjutant-General's meeting, was converted into an Army Board. This, to save confusion, may be called the 1895 Board. It was to consist of the Commander-in-Chief and the four other military heads of departments. It met under the Presidency of the Commander-in-Chief, took minutes, and had fairly regular meetings.

Apart from this there existed the formal War Office Council constituted by Mr. Cardwell, which met under the Presidency of the Secretary of State for War, was summoned only when he thought a meeting necessary, and, speaking in general terms, worked only on his agenda.[1]

When the South African War broke out, Lord Lansdowne first called up the War Office Committee for Mobilization. He speedily found, however, that this Committee of nineteen members was far too cumbrous for war-time measures. He therefore formed a new Army Board (hereinafter referred to as the 1899 Board) which consisted of the five members of the 1895 Board together with the Accountant-General and the Assistant Under-Secretary of State. Both these added officials came from the civil staff at the War Office.

Then Mr. Brodrick took office in November 1900, and altered the situation once again by restoring the importance of the War Office Council.[2] It was, in future to meet regularly, and any member of the Council could bring up any subject that he wished. The Army Board in its 1899 form Mr. Brodrick considered to be 'imperative in any case of war', and his Army Council proposals were not affecting its work as far as concerned its mobilization functions. He did not, however, think that continuous sittings of the Army Board would be necessary in peace-time.

A War Office Committee under the presidency of Mr. Clinton Dawkins had been appointed on January 8, 1901, to conduct an enquiry into the conduct of official business at the

[1] E.C., q. 21477. [2] E.C., q. 21595.

War Office.[1] Among other matters it was asked to point out any amendment of procedure which in its opinion 'would bring the work of the War Office more into harmony with that of large business undertakings'.

In paragraph 131 of their Report issued on June 8th, the Dawkins Committee proposed 'to establish a War Office Board on a permanent basis, with clearly defined duties and powers, which, acting under the authority of the Secretary of State, and without in any way detracting from the individual responsibilities of the Commander-in-Chief and of the Military Heads of Departments, would control and supervise the business of the War Office as a whole'.

Though Mr. Brodrick claimed in his evidence before the Elgin Commission that, in his newly revived War Office Council, he was carrying out the recommendations of the Dawkins Committee, the Commission in its Report doubted whether the Secretary of State's Council was in fact equivalent to the powerful Board envisaged by Mr. Clinton Dawkins and his colleagues.

The Report of the Elgin Commission, and, as has been seen, particularly the annexe to the Report signed by Lord Esher, provided powerful argument for a change.

Lord Esher's recommendations were:

First to reorganize the War Office Council and to define more clearly their functions as an advisory and executive Board, presided over by the Secretary of State in whom however final responsibility to Parliament must be reserved.

Secondly, to decentralize internally the War Department by a rearrangement of duties, under the important members of the Board, abolishing the cross jurisdiction now existing.

---

[1] The members of the Committee were:

Mr. Clinton Dawkins (Chairman).
Colonel Sir George Clarke, K.C.M.G.
Mr. G. S. Gibb.
Mr. W. Mather, M.P.

Colonel H. G. S. Miles, C.B., M.V.O.
Sir Charles Welby, Bart., C.B., M.P.
Secretary: Mr. H. J. Gibson.

The Report of this Committee on War Office Organization was published as Command Paper 581 of 1901.

Thirdly, to abolish the Commander-in-Chief and to appoint a General Officer Commanding the Army, responsible to the Secretary of State for the efficiency of the military forces of the Empire.[1]

The Report of the Royal Commission on the War in South Africa was signed on July 9, 1903. The Cabinet was in the throes of political controversy. Resignations were being steadily announced all through September, and it was not until October 6th that the more important ministerial changes could be announced.

In Chapter 9 the story has already been told of the manner in which the small Esher Committee was launched upon its task with a very special manifestation of royal and Cabinet support. Indeed, the work achieved by these three, or rather four, men was so great, and in nearly every respect, so enduring, that the personalities concerned repay some slight study. Each contributed an individual share to the total result. The three members of the Committee were: Reginald Viscount Esher, Admiral Sir John Fisher, Colonel Sir George Sydenham Clarke. The Secretary was Lieutenant-Colonel G. F. Ellison.

Esher had already made his mark by his work as a member of the Royal Commission on the South African War. He was determined above all things to get into the War Office his scheme for an Army Board and to create, for the War Office, a General Staff, similar, in some respects to the Generalstab of Berlin, to which his journals so often refer.[2] Fisher, a man of famous, and powerful, personality was chiefly notable, so far as this Committee was concerned, for his cheerful and all-embracing preference for Naval methods. He bombarded the Secretary with characteristic, largely written, notes upon many subjects not all within the terms of reference of the Committee. He disliked the 'double entry' of Sandhurst and Woolwich existing side by side. He disapproved of the Regimental

---

[1] E.C., p. 146.
[2] It appears likely that he was influenced by the evidence given before the Elgin Committee by Sir John Ardagh.—Esher Journals, vol. i, p. 360.

system. Naturally he was a powerful supporter of the Esher plan for government by an Army Board. Clarke, who did not return to England from Australia till Christmas, was the financial member of the group.[1] Although he did not do much work upon the earlier stages of the Report, the chapters, in the later parts, dealing with Military Finance, were almost entirely his work. Ellison was the trained Staff Officer, and was responsible for the very complete and detailed distribution of staff duties to be found in Parts II and III of the Report.

In fact internal and external evidence alike combine to indicate that the famous report was, in its fullest aspect, the work of two men, Esher and Ellison, with Clarke contributing the financial paragraphs. There are complete phrases in the Report which may be compared with earlier entries in the Esher Journals or with the minority report contributed by Esher to the Report of the Royal Commission upon the South African War. As for Ellison, events had already directed his mind towards Staff Organization. In the early days of 1902, he had been assisting Colonel Henderson at Winchester House. Lord Roberts, at that time, instructed Henderson to prepare a simple manual dealing authoritatively with the British Staff System in war.[2] Henderson was at that time engaged upon the task of writing 'Infantry Training', a revised form of the old Infantry Drill Book. After Henderson's death, and after 'Combined Training' had been brought out,[3] Ellison had an opportunity to return to the task of drafting rules for staff organization. Therefore when the Esher Committee was formed, Ellison was able to produce for Esher a great deal of preliminary work upon staff organization.

One important change was however made in the original plan. Ellison's first division had been triple. He intended to convert the Quartermaster-General's branch into an Opera-

[1] He had served, it will be remembered, as Secretary to the Hartington Commission and as a member of Mr. Clinton Dawkins' Committee.
[2] .'Lord Roberts and the General Staff'.—'Nineteenth Century Review', No. 670, 1932.
[3] See Chapter 2.

tions branch, and for the Administrative side would revive the old Peninsular title of Commissary-General.[1] His staff plan would thus have the three main departments of the Quartermaster-General, the Adjutant-General, and the Commissary-General. Esher had, however, in previous writings, urged the style of 'General Staff' and it is likely that it was upon his promptings that the division was made into the three branches of General Staff, Adjutant-General, and Quartermaster-General. Fisher, however, pointed out that in the Army Council there should be four military members. For one thing there were four Naval members on the Navy Board; there was, moreover, the added reason that there were to be three civil members on the Army Council, and if there were four military members the soldiers would be in a majority. Esher accepted this view, and the fourth member of the Army Council came into being with the style of the Master-General of the Ordnance.

The Committee examined few witnesses, took no written evidence and published no minutes. It certainly worked with great speed. It had been constituted on November 6th. By December 30th Lord Esher was able to write to Mr. Balfour that the proposal was:

'To formulate
1. The demand for a Department for the Defence Committee under the Prime Minister.
2. A War Office Army Council, with 4 military members and three civilians constituted by Patent, to be set going at once as a representative body.

. . . . .

I wish to impress on you the vital and urgent importance of getting these two points,
        (*a*) Defence Committee
        (*b*) New Army Council
settled before February 2nd.'[2]

[1] The Quartermaster-General's branch had provided the Operations Staff for the Duke of Wellington in the Peninsula.
[2] Esher Journals, vol. ii, p. 34.

THE FORMATION OF THE ARMY COUNCIL

There was another matter that had to be tackled. The Hartington Commission, and Lord Esher's own Report had recommended the abolition of the post of Commander-in-Chief. On January 3, 1904, Lord Esher was writing to Mr. J. S. Sanders, Mr. Balfour's Private Secretary: 'I mention this, as you well know the insurmountable obstacle which Lord Roberts' retention of the Command of the Army would place in the way of War Office Reform. His retirement unfortunately is the condition precedent upon which our scheme hinges.'[1] It was of course clear that the Field-Marshal would have to go, and on the whole he showed himself very willing to aid Army Reform.

The first Report from the Committee of Three was published on February 1, 1904, one day before Parliament reassembled. Never before, perhaps, had there been a Report of such a concise, and, at times, devastating nature. The opening sentences of the First Section of the Report set the pace of the whole of this Committee's work.

'We have been directed to make recommendations for the reconstitution of the War Office. Our task, as we understand it is specially difficult from the fact that for many years this Department of State has been administered from the point of view of peace. It is necessary to make a complete breach with the past, and to endeavour to reconstitute the War Office with a single eye to the effective training and preparation of the Military Forces of the Crown for War.'

There were, in all, three sections of the First Part. Section I dealt with the constitution of the Defence Committee—it might almost be described as pure Esher, Section II with the formation of an Army Council upon the general lines which had been adopted for many years by the Navy Board, Section III with Decentralization and the functions of the Inspector-General. This Section commenced with two decisive sentences:

[1] Esher Journals, vol. ii, p. 35.

'The reconstruction of the War Office, and the readjustment of its relations with the Army demand a large measure of decentralization. Many existing evils can be traced directly to the attempt to perform in the Central Office duties which should be delegated to the Executive Commanders at home and abroad.'

The appointment of an Inspector-General was recommended, whose duties would be 'those of Review and Report upon the practical results of the policy of the Army Council within the financial limits laid down by the Cabinet. His field of action would cover the United Kingdom and those portions of the Empire where troops under the control of the Home Government are stationed'.

Action by the Government was taken rapidly. The Report was published on February 1st. On February 8th, Letters Patent under the Great Seal were issued to the following to be members of the Army Council:

The Secretary of State . Right Honourable H. O. Arnold-Forster.
First Military Member . Lieutenant-General Honourable Sir N. G. Lyttelton, K.C.B.
Second Military Member Major-General C. W. H. Douglas.
Third Military Member Major-General H. C. O. Plumer, C.B.
Fourth Military Member Major-General Sir J. W. Murray, K.C.B.
Civil Member . . Earl of Donoughmore, Parliamentary Under-Secretary of State.
Civil Member . . W. Bromley-Davenport, Esq., D.S.O., M.P., Financial Secretary.
Secretary . . . Colonel Sir E. W. D. Ward, K.C.B., Permanent Under-Secretary of State.

As for the Inspector-Generalship, this was in the first instance offered to Lord Roberts. While the offer was made, it was accompanied by the suggestion, from His Majesty, but heartily echoed by the Committee, that an ex-Commander-in-Chief could hardly become an Inspector-General. Lord Roberts, as was hoped, refused the post of Inspector-General and accepted a seat upon the new Defence Committee, where-

THE FORMATION OF THE ARMY COUNCIL

upon the Inspectorship was offered to, and accepted by the Duke of Connaught.[1]

So the historic office of Commander-in-Chief passed from the scene. The new organization was in line with the constitutional development of the powers of Parliamentary control. Nevertheless, from the standpoint of the nation's attitude to the Army, something was lost. It is no disrespect to the many able soldiers who since 1904 have filled the position of Chief of Staff, or as it later became, Chief of the Imperial General Staff, to suggest that none of them has filled the same place in the popular imagination as did the three Commanders-in-Chief of a previous era, the Duke of Cambridge, Lord Wolseley and Lord Roberts. In the nation's regard, the Army may indeed have suffered from the absence of one honoured and renowned titular chief. The constant changes in the position of the Chief of the Staff during the Great War should be considered in this connection. For several months Lord Kitchener dispensed with the position of Chief of the Staff altogether.

No sooner had the new Army Council been appointed than the members of the Committee again got to work, this time in consultation with those members of the Council whose department was the subject of particular review.

On February 26th, three weeks after the publication of the First Part, the Second Part of the Report appeared. Well might the members of the Committee in the concluding paragraph of their covering memorandum express their thanks to the Secretary, 'to whom credit for the rapidity with which we have been enabled to present our Report must fairly be assigned'.

Of this Part II, Section I defined the status and duties of the Army Council. Section II dealt with further aspects of Decentralization. Of this Section, paragraph 5 read:

---

[1] Lee, vol. ii, p. 199, and Esher Journals, vol. ii, p. 42. One may also quote: 'Such a scurry to-day . . . our torpedo has exploded and the little C.-in-C. has left the W.O. for good in the devil of a temper.'—Esher Journals, vol. ii, p. 44.

'The natural results of an inordinately centralized system have been the destruction of initiative throughout the Army. Officers have been brought up in peace-time to refer everything to superior authority, and to shun the responsibility of taking action. Remarkable instances of the prevailing reluctance to assume responsibility in regard to trivial matters have come to our notice. The army is tied and bound in the toils of excessively complex and minute regulations drawn up without any regard to the essential requirements of modern war, and needing expert interpretation.'

Section III, largely the work of Sir George Clarke, covered the vexed ground of civil control in the War Office. Some of his paragraphs contained fairly strong expressions of opinion.

'The entire system of War Office finance, which has been built up during many years, and has its origin in a distant past, is based upon the assumption that all military officers are necessarily spendthrifts and that their action must be controlled in gross and in detail by civilians. This theory is largely responsible for the unreadiness for war which has been frequently exhibited as well as for reckless and wasteful expenditure . . . 6. And further the War Office papers teem with minutes proving that the clerks of the Finance branch freely express their opinions on matters of military policy. . . . The power of finding available funds when a policy is favoured and of suggesting financial difficulties in other cases, is one which, in our opinion, should certainly not be wielded by the Accountant-General's branch.'

In Section IV, the first of a series of chapters is reached—the others are Sections I to III of Part III—which for the first time give a picture of staff organization not unlike that which we know to-day. On page 25 of Part II, at the end of the Section dealing with the Chief of the General Staff, there is a chart which, in its main features, shows the Directorates in their present form. For the first time appear as such the Director of Military Operations, the Director of Staff Duties and the Director of Military Training. On page 8 of Part III at the end of the Section dealing with the Adjutant-General's Department is a further chart. There may be found the Director of Recruiting and Organization, the Director of Personal Services, the Director-General of Army Medical Services, the titles of 1936, just as they came thirty years ago from Ellison's pen.

Page 11 shows the Quartermaster-General's staff. There have been changes here, but the main picture has not greatly altered. In 1906 there were the Director of Transport and Remounts—with the Director-General of Army Veterinary Services as an assistant—the Director of Movements and Quarterings, the Director of Supplies and Clothing, and the Director of Equipment and Ordnance Stores.[1]

The Master-General of the Ordnance had the Director of Artillery, the Director of Fortifications and Works, and a Naval Adviser.

Other Chapters of the Third Part dealt with the Civil Member of the Army Council—the Parliamentary Under-Secretary of State, and with the Secretary of the War Office. The important Part IV urged the creation of a properly trained General Staff.

In brief, a complete and comprehensive scheme of Military organization was presented by this threefold report, whose parts appeared within the short period covered by the dates February 1st, February 29th, and March 26th. What had before been tentative approaches to better methods of administration were, by the labours of this small and capable group, gathered together into one coherent scheme. Well might Joseph Chamberlain say to Esher, 'It very seldom falls to the lot of any man to be able to do such good service for his country.'

There is a further testimony from one qualified to judge which demands quotation:

[1] It will be remembered that since the Great War there has been a redistribution of duties between the branches of the Quartermaster-General and the Master-General of the Ordnance.

'*March 23rd.*

DEAR LORD ESHER,

... You must be overwhelmed with congratulations on the success of your labour, but I feel sure that no one appreciates what you have done for the Army more than I do. I never believed it possible to get such a thorough reorganization without undergoing first of all some military disaster!

Now, thanks to your energy, things seem on the right road for efficiency. . . .

Yours very sincerely,
DOUGLAS HAIG.'[1]

Contemplating the great changes wrought by this small group, wrought indeed for the most part by one public-spirited peer and one Lieutenant-Colonel on the Staff, the mind is tempted to regard the whole history of the Esher Committee's report as somewhat miraculous in nature. It must, however, be remembered that the two reformers were working in a congenial medium. Not only were they assured of powerful support from the Monarch and the Prime Minister, but they also had powerful support within the Army. Enlightened officers, from the Commander-in-Chief downwards, were convinced of the need for reorganization and reform. The Report of the Esher Committee was the executive word of command which set the alterations in motion, but some such command had been anxiously looked for by many for months, even years past.

It was on February 8, 1904, that Letters Patent announced the formation of the Army Council. On August 10th the same year, an Order in Council laid down the Constitution and the duties of the new body, and the individual responsibility of the members thereof.[2]

Other action along the lines of the Esher Committee's recommendations followed in 1905. By Army Orders 30, 87, 110, 150, 169, and 231 of that year, the Six Army Corps system was completely reorganized, and was replaced by a

[1] Esher Journals, vol. ii, p. 51.   [2] Printed as Appendix I.

system of Commands not very different from that obtaining at the present day. There were seven Commands—Aldershot, Southern, Eastern, Irish, Scottish, Northern and Welsh and Midland, and a London District.[1] A General Officer Commanding-in-Chief was placed at the head of each Command, assisted by officers of the Staff, whose duties at the Headquarters of Commands were subdivided among the branches of the General Staff, the Adjutant-General and the Quartermaster-General.

Finally, at a meeting of the Army Council held on August 9, 1905, certain general conclusions with regard to the formation of a General Staff were reached, and these were embodied in a Memorandum on the General Staff which, issued by Mr. Arnold-Forster on November 22, 1905, was, as events turned out, the very last contribution made by that Secretary of State to the work of Army Reform.[2]

The Committee of Imperial Defence

In the late autumn of 1899 there existed within the Cabinet what was known as the Committee of National Defence.

It consisted at the time of:

The Duke of Devonshire, President of the Council;
The Marquis of Salisbury, Prime Minister;
The Marquis of Lansdowne, Secretary of State for War;
The Right Honourable C. J. Goschen; Chancellor of the Exchequer and The Right Honourable A. J. Balfour,[3]

all of whom were of course Cabinet Ministers. In some form or another a Defence Committee had existed in the Cabinet for years but it was chiefly, indeed only, concerned, in peace-

[1] By Army Order 89 of 1906 the Western Command took the place of the Welsh and Midland. It took over the Lancashire Regimental District from the Northern Command in exchange for the North Midland Regimental District.—'Chronology', pp. 96 and 100.
[2] 'Memoirs of H. O. Arnold-Forster', p. 293.
[3] There is an interesting black-and-white drawing of this group in 'With the Flag to Pretoria', vol. i, p. 59, Harmsworth, 1900.

time, with two classes of business. This Committee considered the Service Estimates before they came before the full Cabinet and they acted as the medium for the reconciliation of conflicting claims between the Navy and the Army.[1] It had nothing to do with the War Office.[2]

In 1902, Mr. St. John Brodrick, in consultation with Lord Selborne, the First Lord of the Admiralty, decided that it was essential that the Defence Committee should be put upon a broader basis. They put these views strongly before Mr. Arthur Balfour, then Prime Minister, who was in the first instance not greatly impressed. The two colleagues were, however, insistent that without some such committee, it would not be possible for them to carry on their responsibilities. Thus stirred to the examination of the problem, Balfour showed his habitual grasp of essentials, and on February 11, 1903, while the Elgin Commission was still sitting, a new Defence Committee came into being. Lord Roberts, the Commander-in-Chief, had been giving evidence before the Elgin Commission the previous day, and his replies clearly showed the tentative nature of the new plans. 'We meet to-morrow for this purpose', he said; he had not been present at past meetings of the Defence Committee, 'but at this reorganized one I must be . . . in future I understand I am always to be present, and also a representative of the Admiralty. I think Mr. Balfour promised to announce the arrangement.'[3]

It was in fact not until March 5, 1903, that Mr. Balfour moved in the House of Commons the following resolution: 'That in the opinion of this House, the growing needs of the Empire require the establishment of the Committee of Defence on a permanent footing.' In the course of his speech Mr. Balfour explained the limitations of the old Committee. 'The old Defence Committee was, in the strictest and narrowest

[1] E.C., Evidence of Mr. Brodrick, q. 21732.
[2] 'I know nothing of the Defence Committee, except that the Duke of Devonshire I believe is the President of it.'—Evidence of Lieutenant-General Sir W. G. Nicholson, Director of Military Intelligence, E.C., q. 120.
[3] E.C., qq. 13223, 13225, and 13226.

THE FORMATION OF THE ARMY COUNCIL

sense of the word, a Committee of the Cabinet, and like all ordinary Committees of the Cabinet, it kept no records and admitted to its councils no outsiders.'[1] He added, 'The new Defence Committee is more ambitious in its scope—at all events at this early stage I have no right to use any other word. The idea the Government had in establishing it is not to take up from time to time questions referred to it by the Cabinet, but to make it its duty to survey as a whole the strategical military needs of the Empire.' Continuing his speech, Mr. Balfour dealt with the composition of the Committee. 'Our view is this—that there must be a fixed nucleus in this Committee—. . . . The permanent nucleus which we have tentatively, provisionally at all events, determined upon, makes the Cabinet members of the Committee consist of the Lord President, the Prime Minister, the Secretary of State for War and the First Lord of the Admiralty. It makes the non-Cabinet members of the Committee the First Sea Lord, the Commander-in-Chief, the Head of the Naval Intelligence, and the Head of Military Intelligence.' He made it clear also that there would be no strict limitation upon the additional members who might be called in for consultation and particularly mentioned the Chancellor of the Exchequer and the Secretary of State for India as members of the Cabinet who might from time to time be called upon to take part in the deliberations of the Committee of Defence.

In reply to a question a few days later Mr. Balfour said that it was proposed that the minutes of the Committee of Defence would be kept at the Foreign Office.

The work of this Committee of Defence thus formed in 1903, was to be seen in the succeeding years, though it was not until 1905 that Mr. Arthur Balfour made a speech of considerable importance wherein he brought into the open for the first time the mature reflections of the Committee. In preparation for this speech Lord Esher and Admiral Fisher had discussed the problem and Lord Esher quotes in his letters

[1] A.D., 1903, p. 379.

a draft 'Exordium' (such is his own word) for Mr. Balfour's speech. It runs as follows:

'The Army is maintained for offensive-defensive purposes of the Empire. It is not to be organized for the defence of these shores but is intended to take the field, at any threatened point, where the interests of the Empire are imperilled, and especially on the north-west frontier of India.'[1]

So on May 11, 1905, in the House of Commons, Mr. Balfour reviewed the tasks of the British Army as conceived by the Committee of Defence.[2]

He reviewed in the first instance the work of the Committee and pointed out in what respect it was an improvement upon what had gone before.

'Of course from time to time the sort of questions with which this Committee has to deal have been confided to successive Committees appointed *ad hoc* consisting of eminent sailors and soldiers, and no doubt in many cases a strong civilian element. These Committees, and this is the main point to be remembered, kept no continuous record.'

In the past there had been no co-ordinating authority which could adjudicate between various schools of thought.

'But though everybody realizes that there is this central problem of Imperial and national defence, we go on year after year with something of the nature of a profitless wrangle between the advocates of different schools.'

Then he turned to the conclusions arrived at by the Committee. Empire Defence was to be regarded as a whole. The British Fleet and the British Army, the mainstays of Imperial Defence, were not to be scattered throughout the world in small units without fighting value.

---

[1] Esher Journals, vol. ii, p. 75, February 21st.
[2] The speech was delivered on the Civil Service Estimates, Class II, Committee Stage, the vote for the Committee of Defence being carried at that time on the Civil Estimates.—A.D., 1905, p. 1423.

THE FORMATION OF THE ARMY COUNCIL

'As the British Fleet and British Army should be available for the Defence of the British Empire in all parts of the world, our force should be as far as possible concentrated at the centre of the Empire.'

As for the problem of an invasion, the Committee, after careful consideration, had placed on record their views that the smallest force which would be landed on these shores with any possibility of success would be one of 70,000 men. Such a force would require not less than 210,000 tons of sea-going shipping, and the provision of this shipping, the Government considered, would require such elaborate preparation that a surprise attack was unthinkable.

The major military problem for the British Army was the defence of India. Lord Kitchener had put on record his opinion that the defence of the north-west frontier against a Russian advance through Afghanistan might require the reinforcement of the existing Army in India by eight divisions from home. Such a reinforcement could of course never be sent unless this country had command of the seas. Government regarded the dispatch of Regular Army reinforcements from this country to India as the most important military task which confronted them. The speech was well received. It was a first-class testimony to the value of the existence of the Committee of Defence, and it drew a most significant testimony from the opposite Benches; Mr. Haldane, after paying a well-merited tribute to the work of the Prime Minister to whom he gave the credit for the formation of the Committee of Defence, closed with these words, 'In other words, an element of continuity must run through Imperial policy however great Party changes might be'.[1]

[1] A.D., 1905, p. 1479. It is perhaps interesting to note that the relative importance of policy and Party as indicated by the capital letters are so shown in the official report of the debate.

CHAPTER 11

RETROSPECT

THE interval of time between the summer of 1900 and the close of 1905 has here been called a 'Period of Attempted Reforms'. There may be some advantage in pausing at the end of the Balfour regime to take stock of what had actually been accomplished during those difficult post-war years.

The geographical distribution of the British Army had, to some extent, changed since the last survey in 1899. As a result of Mr. Brodrick's costly and criticized programme of barrack building, a degree of concentration had been effected.

The main portion of the Army was quartered at Aldershot.[1] Here Lieutenant-General Sir John French had an Army Corps consisting of the 1st Cavalry Brigade, and the 1st and 2nd Divisions, each of two Brigades of four battalions.[2] The 3rd Division did not exist in peace, but would be formed on mobilization; the 5th Brigade of this Division was stationed at Bordon. In the Eastern Command there were two Cavalry Brigades, the 2nd then commanded by Brigadier-General Honourable Julian Byng and the 3rd commanded by Brigadier-General Allenby. In this Command the 5th Division had its two Brigades based on Shorncliffe and Dover, but the 6th Division had, in peace-time, only the 11th Brigade at Colchester, the 12th Brigade was to be formed on mobilization by two battalions from Lichfield with two battalions of the Brigade of Guards from London. In the London District, with its Head-

---

[1] Army List, December 1905.
[2] The 1st (Foot Guards) Brigade had four battalions of the Brigade of Guards.

quarters at 23, Carlton House Terrace, were six battalions of the Guards, not organized in any part of the Divisions. There were no divisional formations in the Northern or Scottish Commands. The Southern Command, from its comparatively new Headquarters at Salisbury, had the 4th Division, with the 7th Brigade at Tidworth and Portland, and the 8th Brigade, only two battalions strong, at Devonport. In Ireland the 7th Division had its two Brigades divided between Dublin and the Curragh, while the 8th Division had the eight battalions of its 15th and 16th Brigades scattered over a number of single battalion stations in the Fermoy–Cork–Tipperary area. The 17th Brigade at Belfast was attached to the 8th Division.

Thus the 1st and 2nd Divisions at Aldershot and the 5th Division of the Eastern Command might be said to be fairly well organized for mobilization, each Division, be it remembered, of two Brigades only. All the other Divisions contained some element which required post-mobilization improvisation. Moreover, even in the best cases there were grave shortages in the services. Though the infantry and the artillery might be available, the medical and supply units were very weak, and below what was required for war.

Abroad, the most important new factor affecting the situation was the garrison of twelve battalions in South Africa.[1] The general distribution of the British Army at this time is shown in Appendix C where it may be compared both with the distribution of 1899 and with that of 1935.

As concerns the senior arms of the Service, there had been no important change in the numbers of the Cavalry Regiments. In the Artillery, however, there had been, as a result of Mr. Brodrick's plans, a notable increase. The 21 batteries of Royal Horse Artillery and 108 batteries of Royal Field Artillery of 1899 had been expanded to 28 and 150 respectively. The proposed conversion of Militia and Volunteer batteries had not proceeded very far. The Army List of December 1905,

[1] One of these was a garrison battalion.

showed only the Lancashire Militia Artillery Brigade of three batteries of Field Artillery.[1]

The Infantry had 10 battalions of the Brigade of Guards and 176 battalions of the Line.[2] There were still remaining two battalions of the Royal Garrison Regiment, two of the West India Regiment, the Chinese Regiment, and three battalions of Mounted Infantry in South Africa. Moreover, there was at Dover a provisional battalion to provide drafts for the Royal Sussex, Essex, and Royal West Kent Regiments, three units of the army which had both battalions abroad.

The frequent changes in organization had had a bad effect on the Auxiliary Forces as a whole. The Militia had declined in strength since the end of the war and was not in a good state. Its supporters could claim, with considerable truth, that in the third year of the South African War, when volunteering for the Service Companies had come to an end, the Militia could, and did, send out many battalions to South Africa to release other Militia units who had gone out in the early days of the war. Usually, however, those who knew most about

[1] This Brigade had a unique and very specialized organization. It had as Commanding Officer, a Regular officer permanently employed. It had a large cadre of regular instructors, gunners, and drivers amounting to 25 per cent of the total strength of the unit. 'So that instead of having a small permanent staff attached to the Militia, you have 75 per cent of the Militia drafted to a Regular Unit.' The Brigade did two months' training a year on Salisbury Plain, and for that reason it was very difficult to get subaltern officers.—Speech of Lieutenant-Colonel W. C. Hyslop, Lancashire Royal Artillery (Militia), R.U.S.I., February 22, 1905. 'R.U.S.I. Journal', vol. xlix, p. 771.

This Brigade cost £21,000 per annum as compared with the £40,000 of a Regular Brigade Royal Field Artillery on the lower establishment.—Mr. Haldane, House of Commons, March 29, 1906.

At £6,500 per battery it compared with the cost of £1,100 per battery of the Honourable Artillery Company.—Haldane's reply to Arnold-Forster, July 9, 1906. A.D., 1906, p. 926.

[2] Three battalions of Grenadier, Coldstream, and Scots Guards, one battalion of Irish Guards. Among the Line Regiments, the Royal Warwicks, Royal Fusiliers, Lancashire Fusiliers, Middlesex, King's Royal Rifles, Manchesters, and the Rifle Brigade had each four Regular Battalions.

the force were loudest to complain of its state. Sir Carne Rasch, speaking in the House of Commons in the spring of 1906, called the Militia 'a force nominally of 90,000 men which had no guns, no transport, and hardly any officers in the junior ranks'.[1]

In the previous year, in the course of a debate at the Royal United Service Institution a speaker had said:

'Why is the Militia not efficient? Simply because it has gradually been removed from its old county locus standi, its old recruiting conditions, from its mother so to speak, and severed from its ancient prestige, tradition and local influences until it has become a comparative nonentity, a recruiting agency for the Regular Army.'[2]

The extent to which this use of the Militia was carried is perhaps explained in part by the conditions attached to bounties paid to recruiters, though certainly to modern ideas the abuse of the system appears fairly obvious. Mr. Arnold-Forster speaking from the Opposition benches in the spring of 1906 said that Recruiting officers got one bounty for 'enticing boys into the Militia' and then a further 2s. 6d. for enticing them into the Regular Army. It was obviously to the advantage of the local depot recruiting staff to carry a boy for two or three weeks as a Militiaman and win a double recruiting reward. 'For some of the depots this happened to 70 per cent of the recruits'; such at least was Mr. Arnold-Forster's view.[3]

Such a method, if method it can be called, was obviously productive of very misleading results, for though in fact the same boys were not counted twice in the final annual returns,

---

[1] A.D., 1906, p. 472. March 29th.
The actual strength of the Militia on October 1, 1905, was 82,883 non-commissioned officers and men.—Command Paper 4058 of 1908.

[2] Colonel W. C. E. Sargeant, C.B., 5th Battalion Rifle Brigade, February 22, 1905. 'R.U.S.I. Journal', vol. xlix, p. 771.

[3] A.D., 1906, p. 473.

there was a definite tendency to associate their enlistment with a certain strength in the Militia organization, whereas, in fact, these recruits were not in any way associated with the traditional militia spirit.

Indeed, the Militia had changed very much since the days when it was taken from the control of the Lords Lieutenant and put under the War Office. The County spirit had gone, the association of Militia rank with county landed estates of a certain calculated worth had no meaning, and the local Militia machinery was an appanage of the local Regular Depot. There the recruits were drilled, there the Permanent Staff lived. 'A Militia Commanding Officer has now to go, hat in hand', said Lord Raglan, 'and ask a major in the Regular Army whether he can look at his recruits.'[1, 2]

The strength of the Volunteers was declining.[3] The force had been disturbed by the various new methods introduced by successive Secretaries of State since the outbreak of the South African War. These improvements were undoubtedly intended to secure greater efficiency, and some of the resentment caused by these attempts to raise the military standard of the force may appear at this distance to be factious and short-sighted. It must, however, be remembered that the financial position of these volunteer units was always a matter of very great importance to their members, to their officers, and, above all, to their Commanding Officers. With all the improvements that had taken place nothing had so far been done to reduce that heavy load of responsibility.

In the days of the French Revolution, and in the days of 1859 the Government was content to regard the Volunteer as a man of substance who was prepared to equip himself

[1] 'R.U.S.I. Journal', vol. xlix, p. 785.
[2] The Earl of Portland, speaking in the House of Lords, May 16, 1906, said: 'I look to the Militia much more as a support and adjunct to the Regular Army for service overseas in time of great national emergency. I look to the Volunteers as the main reserve for our Home Defence.'
[3] Strength on October 1, 1905, 219,351 non-commissioned officers and men.—Command Paper 4058 of 1908.

at his own expense.¹ As has been pointed out already² the difference between the Militia and the Volunteers was a social and financial difference as well as a military one, and that at a time when social distinctions were more powerful than they are, perhaps, to-day. To the purchase of uniform, rifles and equipment were soon to be added in the case of most Volunteer units greater and more permanent obligations in respect of Headquarters, Drill Halls, rifle ranges,³ bands, unit equipment and the like. Eventually Government funds were to some extent forthcoming, but as has been shown, they chiefly took the form of a capitation grant. If the unit were to remain financially solvent, the largest possible grant had to be earned. This undoubtedly did mean that many men were carried on the membership roll of the unit who were thoroughly unfitted, militarily speaking, to belong to the force.

When, however, the War Office in the interests of efficiency proposed to reduce the gross numbers of members by cutting out the inefficients, the point that rose first in the minds of many senior volunteers was the financial effect. 'We have erected headquarters and entered into financial obligations which are still continuing', said one Volunteer, 'and if the Force is deprived of the necessary amount of financial support, it is perfectly certain that in the course of a very short time many regiments in the Service will become insolvent.'⁴

[1] 'The idea then was that the Volunteer was to be one who not only sacrificed part of his spare time, and of the enjoyments of house and social life, to prepare for the defence of his country, but that he should find the money to clothe and equip himself, and pay out of his own pocket for the weapon served out to him, and the ammunition to be used with it.'—Paper at R.U.S.I., 'The Volunteers, 1905', Colonel Right Honourable Sir J. H. A. Macdonald (Lord Kingslaugh), P.C., K.C.B., April 11, 1905. 'R.U.S.I. Journal', vol. xlix, p. 910.

[2] Part I, Chapter 4.

[3] Lord Newton, in a speech in the House of Commons as late as May 28, 1906, instanced a case where £150 had been collected in local subscriptions to help build a Volunteer Rifle Range.—A.D., 1906, p. 758.

[4] Colonel M. B. Pearson, C.B., late 2nd Middlesex Royal Garrison Artillery Volunteers, 'R.U.S.I. Journal', vol. xlix, p. 927.

The law case of Samuel Brothers v. Colonel Wetherby's Executors caused

In pursuance of Mr. Arnold-Forster's scheme, 27 Volunteer Battalions had been selected for the Field Force, and were so noted in the Army Lists. They were grouped in 6 Brigades each of 4 battalions, and 3 battalions were unbrigaded. These nominal Brigades of the Field Force did not, however, correspond with any formation of the peace-time Volunteers. The selected units were drawn from widely separated districts. The peace-time Volunteer Brigades would often contain 5, or 6, battalions.

From the London area 3 battalions were selected for the Field Force. They were the 12th Middlesex Rifle Volunteers (Civil Service), the 16th Middlesex Rifle Volunteers (London Irish), and the 2nd London Volunteer Rifle Corps.[1] Each of these came from a separate London Volunteer Infantry Brigade. The Volunteer Brigades for the Field Force would therefore have to perfect their organization after mobilization, for they had no opportunity of working together during peace.

Since 1901, under somewhat varying regulations, summer camps had taken place, and the training of the Volunteers had benefited greatly thereby.

In an entirely different direction, that of the material equipment of the Army, very substantial improvement had been made. The delivery of the short rifle to the Infantry had commenced. By 1905 substantial progress had been made in this rearmament, though some units in India did not get the short rifle till 1907 and the programme was not completed till 1908.[2]

a good deal of comment at this time. It was held that the private estate of a deceased Commanding Officer of a Volunteer unit was liable for goods which he ordered in his capacity as Commanding Officer, and for the use of his unit. This liability was specifically removed by the Territorial and Reserve Forces Bill.

[1] These units are now the 16th London Regiment (Queen's Westminster and Civil Service Rifles); London Irish Rifles; and 31st (City of London Rifles) Anti-Aircraft Battalion.

[2] 'Annals of the King's Royal Rifle Corps', vol. iii, p. 315, and 'Chronology', 1908, p. 7. A specimen of the new rifle was exhibited in the Smoking Room of the House of Commons in the spring of 1906.—A.D., 1906, p. 597.

The Cavalry had received the short rifle but still carried the old sabre.[1] The lance had been abolished by Army Order No. 39 of March 1903, but this abolition, had not, in fact, been generally carried out.[2] The delivery of the new 13-pounder and 18-pounder guns for the Royal Horse Artillery and Royal Field Artillery had been delayed owing to a difficulty with the fittings to carry the fixed ammunition in the battery limbers. The first design had used brass strip springs; these proved too weak, and the Government of India had to be consulted before wicker fittings could be substituted. By June, 1906, out of 21 Royal Horse Artillery batteries, 8 at home and 6 in India had been completely rearmed, of the 109 Field Batteries, 66 had received the new 18-pounder, 36 at home and 30 in India.[3]

Following the recommendations of the Mowatt Committee the entire army trained in the new service drab uniform which they would wear in war.

In training a new era had dawned. Shortly after his return from South Africa Lord Roberts had instructed Colonel G. F. R. Henderson to prepare a work to be called 'Infantry Training' which would be a revised issue of the old 'Infantry Drill Book'.

Colonel Henderson, while engaged upon this task, was also writing the History of the South African War. To collect material for his history he journeyed to South Africa in 1901, fell ill, and died in Egypt in 1903 while on his journey home. The chapters which he had already written were found to contain a great deal of military doctrine which was common to all arms. A small Committee was assembled at Aldershot

[1] To anticipate, it may be explained that the new pattern sword was considered in 1906, was approved in 1908, and issue was begun in 1909. —A.D., 1906, p. 1461; 'Chronology', 1908, p. 7, and 1909, p. 7.
[2] 'R.U.S.I. Journal', vol. xlix, p. 118, and A.D., 1906, p. 1516.
[3] Speeches of Mr. Arnold-Forster and Mr. Haldane—A.D., 1906, pp. 798–800. This rearmament was completed in the financial year 1907–8. The pattern of the 4·5 howitzer was not approved till 1909.—'Chronology', 1909, p. 7.
See also 'Treatise on Service Ordnance, 1908', p. 366, for contemplated use of R.M.L. howitzers of 9-inch or 10-inch howitzers for siege work.

to carry on the work, interrupted by Colonel Henderson's death, the President of the Committee being General Stopford, and the Secretary Colonel Ellison. It was decided to issue this book under the title of 'Combined Training', and as if to mark the importance of the issue and to emphasize the change in Military thought, Lord Roberts contributed a most important foreword.

'Success in war', he wrote, 'cannot be expected unless all ranks have been trained in peace to use their wits. General and Commanding Officers are, therefore, not only to encourage their subordinates in so doing by affording them constant opportunities of acting on their own responsibility, but they will also check all practices which interfere with the free exercise of the judgment, and will break down, by every means in their power, the paralysing habit of an unreasoning and mechanical adherence to the letter of orders and to routine, when acting under service conditions. All works and regulations which have hitherto dealt with the subject contained in this manual either have been, or shortly will be revised. Meanwhile this manual is to be regarded by the Army as authoritative on every subject with which it deals.—ROBERTS, F. M.'

This was a definite break with the past. Cavalry Training followed in 1904, Infantry Training in 1905, and the Manual of Engineering in 1905. Field Artillery Training was to appear in 1907.

Rifle shooting was assiduously practised, volley firing had disappeared, field firing ranges were installed wherever possible. In his Annual Return for the year 1904, Von Lobell gives a striking testimony to the realist doctrines that were then pervading the British Army:

'In their manœuvres the British Infantry showed great skill in the use of ground. Their thin khaki-clad skirmishers were scarcely visible. No detachment was ever seen in close order within three thousand yards. Frontal attacks were entirely avoided. No attack on entrenched positions was adjudged successful unless with a numerical superiority of six to one. The excessive extension allowed militated against really powerful attack. The machine-guns were too exposed. Volley firing is abolished. Slow fire and rapid fire—the latter not exceeding 15 rounds a minute—being alone used.'[1]

The men of 1914 were already coming to the fore. French was Commanding at Aldershot. At the War Office, Plumer was Quartermaster-General, Grierson was Director of Military Operations, with William Robertson as his A.D.M.O. Rawlinson was Commandant at the Staff College, where the Instructors were Haking, Capper, Kiggell, H. de la P. Gough, Du Cane, Colonel Aston of the Royal Marines, and Lieutenant-Colonel Stopford. With the turn of the year Henry Wilson was to succeed Rawlinson. Douglas Haig was in India as Inspector of Cavalry, Smith-Dorrien commanded the Quetta Division. Among the D.A.Q.M.G.s of the Operations Directorate at the War Office were such names as Brevet Lieutenant-Colonel G. F. Milne, Brevet Lieutenant-Colonel J. H. Haldane, Major R. P. Lee, Major J. E. Edmonds, Brevet Major C. F. Romer, Major W. T. Furse.

These were the men of a newer generation who were to aid Haldane in the development of his ideas. More than any other army in the world, they were putting into practice the lessons learnt in South Africa and reported from Mukden.

Yet towering over all other changes were two new developments which in December 1905, were not yet two years old. At Whitehall Gardens was the permanent office of the Committee of Imperial Defence, while at the War Office, not yet removed from Pall Mall, reigned the Army Council of the Esher Committee's Report, served by the General Staff of Arnold-Forster's November Memorandum.

Arnold-Forster's successor was to have, to carry out his wishes, a military machine such as had been possessed by no previous Secretary of State for War.

Respect for Mr. Haldane's undoubted achievements must never be allowed to underrate the spadework performed by the two Secretaries who preceded him.

[1] Von Lobell's Reports for 1904, quoted in 'R.U.S.I. Journal', vol. xlix, p. 1281.

PART IV

THE HALDANE REFORMS

CHAPTER 12

MR. HALDANE BECOMES SECRETARY OF STATE FOR WAR

RICHARD BURDON HALDANE, in the opinion of Haig 'the greatest Secretary of State for War England has ever had',[1] came to his high office not as a result of notable service in the field, nor by reason of long years of military study expressed in writing and in debate: his appointment was the outcome of the political exigencies of the Liberal Party. He himself wished to be Lord Chancellor, Asquith and Grey thought he had good title to the appointment.[2] The King would have liked Haldane as Chancellor, but realized the senior position of Sir Robert Reid. Campbell-Bannerman, the Prime Minister of the Liberal Party, offered Haldane the post of Attorney-General,[3] and, in the other direction had, through John Morley, sounded Lord Esher on the subject of the War Office.[4] When Esher refused, Campbell-Bannerman's mind had turned to an old Liberal, Herbert Gladstone.[5] The factor

[1] On the night after the triumphal march of British troops through London on July 19, 1919, the Field-Marshal called unheralded at Haldane's house and left a bound volume of his Despatches with the following inscription: 'To Viscount Haldane of Cloan—the greatest Secretary of State for War England has ever had. In grateful remembrance of his successful efforts in organizing the Military Forces for a War on the Continent, notwithstanding much opposition from the Army Council and the half-hearted support of his Parliamentary Friends. HAIG, F.M.'

[2] Autobiography, p. 157.   [3] Letter of December 7th, ibid., p. 169.

[4] Esher Journals, December 1st, vol. ii, p. 122. 'This is ludicrous. To have an offer from one P.M. and a feeler from the other side is an adventure almost unparalleled.' In explanation of Campbell-Bannerman's action it may be pointed out that Esher as Mr. Reginald Brett had been Liberal M.P. for Penryn-Falmouth from 1880 to 1885, and had been Private Secretary to Lord Hartington when the latter was at the War Office.

[5] Ibid., December 7th, vol. ii, p. 124.

that brought Haldane to Pall Mall, was the realization, by all concerned, that Edward Grey had got to be a member of the Cabinet. Without Haldane, Grey would not enter Campbell-Bannerman's Government. Grey and Haldane had each written letters of refusal—both men would make serious sacrifices of income by joining the Government—but after an evening of earnest talk, on December 7th, Haldane went to Campbell-Bannerman and promised to bring in Grey if possible. Grey obviously would have the Foreign Office. Campbell-Bannerman offered Haldane the Home Office. 'I said, "What about the War Office?" "Nobody", answered Campbell-Bannerman, "will touch it with a pole."[1] "Then give it to me. I will come in as War Secretary if Grey takes the Foreign Office, and I will ask him to call on you early to-morrow to tell you his decision, which may, I think, be favourable." '[2] Thus, in a somewhat typically British way, were two great men launched upon their destinies.[3]

The long negotiations which led up to this conversation late in the evening of December 7, 1905, the 'Relugas Compact' and the breaking thereof, are outside the scope of this work, but it is essential that mention should be made, however briefly, of the general conditions under which Haldane assumed office. In an earlier chapter it has been shown how the Liberal Party had been seriously split by the South African War. The Liberal Imperialists, then led by Rosebery, included Asquith, Grey, and Haldane, intellectually probably the strongest men in the Party. In the realm of foreign politics

[1] A similar unflattering comment upon the War Office had been made a few hours earlier by Grey himself. 'If we enter it is not for pleasure's sake, and we must take the most beastly things. I will take the War Office.'—Autobiography, p. 180.
[2] Ibid., p. 173.
[3] Asquith's verdict is of interest. Speaking of the Campbell-Bannerman Government, he said: 'The most striking, and in its international consequences one of the most momentous, of its administrative achievements was the reconstruction of the Army, begun in these years and subsequently developed and completed, by Mr. Haldane.'—'Fifty Years of Parliament', p. 55.

they were much more closely allied to the Conservative viewpoint of Arthur Balfour than to the 'Little Englanders' of their own Party. But they all believed in intellectual Liberalism, especially in the domain of local government, social reform, and in education. After Rosebery's withdrawal and the Liberal victory, the other three had little illusions about the debating strength of their own Party, and they were doubtful of the foreign policy of Campbell-Bannerman. Their first scheme was that Campbell-Bannerman should retire to the House of Lords, and that Asquith should lead the Commons as Chancellor of the Exchequer. Although this plan fell through, the three in the end came in together. Haldane must therefore be regarded as standing in some measure as a 'man of the Centre', known and respected by many Conservatives, watched with some suspicion by the extreme Radical element in his own party.[1]

Haldane's own previous life had been devoted to law, philosophy, and to education. A very successful barrister, he had taken a prominent part in the development of civic universities, notably at London and at Liverpool, and in 1902-4 had delivered the philosophic Gifford Lectures at St. Andrews. Educated at the Universities of Edinburgh and of Göttingen, he had acquired in the highest degree the faculty of critical analysis, and constructive reasoning.[2]

That he came to the War Office with no preconceived ideas was to prove his great advantage. Brodrick and Arnold-Forster both bore the weight of their own previous utterances. Nor, in spite of his remarks to Campbell-Bannerman, was his new post entirely uncongenial. There was about him a Scots

[1] Lord Newton, speaking in the House of Lords, July 24, 1906, emphasized this 'central' position of the Secretary of State for War. He thought it made Haldane a 'dangerous' man.—A.D., 1906, p. 1190.

[2] It is right that a record should be made of the very fine quality of Haldane's character. Mr. A. E. Widdows, C.B., Assistant Under-Secretary at the War Office, who was Haldane's Private Secretary in 1906, said: 'Haldane had a sweet character, it is the only word which describes it properly.' Similar tribute is paid by others who, alive to-day, worked with Haldane thirty years ago.

dourness that loved to wrestle with a difficulty. Two successive Conservative Governments had failed to achieve success in the problem of Army reform. He meant to show what might be achieved by the application of Hegelian principles.

Within the first few days, important steps had been taken. On the 9th the Army Council had been met, and their curiosity dispelled by a jest,[1] and, by the 11th, on the advice of Lord Esher, Colonel Ellison had been secured as a Military Private Secretary.[2] An interesting incident associated with Ellison's appointment shows how new military matters were to Haldane's experience. When Ellison first received Lord Esher's telegram, he asked the question whether Mr. Haldane 'had any preconceived cut and dried plan of his own for the Army'. Ellison, with memories of the two previous Secretaries of State for War, did not wish to be associated with another example of doctrinaire legislation. Lord Esher was able to give the assurance that Haldane's mind was free from any such preconceived notions. The message was apparently conveyed to Haldane, because no sooner had he met Ellison than he emphasized to his assistant the existing state of his ignorance.[3] During the General Election of January, 1906, and after that at Cloan, Ellison was with his chief, providing him with information and reviewing with him the report of

[1] 'Their leader said to me that they all felt that . . . they would all like to have some general idea of the reforms which I thought of proposing to Parliament. My reply was that I was as a young and blushing virgin just united to a bronzed warrior, and that it was not expected by the public that any result of the union should appear until at least nine months had passed.'—Autobiography, p. 183.

Perhaps it was this remark which led to the entry in Douglas Haig's Diary (Haig—Duff Cooper, p. 105), 'French seems to like him (i.e. Haldane) and "The Army Council", Hubert Hamilton writes me, "have the spirits of schoolboys home for the holidays".'

[2] 'Ellison came down . . . had a talk and said yes. There and then I telephoned through to Haldane, who was with Clarke, and he will see Ellison to-morrow.'—Esher Journals, December 10th, vol. ii, p. 126.

[3] 'He confessed that he knew nothing whatever about the elements of military organization, e.g. the composition of units, divisions, brigades, etc., and that he relied on me to explain all such matters to him.'—Ellison, xvii.

HALDANE BECOMES SECRETARY OF STATE FOR WAR

the Esher Committee. Ellison gives a vivid picture of this period:

'During the day-time he was engaged in canvassing and it was not till after dinner that we got busy with Military affairs and then we were often at it till one or two a.m. Hour after hour we would walk backwards and forwards in a big billiard room, Mr. Haldane on one side of the table smoking the best cigars procurable, I on the other.'[1]

On December 16th, Haldane had asked for an audience with the King in order that he might 'take the King's pleasure' on 'matters of importance under consideration', thus commencing a period of close collaboration with the Monarch which was to prove of the utmost value.[2]

The Liberal Party had returned to power in the House of Commons pledged, in varying degree, to a Gladstonian policy of 'Peace, Retrenchment, and Reform'. Many speeches made by leading Liberals at the end of 1905 had specifically dealt with the cost of armaments; others had looked forward to a period of international reconciliation.[3]

Haldane realized that from a large section of his own party would come a demand for a tremendous reduction in the Army Estimates. His own feeling was that 'economy and efficiency were not incompatible'.[4] Upon one subject he had, however, even in December, made up his mind; efficiency must be obtained even if economies could not be made. This much he said in the City of London a few days later.

---

[1] Ellison, xvii.   [2] Lee, vol. ii, p. 494.
[3] Thus Sir Henry Campbell-Bannerman, in his great Albert Hall speech on December 21, 1905: 'While the outlook in foreign affairs was most pleasing, the growth of armaments remained a danger to the world. . . . A policy of huge armaments keeps alive and stimulates and feeds the belief that force is the best if not the only solution of international differences. . . . What nobler role could this great country assume than at the fitting moment to place itself at the head of a League of Peace through whose instrumentality the great work of peaceful arbitration could be effected.'
—J. A. Spender, 'Life of Sir Henry Campbell-Bannerman', vol. ii, p. 20.
[4] Autobiography, p. 186.

Then there ensued a pause while the General Election of January, 1906, was being fought. Balfour had resigned without forcing a dissolution. Campbell-Bannerman on taking office had dissolved Parliament and had appealed to the country for a mandate. He got it. The Liberal majority was large, and the party was quite independent of Irish votes.[1]

During the election Haldane, whose own seat at East Lothian was safe, went to Berwick to give support to his friend and colleague Edward Grey by speaking at election meetings.

There, and during that period, occurred an incident which was to govern the orientation of Haldane's whole military outlook.

'I found that he had ordered a carriage to take us, after the meeting, for a long and private talk. He told me that the French were concerned about the possibility of a German move against them in the summer. How far were we, if an emergency compelling our intervention should arise, prepared with plans for it? Had we compared ideas about preparation with the French Generals?'[2]

It is an idle speculation to wonder how far Haldane's plans for military reorganization had progressed in his mind before the drive with Edward Grey. It is, however, an interesting consideration that this most decisive discussion took place almost at the very commencement of his term of duty at the War Office.

It was on January 13th that this evening drive took place. It was on the 10th that M. Cambon had talked over the situation with Sir Edward Grey.

At the time of the Tangier crisis Lord Lansdowne, then

---

[1] 'The General Election which followed in 1906 was one of the most remarkable in our modern history. The Unionists in the House of Commons were reduced from 369 to 157; the Liberals numbered 379. There were 83 Irish Nationalists and 56 so-called Labour Members.'—Asquith, 'Fifty Years of Parliament', vol. ii, p. 34.

One of the newcomers to Parliament was Mr. Ramsay MacDonald.

[2] Autobiography, p. 189.

HALDANE BECOMES SECRETARY OF STATE FOR WAR 237

Foreign Secretary, had written to M. Cambon a letter which spoke in general terms of 'full and confidential discussion between the two Governments . . . in anticipation of any complications to be apprehended during the somewhat anxious period through which we are at present passing'.[1]

M. Delcassé had been greatly impressed by the evident potentialities of such an offer, but M. Rouvier was at that time hostile to the idea of such a definite entente with England.[2]

In the winter of 1905–6 the situation still appeared menacing to French statesmen. The Algeciras conference was about to take place; the Tangier incident had been a clear warning that Germany was prepared to carry matters with a strong hand. In England a new Liberal Government had taken office and Paris was not certain what might be the views of the men now in authority in England. M. Cambon was therefore charged to curtail his leave and seek from Sir Edward Grey an indication of the position taken by England, should the Algeciras conference fail and serious tension arise between France and Germany.[3] Further interviews took place on

[1] B.D.O., vol. iii, No. 95. This letter is dated May 25, 1905.

[2] Delcassé: 'Consider very carefully the decisions you are about to take, gentlemen. To-day England is boldly espousing your cause. But to-morrow, if she sees you weakening, trembling before the insolent bluster of William, she will lose all faith in you. . . .'
Rouvier: 'Are we in a state to face war with Germany? No, a thousand times no. Even with the help of the English Fleet we should walk into a catastrophe worse than 1870. . . .'—'The Turning Point,' Maurice Paléologue, p. 265.

[3] 'Twenty-five Years', Sir Edward Grey, vol. i, p. 72, where Sir Edward Grey's letter to Sir F. Bertie reporting the interview is printed in extenso: M. Cambon said that he did not believe that the German Emperor desired war but that His Majesty was pressing a very dangerous policy. . . .
'During the previous discussions on the subject of Morocco, Lord Lansdowne had expressed his opinion that the British and French Governments should frankly discuss any eventualities that might seem possible. . . . It had not been considered necessary at the time to discuss the eventuality of war, but it now seemed desirable that the eventuality should also be considered. . . .
I replied that at the present moment the Prime Minister was out of town, and that the Cabinet were all dispersed seeing after the elections; that we

January 15th and 31st. It was this latter discussion which Grey calls 'the critical discussion with M. Cambon'.[1]

Before Christmas however there had commenced a series of unofficial interchanges of opinion upon military matters between British and French representatives. These interchanges were conducted through the medium of Lieutenant-Colonel C. à Court Repington, then the Military Correspondent of 'The Times'. On December 29th Repington had sent Grey an express letter on the subject, and on the following day Grey had replied from Fallodon:[2]

'I am interested to hear of your conversation with the French Military Attaché. I can only say that I have not receded from anything which Lord Lansdowne said to the French, and have no hesitation in confirming it.'

To avoid overloading this text with detail, the time-table of various meetings from December 15th to January 16th is given in Appendix J. It is however clear that on January 13th, at Berwick, Grey knew more than Haldane did about the immediate unofficial conversations.

The first of Grey's two questions, that concerning our own readiness, Haldane was to take time over, the second question, concerning co-operation with the French Generals, took him to London at once for talk with the Prime Minister.

'The Prime Minister asked whether it could be made clear that the conversations were purely for military General Staff purposes and were not to prejudice the complete freedom of the two Govern-

were not as yet aware of the sentiments of the country as they would be expressed at the polls; and that it was impossible therefore for me, in the circumstances, to give a reply to His Excellency's question. I could only state as my personal opinion that, if France were to be attacked by Germany in consequence of a question arising out of the Agreement which our predecessors had recently concluded with the French Government, public opinion in England would be strongly moved in favour of France. . . .'

This letter is given in full in B.D.O., vol. iii, No. 210, p. 170. Its reference was F.O. 371/70, No. 22. Very confidential.

[1] 'Twenty-five Years', p. 78.
[2] 'The First World War', Repington, vol. i, p. 4.

ments should the situation the French dreaded arise. I undertook to see that this was put in writing.'[1]

It was therefore upon the explicit instructions of Sir Henry Campbell-Bannerman that the War Office was authorized to enter into direct correspondence with the French Military Authorities.[2] Once in London Haldane saw both Grierson and Huguet, but the official instructions to the former had actually reached him from the Foreign Office. On January 15th, Lord Sanderson had written:

'MY DEAR GRIERSON,
I showed your letter of the 11th to Sir E. Grey, and he has spoken to Mr. Haldane on the subject. They agree to your entering into communication with the French Military Attaché here for the purpose of obtaining such information as you require as to the methods in which military assistance could in case of need be best afforded by us to France and vice versa. Such communication must be solely provisional and non-committal.

Sir E. Grey sees no objection to similar enquiries being addressed by our Military Attaché at Brussels to the Belgian Military Authorities as to the manner in which, in case of need, British assistance could be most effectually afforded to Belgium for the defence of her neutrality.

Yours sincerely,
SANDERSON.'[3]

That same evening Sir Edward Grey added a postscript to his confidential letter to Sir F. Bertie, our Ambassador in Paris:

'P.S.—As to taking precautions beforehand in case war should come, it appears that Fisher has long ago taken the French Naval

[1] Autobiography, p. 190.
[2] 'The Military conversations had hitherto been through an intermediary: they, too, were henceforth to be direct.'—'Twenty-five Years', Sir Edward Grey, p. 76.
[3] B.D.O., vol. iii, No. 214. The letter is numbered W.O. Liaison I/1 and W.O. 371/70. It is endorsed at the close, '(Approved by Sir E. Grey)'.
General Grierson's letter of the 11th referred to above is included in Appendix J.

attaché in hand, and no doubt has all naval plans prepared. I have now got Haldane's consent to General Grierson being in direct communication with the French Military Attaché, but I am told that 80,000 men with good guns is all we can put into the field in Europe to meet first class troops; that won't save France unless she can save herself. We can protect ourselves of course for we are more supreme at sea than we have ever been. . . .'[1]

On the 16th therefore Grierson saw Huguet in a new and official capacity, and that same day wrote to Lieutenant-Colonel Barnardiston the British Military Attaché in Brussels:

'You tell the Chief of Staff what we are prepared to put in the field in this case, 4 Cavalry Brigades, 2 Army Corps, and a division of mounted infantry, and you know from our conversations the general lines on which you should go. The total numbers will be about 105,000 and we shall ferry them over to the *French* coast—Calais, Boulogne, Dieppe and Havre, railing them afterwards if necessary to Belgium and then, when command of the sea is assured, changing our base to Antwerp.'[2]

There were of course several alternative schemes for the employment of British forces, the discussions envisaged various possibilities, and went into considerable detail. The time-table of General Grierson's work as revealed in his diary,[3] shows almost daily conferences after December 15th, either with the Navy—Ottly, the Director of Naval Intelligence or Ballard, the Director of Operations at the Admiralty —or else with Colonel Huguet, General French, or members of the Committee of Imperial Defence.[4] On March 2nd he

---

[1] B.D.O., No. 216. Dated January 15th.

[2] B.D.O., No. 217B. The reference is: Major-General J. M. Grierson to Lieutenant-Colonel Barnardiston, W.O. Liaison I/3. Secret.

[3] Macdiarmid, pp. 215, 216, 217.

[4] A good deal of this work was done before the official instructions of January 15th. On January 14th Grierson wrote to his sister: 'Since I came back I have been very busy, for no one knows what is going to come out of this conference about Morocco. The French fear that the Germans will force war upon them over it, and in that case we shall be in it in the French side, and J. M. G. is not going to be caught napping.'—Ibid., p. 123.

crossed to France, met Huguet there, and together they examined the port facilities of Calais. On March 10th a second journey was made, this time with Robertson via Valenciennes and Charleroi, to Namur and the Ardennes.

The events of January, 1906, must, however, be chiefly considered, not in their relation to the officers of the British General Staff. It is the business of the General Staffs of all Armies to prepare schemes and plans for all contingencies. The great effect of the French message was upon the British Statesmen, and, above all, upon Haldane himself.

To the Prime Minister the situation had come as a shock. How far the Algeciras crisis and the fall of Delcassé had been appreciated at their true worth by the Liberals while they were in opposition is not clear.[1] At any rate, M. Cambon's intimation of his Government's grave fears was taken very seriously by Grey and by the Prime Minister.[2]

The effect on Haldane was strong. He had, at once, set before him, a main problem, a story as old as British history, the vital need to this country of the security of the 'Channel Ports'. Thus he wrote in his Autobiography:

'The continued occupation by a friendly nation like the French of Dunkirk, Calais and Boulogne, the vital Northern Channel ports of the Continent, was therefore an objective upon which to concentrate. The accomplishment of this implied that we should have an Expeditionary Force sufficient in size and also rapidity of mobilizing power to be able to go to the assistance of the French

[1] 'The outgoing Ministers apparently had not taken their successors into their confidence about foreign affairs . . . for if they had, Sir Henry Campbell-Bannerman could scarcely have said, as he did in his first speech as Prime Minister (Albert Hall, December 21, 1905) that "the outlook abroad was most pleasing". By the beginning of January the new Foreign Secretary, Sir Edward Grey, had discovered that it was most unpleasing.'—J. A. Spender, 'Fifty Years of Europe'.

[2] 'Sir Henry Campbell-Bannerman was still receiving the resounding acclamations of Liberals, peace-lovers, anti-jingoes and anti-militarists, in every part of the country, when he was summoned by Sir Edward Grey to attend to business of a very different character.'—Winston Churchill, 'World Crisis', vol. i, p. 7.

Army in the event of an attack on the Northern or North-Eastern parts of France.'[1]

This was a most momentous conclusion. Moreover, as far as can be judged, it was reached by Haldane out of his own appreciation of the situation, and was not imposed upon him by any adviser. It is, in any event, very significant that Arthur Balfour, speaking in the House on May 9, 1906, on Mr. Vivian's motion on the reduction of Army Expenditure, still looked to the East as the main military preoccupation of the realm. 'In regard to military operations, I think our danger is not within these islands at all, but on the frontier of India.'[2] Haldane saw a danger nearer home than that.

Military aid to France in the days of Lansdowne and Arnold-Forster was conceived in vague terms; the conversations which Grierson had with Huguet were very much along the lines of doing the best we could with the material at our disposal. The creation for one definite objective of an overseas striking force of such dimensions was Haldane's bold conception.[3]

[1] After the Great War was over, Haldane, in the following speech, rephrased his decision of 1906. The allusions to submarines and air fleets are of course an anachronism; neither arm, in 1906, merited very serious consideration. The problem of the Northern Ports was, however, the vital factor. 'We had no doubt that the Germans could not, in face of our magnificent and superior fleet, invade this country directly: we knew them too well to think they were likely to try. But they had other means. If they could get possession of the northern ports of France, Calais, Dunkirk, and Boulogne, then, with long-range guns and submarines, and with air fleets, they might make the position of this country a very precarious one in point of safety. That problem had to be thought out, and after surveying the whole Army, I took it upon myself to ask Lord Haig, who was then in India, to come over to this country and think for us.'—Haldane, speaking after Haig's death. Quoted Charteris, pp. 34 and 35.
[2] A.D., 1906, p. 659.
[3] According to M. Paléologue, 'The Turning Point', p. 314, notes of December 22, 1905, General Grierson, in conversation with Colonel Huguet, had said: 'We have got out a scheme for landing 115,000 men (three army corps and four cavalry brigades) at Antwerp. This army could cover Brussels between the twelfth and twenty-first days of mobilization. . . . We have

'We had therefore to provide for an Expeditionary Force which we reckoned at six great divisions, fully equipped, and at least one cavalry division. We had also to make certain that this force could be mobilized and sent to the place where it might be required as rapidly as any German force could be.'[1]

With these words the Stanhope Memorandum was torn up for good and all. That document had provided for two complete Army Corps for dispatch on foreign service, but the very provision was secondary to the needs of Home defence and 'their employment in the field in any European war is sufficiently improbable'. Under the new regime of a Liberal Government, six divisions were to be specially prepared for rapid intervention in a European war.[2]

also provided that two divisions drawn from Gibraltar, Malta and Egypt could land at Marseilles on the eighteenth day of mobilization.'

The two divisions last named would clearly be improvised formations, and from the facts of the case would consist of little more than infantry units. In December 1905 there were three Battalions at Gibraltar, eight at Malta, and four in Egypt. There was no Field Artillery at all, only garrison artillery manning the fixed defences. There were no Field Companies Royal Engineers and only one company of Army Service Corps at each station.

When General Grierson wrote to Lieutenant-Colonel Barnardiston on January 16th (see p. 240) he said it was not possible to give a date for the arrival of the mounted infantry division as the cobs would have to be bought after mobilization.

[1] Autobiography, p. 188.
[2] In 'Before the War', which Haldane published in 1920, he describes the development of their idea in the following words: 'Sir Edward Grey consulted the Prime Minister, Sir Henry Campbell-Bannerman, the Chancellor of the Exchequer, Mr. Asquith, and myself as War Minister, and I was instructed, in January 1906, a month after assuming office, to take the examination of the question in hand. This occurred in the middle of the General Election which was then in progress. I went at once to London and summoned the heads of the British General Staff, and saw the French military attaché, Colonel Huguet, a man of sense and ability. I became aware at once that there was a new army problem. It was, how to mobilize and concentrate at a place of assembly to be opposite the Belgian frontier a force calculated as adequate (with the assistance of Russian pressure in the East) to make up for the inadequacy of the French armies for their great task of defending the entire French frontier from Dunkirk down to Belfort, or even farther south, if Italy should join the Triple Alliance in an attack.' (Pages 30, 31.)

Foch used to say, 'De quoi s'agit-il?' Haldane wrote: 'The first question was what must be our objective, and what was required for its attainment?'[1] The answers, as they forced themselves out of his reasoning gave, as the potential enemy, Germany, as the field of battle, Northern France, and as the British contribution, the Expeditionary Force of Six Divisions.[2]

It is in no sense a detraction from Haldane's great service to point out how emphatically his first decision led on to the various developments with which his name is associated. The Expeditionary Force and the Territorial Force did not spring fully armed from Haldane's brain; they were evolved as the logical sequence of his train of thought. It might be possible to argue that if there had been no evening drive with Edward Grey in the environs of Berwick, there might have been no Expeditionary Force as history knows it. Haldane himself suggests as much.[3] Had the problem been different, had the peril to the North-West Frontier remained as the greatest of our military questions, the reformed instrument forged by Haldane might well have taken on a very different shape.

As it was, the character of the problem determined in many ways the form of the solution. In the days when British troops were employed many weeks' sail away from the Home Country, when vessels were small, and at the mercy of bad weather or indifferent engines, when ports of disembarkation were cramped, or scattered, then there was at least some excuse for being content with a system which shipped off individual units, and grouped them into larger bodies in the overseas

---

[1] Autobiography, p. 187.

[2] Repington claims to have invented the title: 'I believe that I first suggested the name of the Expeditionary Force It was first called the Striking Force and I thought that this would alarm the Radicals unduly.'—'First World War', p. 14.

It is true that in his speech in the House of Commons on the Estimates Haldane spoke of a Striking Force (see post, p. 250).

[3] Autobiography, p. 191.

theatre of war, forming Highland Brigades, Irish Brigades, or Light Divisions as the case might be.

A casual arrangement like this would not do for this new conception of the employment of British troops. It was to be but a ferry journey to the scene of the campaign, and fifteen days was allowed for mobilization. It was clear therefore that the larger units must be organized in peace-time and not improvised to meet the emergency. Moreover, as for the first time for years, our Army was to prepare to meet European formations, a grouping more suitable to Continental warfare, the 'great' division, of twelve battalions, was to be adopted.

Such were the resolutions taken by Haldane in the early spring of 1906, resolutions of the greatest gravity for the country. In his consideration of the various factors he had, to aid him, Lieutenant-Colonel Ellison, and for his financial plans, Charles Harris, whom he made Permanent Head of the Financial Department of the War Office.[1] The directing brain was clearly that of Haldane himself.

The decision to commit the British Army in advance to a continental intervention was a very serious one. It raised questions of policy and control which far transcended the merely military aspect of the problem. It meant that Britain would be a partner with one or more Allies, and that questions of command and direction might be raised. Indeed they were already being raised, for the French reply to Colonel Reping-

[1] When Haldane came to the War Office Sir Guy Fleetwood Wilson was Permanent Head of the Finance Department, with the title of Director of Finance, and Mr. Harris was Principal Clerk in charge of the Estimates Branch. His title was changed to Director-General of Finance in 1907 and a rank of Director introduced between him and the Principal Clerks. When Sir Guy Fleetwood went to India in 1908 as Financial Member of the Supreme Council of India, Haldane 'leapfrogged' Mr. Harris from Principal Clerk to Wilson's post, but with the altered title of Assistant Financial Secretary (the Financial Secretary being a minister).—MS. evidence, Sir Charles Harris.

In discussing Mr. Haldane's methods, Mr. A. E. Widdows said: 'If he found anyone doing his work well, whatever his position, Haldane dealt with that man.'

ton's questionnaire clearly indicated French preference for a unity of military command.¹

In the Peninsula, Wellington's Army had been the most important fighting force among the Allies, at Blenheim, as at Waterloo, there had been a British Commander of the combined forces of many powers. Even on the Crimea, the British had been but slightly junior partners. On the continental field, however, armies of a far greater size would be met. To send six British Divisions to fight alongside sixty divisions of our Allies, against some eighty divisions of our foes, this was to create fresh problems for the nation.

For the moment however the full implication of the new policy was not grasped, nor was the situation as dangerous as it would become later. With General Grierson at the War Office a British Force for the defence of the Northern Ports was a controllable factor, it was not until General Henry Wilson came to the War Office with his devotion to French doctrine and French leadership that the British Expeditionary Force became tied to a preconceived French plan.

At all events, faced with the facts as he saw them, Haldane had made up his mind, and for six years was going to follow one definite course of action.

'Had we organized the requisite Expeditionary Force? Clearly we had not.'²

His enquiries showed him that to put even 80,000 men on the continent would take two months.³

It was clear that before the Expeditionary Force of his plans could be realized there would have to be considerable recasting of the Standing Army.

He was, however, resolved to proceed carefully. The prevalent feeling of the newly elected House of Commons had to be considered. Therefore, when in March 1906, he pre-

¹ See Appendix K.   ² Autobiography, p. 187.
³ This obviously differs from Grierson's suggestion to Belgium to have 105,000 men in Antwerp in thirty-two days. Probably the completeness or otherwise of the transport accompanying the force accounts for the different estimates.

sented his first estimates, they contained little that was sensational.

The Memorandum of the Secretary of State which accompanied the Estimates gave the key to Haldane's conception of his duty. He was going to take time to study his problem.

'The Army Estimates of 1906–7, viewed as a whole, embody no far-reaching changes of new departures but provide the money necessary to carry on the army on its present footing for another year. I do not desire to attempt the introduction of serious changes in policy without taking full time for their consideration.'[1]

Certain economies were, however, to be made, and there was to be a reduction in the establishment of 5,300 officers and men. This was caused by the disappearance of the Royal Garrison Regiment, by the transference of Submarine Defences to Naval Control, and to the disbandment of certain Colonial units. There was a slight decrease (£17,000) on the Estimates of the previous year. An important step in the development of Dominion responsibility for Defence was announced in these Estimates. The fortified Naval coaling stations of Halifax and Esquimault were being handed over to the Dominion of Canada and the British troops were to be withdrawn from these garrisons.

An interesting experiment was to be tried with the Militia. Twenty selected battalions were to train for six months with their own Militia officers, and in the case of these units no Militia recruits were to be allowed to enlist into the Line until one annual training had been completed.[2]

When the time came for Haldane to open his case in the House of Commons, the same prudent caution was manifest. He opened modestly:[3]

[1] Command Paper 2694 of 1906. Dated March 2, 1906.
[2] This development of the Militia idea had been strenuously urged by the Duke of Bedford. Before the scheme could be properly tried out the whole force had disappeared.—MS. evidence, Sir Charles Harris.
[3] A.E., 1906–7; A.D., 1906, p. 42.

'I address this House with unfeigned diffidence. My predecessors, or many of them, have been people of great military knowledge, or, at any rate, knowledge with regard to military matters. Never did a Minister rise to address this House on subjects connected with his department with less prepersuasion. Whether that is a merit or not it has at least allowed me to approach the questions which I had to face in the beginning of last December with an open mind. . . . Let me say at once—and this is the only personal reference that I have to make—that I have found my task a fascinating one. There is no part of the question connected with the army which does not possess peculiar interest. . . . The men one comes across, the new school of young officers—entitled to the appellation of men of science just as much as engineers or chemists —were to me a revelation; and the whole question of the organization of the Army is fraught with an interest which, I think, is not behind that of the study of any other scientific problem.

A new school of officers has arisen since the South African War, a thinking school of officers who desire to see the full efficiency which comes from new organization and no surplus energy running to waste.'

He touched on some of the difficulties of the British problem.

'To-day there are some 60,994 men of the infantry of the line at home and 83,292 abroad. . . . In South Africa on the first of this month we had 20,370. When you consider that no man in South Africa costs much under £150 a year, you will see what an enormously increased charge that is.'

Then came a most important declaration. Arthur Balfour a year earlier had definitely decided in favour of the 'Blue Water School', and against those who feared large-scale invasion. Haldane was now to come to the same decision. Having made his statement he showed the result. Speaking in a lighter vein, he described a visit paid to a mobilization centre near Dorking, one of the forts built towards the end of the last century to defend London. These were the centres upon which were to be based the numerous bodies of London

HALDANE BECOMES SECRETARY OF STATE FOR WAR

Volunteers, and in these centres were stacked enormous masses of stores which might be required in such an emergency. Haldane pointed out the wastage and loss involved. 'What an advantage it is when you can get rid of these things root and branch by the aid of the first principle.'

After announcing the Government's decision to abolish the garrison at St. Helena, and to disband the Chinese Regiment,[1] he made a passing reference to the General Staff. 'The late Government laid the foundation of a General Staff, we have got it to work.' Then came a passage which served—and still serves—as a masterly summary of the military problem of Great Britain. Comparing our problem with that of other countries he said:[2]

'They have only one war to contemplate on a large scale, and that is with their neighbours across the border. They have to be ready to mobilize and fight within perhaps ten days from the time of the order being given. Therefore they must be ready. It is absolutely necessary that their reserves should be trained up to the eyes and be ready when called upon to take the field at once. But the British Army is not like that. We live on an island, and our coasts are completely defended by the Fleet. Our Army is wanted for purposes abroad and overseas. It is necessarily a professional Army; we could not get such an Army by conscription. It must be of high quality; but because of the limited nature of its functions—to strike at a distance—it ought to be of strictly limited dimensions.

Have we ever thought, scientifically and clearly, what those dimensions ought to be? I do not think so. I know that certain things have been worked out, but I do not think that the whole problem has been dealt with in its entirety. Here is an island, the striking force of which does not exist for the defence of these coasts—it does not exist merely for our own insular interests.

This island is the centre of an Empire consisting of nearly

---

[1] The Chinese Regiment was reduced to four Companies in 1902, and the remaining four Companies were disbanded in June 1906; the reduction of Establishment (about 550) was shown in Vote A, 1907–8.—MS. evidence, Sir Charles Harris.   [2] A.D., 1906, pp. 59, 60, 61.

12,000,000 square miles, and including some 400,000,000 of population and we have to protect the distant shores of that Empire from the attacks of the invader.

We want therefore an Army which is very mobile and capable of rapid transport. For fighting which has to be at a distance and cannot be against large masses of men it ought to be on a strictly limited scale, and perfect rather in quality than in expanded quantity. There never has been enough careful thinking about this problem. If the Army is something which is not wanted for Home Defence then its size is something which is capable of being calculated. The size of the striking force is the principal ingredient in the present cost of the Army. . . .

I do not think you will ever satisfactorily reduce your striking force, even if you have solved the scientific problem, how much you require for action abroad, unless you provide some power of expansion behind it in this country. . . .'

Such was the speech of the new minister, modest in tone, excellent in manner, making clear, to all who cared to observe, three lines of thought which Haldane meant to pursue: The Expeditionary Force, Expansion from the Territorial Forces,[1] and the Technical Education of the Army.[2]

Each problem was large in itself; each was in the event to require about a year's work; each will need to be made the subject of a separate chapter.

[1] 'Is it possible to shrink this vast and costly organization? Yes, I think so, if that skeleton of expansion of which I have spoken is lying behind, which will become a very real expansion in time of national emergency, and which, until a time of national emergency, need not be made a real expansion.'
'. . . if the Colonies would follow suit with the creation of a potential Army.'
[2] 'Why should there not be a B.Sc. degree in the science of war?'

CHAPTER 13

THE FORMATION OF THE EXPEDITIONARY FORCE

THE man who planned to send abroad in fifteen days the largest force ever possessed by the country commenced his work by reducing the strength of the Regular Army. To some of his critics this seemed the only action by Haldane that was ever worth taking into account. Yet it was quite logical. He had made up his mind to have six great Divisions; anything that was surplus to that need was available to be disposed of, bartered, if need be, for something that was necessary to the Expeditionary Force. It was not easy to persuade the sentimentalists to balance battalions of famous regiments against drivers of the Divisional Train.

Moreover, he had got to make some reductions in the Estimates to make it even possible for him to secure the support of his own party.

Obstacles appeared soon enough. By April, even such a reformer as Esher was writing to the King about Haldane's proposals to reduce the Brigade of Guards by taking away two battalions from the existing Guards Brigade at Aldershot.

'In the course of the discussion which took place yesterday Sir John French told Mr. Haldane that if reductions are absolutely necessary, much as he would dislike it, he would far rather see four batteries of artillery reduced than lose the Brigade of Guards, from a force of three Divisions which he would have to command in the field.'[1]

King Edward made his powerful influence felt in the same direction, writing, on March 23rd:

[1] Esher Journals, vol. ii, p. 157.

'I understand that Mr. Haldane contemplates making many reductions of troops in the Colonies, but I hope that he will clearly understand that I cannot give my sanction to the reduction of any garrison in South Africa.'[1]

On the other side, a Private Members' motion in the House of Commons served to remind Haldane, if reminder were needed, that a large section of his party looked for reductions in the Army Estimates, with little regard to what such reductions might entail. On May 9th, Mr. Vivian moved 'That this House of Commons is of opinion that the growth of expenditure in armaments is excessive and ought to be reduced'.[2] Moreover, the motion, which was not carried to a division, was not seriously contested; even from the Conservative benches came general support of the basic principle of economy in military budgets. It was fairly obvious that if Haldane wished to get his scheme of reorganization approved by his own party the scheme would have to show economies as well as improvements.

In the meantime, he formed a Committee for his own guidance, which was to study the formation of the Territorial Force.[3] Leaving this Committee to study at some leisure the problem of the second line formations, he devoted himself

---

[1] Lee, vol. ii, p. 485.

Sir Sidney Lee's own footnote is: 'For the moment the King's strenuous opposition prevented any further reduction of the South African garrison, but in 1908 . . .'

Sir Sidney Lee is, however, not quite correct, for there was a reduction of three battalions as a result of the Government's policy, and though this reduction was temporarily balanced by the arrival of an extra cavalry regiment, even this addition to the mounted strength faded away in 1909.

See also Esher Journals, July 10, 1906, p. 170. 'We had a Douma this morning and a Defence Committee this afternoon. At the latter Grey insisted that the garrison of Egypt should not be reduced. This throws out Haldane's plan somewhat, as he had counted on withdrawing a line Battalion from there which must now be supplied from Malta.

The King is perfectly furious about the reduction. It is a pity he did not boil himself up earlier in the day. . . .'

[2] A.D., 1906, p. 659.

[3] Mr. Haldane, in answer to a question, May 18, 1906.—A.D., 1906, p. 739.

THE FORMATION OF THE EXPEDITIONARY FORCE

in the late spring of 1906 to the re-modelling of the Regular Army. He saw clearly enough that in 1906, as now, 'the expeditionary force is a by-product of the Cardwell system'.[1] The force which was to be sent into a continental war would have to be created, as far as the more important fighting units were concerned, out of that part of the army at home which balanced the other part employed on garrison duty abroad. Had there been enough at home to find seven great Divisions, then, perhaps, Haldane might have formed seven. As the resources at his disposal would only make six, anything that lay in the margin between six and seven was clearly redundant.[2]

It will be remembered that in his speech on the occasion of the presentation of the Army Estimates the new Secretary of State for War had asked for time. By midsummer he had so used that time that he was ready to place his scheme before the House of Commons. Accordingly, on July 12th, on one of the Supply days allotted to Army votes, he rose in his place to announce the Government's intentions. Two days before, in the House of Lords, Earl Roberts had spoken upon the unpreparedness of the nation for war.[3] There was no lack of interest in Mr. Haldane's speech. The House and the galleries were crowded with those who awaited the scheme which the Liberal Government were to produce for the Army.

Mr. Haldane commenced on a grave note. 'There is', he claimed, 'hardly a member who is not profoundly convinced that the state of our national forces is highly unsatisfactory.' The public were shaken in their trust in the Army and in the

---

[1] This illuminating phrase is used by Major G. H. Cole, M.B.E., in one of his lectures.
According to Mr. Amery, House of Commons, March 12, 1936, the phrase was used by Mr. Haldane.

[2] 'Lord Haldane's thesis can be expressed quite simply: a striking force which can be mobilized quickly is better than a force which cannot be mobilized at all, even if the latter be a little larger.'—'The War Office', Hampden Gordon, p. 84.

[3] A.D., 1906, pp. 656 et seq.

War Office.[1] 'Before you can restore public confidence in the Army you must make people feel that they are getting value for their money.' He then quoted the prevalent army feeling, the feeling of the newer generation of officers. They were, he claimed, reconciled to the necessity for economies, but they felt that it was their duty to see that 'every penny spent on the Army is spent on fighting efficiency'. The proposals which he was about to submit had secured the full approval of the Army Council. They would 'result in a large reduction of men and of money, and yet, by the reorganization of the Army as a whole, the result is produced in a form in which, if we have to pare down, we have also used our materials in building up and completing the structure so that at last it is homogeneous'.

Haldane laid down certain conditions upon which he had worked. First of all he made it clear that the Regular Army was for war overseas. It was not for Home Defence, and therefore anything that had in the past had a meaning only in connection with Home Defence was clearly redundant. He was 'rigidly adhering to the policy of casting off everything useless for war purposes, by applying strictly the principle of organization for war'.

In the total of an army required for a modern war there were a number of functions which did not differ very greatly from those which were a part of ordinary civil life. It was not necessary that the country should maintain in peace-time, upon a professional basis, all the men who would be required to minister in an ancillary capacity to the needs of the fighting portion of the Expeditionary Force. Therefore he proposed that a great portion of the 'services', of the Expeditionary Force which he planned, would be manned on a Militia basis.

He proposed a Force of six great Divisions.[2] It would

---

[1] 'The House of Commons believes instinctively that the Army is administered extravagantly. That is true. But they also think there is a short cut to economy. That is false.'—Esher to Lord Knollys, May 27, 1906. Esher Journals, vol. ii, p. 166. [2] A.D., 1906, p. 992.

THE FORMATION OF THE EXPEDITIONARY FORCE

consist in round figures of 150,000 men. Of these, 50,000 would be men with the colours, 70,000 would be reservists, and 30,000 would be on a Militia basis.

After the needs of this overseas force had been completely provided for, there would be a surplus of units both in the Artillery and the Infantry, and he proposed reductions in both these arms. The Cavalry would not be touched.

In the Artillery he had found a somewhat strange position. The expansion, arranged by Mr. Brodrick in order that the six Army Corps should all have Regular Field Artillery, had provided guns but had not provided the men to man the guns. Moreover, the new quickfirers would require very much more ammunition in the Brigade Ammunition Column—a Royal Artillery unit—and therefore would require longer columns and more men to man them. With the result that though there were nominally 93 batteries in the country, it would only be possible, in the event of mobilization, to man 42 of these, together with the necessary Brigade Ammunition Columns. To cope with this very serious deficiency he proposed to carry out a survey of the Militia Royal Garrison Artillery. Owing to the reorganization of coast defence—and also incidentally owing to the adoption by the Government of the general principles of the 'Blue Water School'—there were 300 guns on the strength of the Militia Royal Garrison Artillery which were now either obsolete or not required. He proposed to ask these Militia men to accept service in the ammunition columns of the Expeditionary Force.[1] In the meantime, he proposed to reorganize the artillery at home so

[1] It appears that some such plan had been in the mind of the former Administration.
The Earl of Donoughmore, former Under-Secretary of State for War, speaking in the House of Lords on July 24, 1906, quoted a decision of the Army Council at its 70th Meeting on November 28, 1905: 'There are about 124 companies of Militia Garrison Artillery not allotted to coast defence and surplus to requirements. A scheme is to be formulated showing how these artillery might be used (*a*) as a reserve for the Regular Siege Artillery, (*b*) to supplement deficiencies of the Reserve in Horse and Field Artillery by the formation of ammunition columns.'—A.D., 1906, p. 1155.

as to provide 81 batteries on a four-gun basis and 18 batteries on a two-gun basis in peace. In both cases the war strength of the batteries would be six gun, and the war equipment would be kept in readiness. The number of field batteries required for the Expeditionary Force of six Divisions would be 63, which would leave him 36 batteries in reserve. The eighteen batteries which were on the two-gun basis would perform the task of training the Militiamen who would serve the ammunition columns.[1] The 15-pounders, which were being replaced by the new 18-pounder, would be converted to quickfiring guns and would be handed to the Volunteers.

He proposed to use the Yeomanry as Divisional Cavalry for the Infantry Divisions of the Expeditionary Force.

In the case of the Infantry he proposed a reduction of eight battalions of the line and two battalions of the Brigade of Guards. The reduction in strength would be chiefly effected by the withdrawal of troops from certain overseas garrisons. At that time there were 52 battalions in India, 32 in the Colonies and 72 at home. It was proposed to withdraw three battalions

[1] This was the scheme as set out by Mr. Haldane in his speech. Actually the artillery training brigade scheme passed through several stages. In the Estimates of 1908-9 it was shown that the R.F.A. at home had:

21 batteries on a 6-gun Establishment
45 batteries on a 4-gun Establishment
33 batteries on a 2-gun Establishment
99

It will be realized that at the outset the scheme had to train as field artillerymen a large number of special reservists who had previously been Militia garrison gunners. After this first contingent had received their training it was no longer necessary to cater for such a large capital intake; it was only a question of dealing with the annual influx of Special Reservist recruits.

Therefore by 1909-10 it had only become necessary to have six training brigades of eighteen batteries. At the same time, it had been found possible to take in more recruits for the R.F.A. on a three-year colour service, and these fifteen batteries were put back to the four-gun basis, making sixty in all. Six of these went to the Divisions as extra Howitzer batteries; the remainder were surplus and were used for Territorial training.—MS. evidence, Sir Charles Harris.

THE FORMATION OF THE EXPEDITIONARY FORCE 257

from South Africa, where they would be replaced by one Cavalry Regiment, two from Malta, one from Gibraltar, and one from Ceylon.

The third battalions of the Coldstream and Scots Guards would be disbanded, in the case of the Coldstream Guards after one short tour of duty in Egypt. After careful consideration it had been decided to disband the third and fourth battalions of the Northumberland Fusiliers, the Royal Warwicks, the Lancashire Fusiliers, and the Manchester Regiment. These battalions were fairly recent creations, and most of them were under strength.[1] The First Guards Brigade at Aldershot would contain only two Guards Battalions, but there would be created a new Fourth Guards Brigade out of the Guards Regiments stationed in London, this Brigade to form part of the Second Division on mobilization.

With regard to the Auxiliary Forces, the Government intended to put to them exactly the same searching question as had been applied to the Regular Army: 'What purpose do you serve in War?' The Militia had fallen in ten years from 113,000 men to 90,000 and yet to-day it was costing £480,000 more than ten years previously. The Yeomanry had increased in strength from 9,600 to 25,000, but at a greatly increased cost. To the Militia Haldane put a very direct challenge. They must 'either fall back to Volunteer work in which case they would not be paid more than Volunteers are paid, or they must take upon themselves the same obligation as the Regular Soldier, that is to be ready to serve abroad in case of war'. It will be remembered that the last Conservative administration had tried to bring in this very proposal, the service of the Militia overseas in the event of war, and that Lord Lansdowne in face of the hostility of the Militia members in the House of Lords had been compelled to drop the Bill. Now Mr. Haldane was to bring it forward again. But he made,

---

[1] A return (Command Paper 198) in answer to a question by Lord Portsmouth, August 1, 1906, shows that these battalions were indeed, taking the eight together, 1,199 O.R. under establishment.

S

on this occasion, an important proviso: 'That men would go abroad in units, not lower than companies, and often in battalions, with their own officers.'[1]

As for the Volunteers, the Government considered that they had three functions. The first was to man the coast fortresses when the Regulars left them to go overseas. The second was to repel raids on the country in the absence of the Regular Army. Such raids the Government thought would not be of greater force than about 10,000 men. The third function was to act 'as a sort of second Reserve for the Regular Army'. He envisaged the creation of 'some kind of Association in the counties' to assist in the raising and administration of the Volunteers. In this connection, however, he added: 'We are still in a state of consideration about the Auxiliary Forces, but about the Regular Army and the Militia our principles and propositions are clear.'

He had spoken for three hours, the total time allowed for the debate was six. There had been rumours of reductions in Army strength, but on the whole the secret had been kept, and the scope of the plan was a surprise. There was a good deal of criticism, in general as to the proposed reduction of 20,000 men, in particular as to the reduction of the Artillery and the Coldstream Guards. From the Conservative benches came protests and requests that nothing final should be done until Parliament had had fuller opportunity of studying these momentous proposals. Haldane, however, would not give way. 'I am sent here', he said, 'to act, and not to sit still.'

There was, however, one more attempt by the Opposition to hold up the programme of Army reform. On July 19th, Mr. F. E. Smith moved the adjournment of the House on 'the avowed intention of His Majesty's Government to commence forthwith reductions in His Majesty's Armed Forces which have not received the sanction of Parliament'. There were confused arguments as to what Haldane had or had not pro-

[1] Mr. Haldane at this time hoped that the Militia would fall into his two-line Army scheme. By 1907 he had realized that such a hope was vain.

THE FORMATION OF THE EXPEDITIONARY FORCE

mised in his opening Estimates speech, but indeed the effort of the Opposition was in vain, for the truth of the matter was bluntly told by Haldane when he said: 'But there is this difference between our scheme and his' (Arnold-Forster's), 'we are fairly agreed on this side of the House.' Haldane had secured the approval of the Cabinet to his propositions, and by his economies had fended off the criticisms of the Radical wing. The solid benches of the Liberal Party assured the safe passage of their Secretary's plans. The motion for the adjournment lapsed 'without question put'.

There was one more attempt in the House of Lords on July 24th, when most of the supporters of the Militia of the past, and the protagonists of National Service, paraded their dogmas. The reply made on behalf of the Government by the Earl of Portsmouth, Under-Secretary of State for War, was perhaps even more categorical than the suaver words of Haldane in the Lower House: 'Our mandate from the country is to spend less money, therefore we must have fewer men.'[1]

On July 30th Haldane published his Memorandum on Army reorganization.[2] In the main this important Memorandum traversed the ground of his speech of July 12th. There were, however, one or two points which were new or at least received new emphasis. In a table attached to the Memorandum he showed the distribution of the men who would be required to fill up the Expeditionary Force but would be on a 'non-regular' basis. It is to be noted that the word now was 'non-regular' not the 'Militia' of his speech, and, indeed, there was little of the old Militia element in this 30,000.

The distribution was:

Cavalry	3,240 (Yeomanry)
Artillery	10,337
Engineers	2,425
Infantry	nil
Army Service Corps	10,775

[1] A.D., 1906, p. 1193.   [2] Command Paper 2993 of 1906.

Royal Army Medical Corps . . 3,098
Army Veterinary Corps . . . 541
Army Ordnance Corps . . . 441

Note 2 to the Appendix described these as 'partly men trained on a Yeomanry or Militia basis, partly of Reservists paid retaining fees but not trained, and partly of civilians to be specially engaged on mobilization'. The only Militia units involved were the Artillery.

Concerning the Militia Infantry, the Memorandum was a little more clear than the speech.

'Similarly the Militia Infantry Battalions, although drawn closer to the Regular Battalions of the Territorial Regiments of which they form part, will be trained as units. What is hoped for is that it will be possible to send them abroad in their units, to render such services as may be required of them. The leading military authorities are agreed, however, that it would be wrong to give a pledge that they shall never be asked to go abroad otherwise than in battalions. National necessities may arise, paramount to every special interest, and it is, therefore, right that there should be reserved, at least for possible exercise, a power to make the same call upon these battalions as is often made upon Regular Battalions, that is to say, to send out companies with company officers to join another battalion of their Territorial Regiment. I need hardly, however, add the observation that the last thing the Government desires is to revert to the old system under which Militia battalions were ruined by being bled white of their best officers and men, before being called upon as units to take the field. To obviate the necessity for this, and to make provision for the maintenance of the Regular Battalions, a depot battalion will, on mobilization, be formed for each Territorial Regiment, from which drafts to replace the wastage of war may be furnished.'[1]

Even to send out Militia Companies under their own officers would require an alteration of the existing laws. Moreover, as was pointed out by the Duke of Bedford,[2] to say that Militia Companies were to go abroad under their

[1] Paragraph 11 of the Memorandum.   [2] A.D., 1906, p. 1191.

own officers was no real protection, for Militia officers were junior to all Regular Officers of the same rank, and, therefore, the Militia Captain in charge of the Company would always be the junior in the Regiment and every single other Regular Captain would be able to order his Militia Company about.

As will be seen, before many months were out even this concession to the old Militia ideas was to fade away. However, the essential present fact was that whereas the reductions in the Regular Army could be made by the mere fiat of the Secretary of State for War, any change in the status of the Militia[1] had to be carried through by Act of Parliament. This Act Haldane's draughtsmen were already considering.

While the reorganization of the Regular Army did not involve new legislation, the amount of detail involved was, of course, very great. Haldane was fortunate to have, as his principal War Office helper in this work, General Douglas,[2] 'one of the most energetic and single-minded administrators we have ever had at the War Office'.[3]

Even so, the task took up the whole of the remainder of the year 1906. It was on January 12, 1907, that the War Office issued a Special Army Order, itself dated January 1st, which set out the new organization to be adopted by the Army. This was accompanied by a memorandum from the Secretary of State which was intended to explain, in some cases, the ideas underlying the changes.

Paragraph 5 of the memorandum dealt with the grouping of the Cavalry. The four Cavalry Brigades were to be grouped into one Division for use in, if necessary, an independent role.

In order that the absence of the Cavalry Division in a strategic role should not deprive the main body of the Army of reconnaissance troops it was intended to form, from four Mounted Infantry Battalions and two Cavalry Regiments,

[1] It is to be noted that an *increase* in the Regular Army, involving as it does an increase in Vote A of the Army Estimates, requires the consent of the House.
[2] Lieutenant-General C. W. H. Douglas, C.B.
[3] Autobiography, p. 189.

not required for the Cavalry Brigades, two mounted Brigades to operate 'in advance of the main body of the Army'.[1]

Paragraph 6 explained that under the new organization all the Artillery in the field was allotted to Divisions, none was retained as Corps Artillery. Paragraph 7 referred to the very important changes in telegraph and bridging equipment.

It was not until May 1907, that the Army List contained a small printed memorandum explaining that 'the alterations necessitated by Army Order No. 28 of 1907 (Reorganization of the Regular Army and the United Kingdom), have been carried out in this issue'.

What these reorganizations were had best be told in tabular form.

ALDERSHOT COMMAND

1st Cavalry Brigade (Byng)

1st *Division* (Grierson)	2nd *Division* (B. M. Hamilton)
1st Brigade Aldershot	4th (Guards) Brigade London
2nd Brigade Blackdown	5th Brigade Aldershot
3rd Brigade Bordon	6th Brigade Aldershot
Three Fd. Arty. Bdes. each three batteries	Three Fd. Arty. Bdes.
One Fd. Arty. (How.) Bde.	
Two Fd. Coys. R.E.	Two Fd. Coys. R.E.
Two Div. Tel. Coys. R.E.	

[1] It will be remembered that in actual practice this was not done. The British Expeditionary Force went to France with one Cavalry Division of four Brigades and an independent 5th Cavalry Brigade. In fact, however, it was speedily found that such a large Cavalry command was unwieldy even for General Allenby. The 5th Cavalry Brigade in the days of the retreat from Mons nearly always acted directly under the orders of the I Corps. On September 16, 1914, the existing Cavalry Brigades were grouped into the 1st Cavalry Division (1st, 2nd, and 4th Brigades), General Allenby, and the 2nd Cavalry Division (3rd and 5th Brigades), General Hubert Gough. The mixed Cavalry and Mounted Infantry Brigades were never formed. As Divisional Cavalry the British Expeditionary Force had with each Division a Squadron, in the case of the 1st, 2nd, and 3rd Divisions from 15th (King's) Hussars, in the case of the 4th, 5th, and 6th Divisions from the 19th (Queen Alexandra's Own) Hussars. As Army Troops there went overseas with the British Expeditionary Force three squadrons of Irish Horse, two from the North Irish Horse, one from the South Irish Horse.

THE FORMATION OF THE EXPEDITIONARY FORCE 263

Army Troops
1st and 2nd Air Line Coys. R.E.
1st and 2nd Cable Tel. Coys. R.E.
1st and 2nd Wireless Tel. Coys.
1st and 2nd Balloon Coys. R.E.
1st and 3rd Bridging Train.

EASTERN COMMAND

2nd Cav. Brigade (Fanshawe) Canterbury
4th Cav. Brigade (Allenby) Colchester

4th Division (Stephenson)
10th Brigade Shorncliffe
11th Brigade Colchester
12th Brigade Chatham
Three Fd. Arty. Bdes.
One Fd. Arty. (How.) Bde.
Two Fd. Coys. R.E.

IRISH COMMAND

3rd Cav. Brigade Curragh
5th Division (Plumer)

13th Brigade Dublin
14th Brigade Curragh
15th Brigade Belfast

Three Fd. Arty. Bdes.
One Fd. Arty. (How.) Bde.
Two Fd. Coys. R.E.

6th Division Cork (Parsons)

16th Brigade Fermoy
17th Brigade Tipperary
18th Brigade (In Northern Command with Bns. at York, Lichfield (two) and Sheffield)
Three Fd. Arty. Bdes.
One Fd. Coy. R.E.

SOUTHERN COMMAND

3rd Division Bulford (Franklin)

7th Brigade Tidworth
8th Brigade Devonport
9th Brigade Portsmouth

Three Fd. Arty. Bdes.
One Fd. Arty. (How.) Bde.
Two Fd. Coys. R.E.

1st Heavy Brigade R.G.A.
2nd Heavy Brigade R.G.A.

The Heavy Brigades of the Royal Garrison Artillery at Fareham, which, under the old plans would be the Corps Artillery of the 1st and 2nd Army Corps, were now in mobilization to send their batteries, armed with the new 60-pounder gun, one to each of the six Divisions.

The expansion in Royal Engineer units was carried into effect by Army Order No. 64 of 1907, to take effect from April 15, 1907. This created out of the old Nos. 1, 2, and 3 (Cadre) Telegraph Companies:

    1.2. (Air Line) Telegraph Coys.
    1.2. (Cable)   Telegraph Coys.
    1.2. (Wireless) Telegraph Coys.
    1.2. (Cadre) 3.4 (Cadre) 5.6. (Cadre) and 7 (South Africa) (Divisional) Telegraph Coys.

Just previously Army Order No. 63 had established new titles for the officers of the General Staff by creating the rank of

    Major-General   General Staff
    Brigadier-General   General Staff
    G.S.O.1.
    G.S.O.2.
    G.S.O.3.

Within a few weeks, moreover, new mobilization store tables had been issued for all the new formations, including those for an Army Corps staff.

Yet all this great work had been carried out without any increase in the Estimates. On February 18, 1907, Haldane issued his Estimates for the year 1907-8. There was a decrease of £2,036,000.[1] The size of the Field Force was now as he

[1] Memorandum of Secretary of State relating to Army Estimates for 1907-8. Command Paper 3293 of 1907.

It should also be noted that expenditure of borrowed (not voted) money on works which had become habitual and had averaged over one and a half million pounds annually in the last ten years, was stopped. Haldane had to find on the votes a sum of over a million a year for annuities to repay the borrowings of his predecessors, and at the same time to take any fresh expenditure, of the kind for which they had borrowed, on to the votes direct.

THE FORMATION OF THE EXPEDITIONARY FORCE 265

explained, 'limited by the establishment necessary to preserve in order to find drafts and reliefs for the force abroad'. Haldane had managed to combine efficiency with economy. He had placated his own party and secured their goodwill for his further schemes; on the other hand he had not sacrificed anything that was essential.

For the Regulars the shifting kaleidoscope of Army reshuffling had ceased and the Army took shape, a shape that was to endure, with but little alteration, through seven years to come, till the day of mobilization sent six great Divisions, and four Cavalry Brigades, as Haldane had foreseen, across the seas to fight against Germany, on the soil of Northern France.[1]

[1] One important development took place in subsequent years. In the year 1910 formation of the Air Corps, to consist in the first instance of 14 officers and 160 men, was approved ('Chronology', 1910, p. 9), and this was followed in 1912 by the formation of the Royal Flying Corps, which took the place of the Air Battalion, Royal Engineers, and consisted in the first instance of No. 1 Airship and Flying Squadron and Nos. 2, 3, and 4 Aeroplane Squadrons. Land was purchased and buildings erected on Salisbury Plain for a Flying School, and the first course of instruction commenced on August 12, 1912.—'Chronology', 1912, p. 4.

In 1913–14 (Seely's first Estimates) this became Royal Flying Corps (Military Wing)—there being also a Naval Wing—with a joint Flying School on Salisbury Plain. Establishment, 1,005 all ranks.

In 1914–15 the Establishment was increased to 1,429, and the total provision for 'aviation' services, under all votes, rose from £520,500 in 1913–14 to £1,000,000 in 1914–15, by express order of Seely as Secretary of State.
—MS. evidence, Sir Charles Harris.

CHAPTER 14

THE TERRITORIAL AND RESERVE FORCES ACT

THE winter days at Cloan, which saw the creation, in Haldane's mind, of the Expeditionary Force, also saw the evolution of his plan for a second line volunteer formation of a novel type. It was to be a Territorial Force based upon County Associations. This title Haldane undoubtedly derived from his memory of the Roundhead organization which maintained Cromwell's troopers in the field,[1] though in the interests of historical accuracy it may be noted that the Haldane usage of the term did not strictly correspond with the precedent of 1643. For the 'Eastern Counties Association' of that year was an association of the shires of Norfolk, Suffolk, Essex, Cambridge and Huntingdon, not an association of men within the counties.[2]

The names and the organization were definitely settled before Haldane and Ellison came south in the early days of February 1906; indeed the whole scheme was embodied at this early date in a minute to the Army Council. There were minor alterations made in the months to come, but substantially the main outlines sketched by the end of January endured in the final Haldane Scheme.[3] There is a letter written by Esher to the King on December 10, 1906, which was intended as a rebuttal of the accusation that Haldane had acted without consulting his Military Members of Council. It shows that Mr. Haldane wrote his first memorandum in January,

---

[1] 'We call them "associations" because that is a good old term invented by Oliver Cromwell.'—Haldane, February 25, 1907. A.D., 1907, p. 77.
[2] Oman, 'History of England', p. 386.
[3] Ellison, xvii, and the evidence of Mr. A. E. Widdows.

THE TERRITORIAL AND RESERVE FORCES ACT 267

and followed it by five others, the last dated November 8th. There was no change in the first plan, but there was a gradual development.[1]

Unlike his less fortunate forerunners in office, Haldane was content to proceed slowly and to sound his ground. As a first step he formed a committee of eminent men chosen from the Regular Army, the Militia and the Volunteers.[2] To this assembly he put certain questions and certain schemes, in order to see whether it might be possible to carry through the reorganization of the Auxiliary Forces by consent rather than by enactment. The Chairman of the Committee was Lord Esher—a fact which has increased the confusion caused by many references to this body also as 'Lord Esher's Committee'. The official style was 'The Territorial Force Committee', but at a very early stage it took to itself the nickname of 'The Duma', a word well-nigh unknown to-day, but, in 1906, of international importance as the title of the somewhat experimental representative assembly in Russia.

Other prominent members of the Duma were Lord Bingham,[3] F. Freeman-Thomas,[4] J. E. B. Seely,[5] the Duke of Bedford, Lord Chesham, Lord Lovat, Lord Stanley,[6] and Colonel Sir Howard Vincent. From the Regular Army came Lord Roberts, Lord Methuen, and Colonel Ellison. General Sir Frederick Stopford was the official representative of the War Office. In all, there were forty-five members of this Committee, which it is important to note, was a body summoned solely upon the initiative of the Secretary of State for War. It was constituted by no Royal Warrant, issued no Minutes of Evidence, and prepared no Report.[7]

---

[1] Esher Journals, vol. ii, p. 206.
[2] The Committee first met on May 22nd. The list of members was published in the Press before it was submitted to the King. Haldane had to make his peace with the Monarch.—Ibid., and Lee, vol. ii, p. 500.
[3] Now Earl Lucan.   [4] Now Lord Willingdon, late Viceroy of India.
[5] Now Lord Mottistone.   [6] Now Earl Derby.
[7] A.D., 1906, p. 739. Also Ellison, xviii. See also 'Chronology', p. 102: 'This Committee, which consisted of a large number of representatives of

In fact before very long it became apparent that there was little likelihood of any agreed solution being reached.

There were, of course, two different problems. The first, what to do with the Militia, the second, what to do with the Volunteers. The first problem was by far the more difficult of the two. Some of those who were most keen in their support of the Militia, and most influential in Parliament and in the country, could hardly yet realize the great change that had been made in the status of the Militia since Mr. Cardwell first brought it under the control of the War Office, and linked Militia Regiments to the Regiments of the Regular Army. Men like the Duke of Bedford and Lord Ampthill vainly looked back to a condition of things,—which, in sober truth had not existed for scores of years,—when the Militia was a local force of landed officers and full-grown men, assembled and trained for the home defence of their native land. The facts of the case, as opposed to romantic theory, show that the Militia had become an avenue for the entry of young men into the Regular Army, and through the medium of the Militia Reserve it had provided a reservoir of more mature men who could be drafted away to the Regular Army on the outbreak of war. Now that the Militia Reserve had ceased to exist,[1] the Militia had, from the purely selfish point of view of the Regular Army, declined in value, and yet, from the youthfulness of its members, the transient nature of its population, and its rudimentary training, the Militia was of doubtful value as a fighting organization for Home Defence.

Haldane had already made up his mind that the military organization of the country was to consist of two echelons only, and not of three. In other words, the Militia was brought

the Auxiliary Forces and others, rendered no formal report, but passed numerous resolutions which were departmentally considered.' Also the speech of Sir Howard Vincent, A.D., 1907, vol. i, p. 827.

[1] The reference here is to the 'old' Militia Reserve, described in the earlier chapters of this book. The 'new' Militia Reserve, formed from the Royal Garrison Regiment and described on p. 134, had hardly ever formed an important part of the military machine.

face to face with the dilemma which had been threatening the force ever since the days of Cardwell.

Either it would have to join in the new Territorial Force, or it would have to merge its individuality even more closely into that of the Regular Army.

The fervent supporters of the Militia could not see the problem in that light. Their claims were perhaps overmuch bound up with history and tradition. Nevertheless they honestly felt that better terms ought to be secured for a force which had played such a notable part in the development of the British Army.

As for the Volunteers, though the problem was easier, there were a number of their Commanding Officers who disliked the prospect of surrendering the very great independence possessed by individual volunteer units, and placing themselves under the financial control of the suggested County Associations.

It soon became apparent, therefore, that it would not be possible to reach the solution desired by Mr. Haldane by any method of voluntary agreement. In July 1906 the meetings of the Duma came to an end, and Esher explained in a letter to the King the distance that had so far been covered by the work of the Committee.[1] Before the sittings of the Territorial Committee were suspended, there were meetings at the War Office on June 26 and 27, 1906, between a number of senior War Office officials and a group of representative Militia Colonels.

Major-General Mackinnon, upon the instructions of the Secretary of State, had arranged the conference. Lord Esher

---

[1] Esher Journals, p. 167. This letter confirms that at this stage the Militia was excluded from the Territorial Army. It also confirms the use of the phrase 'Territorial Army'. It appears that there was at one time a proposal to recall the Duma for further consultation; on October 17th all members of the Committee received a circular from the Secretary of State in which he expressed his hope that he would soon be able to summon the conference and resume discussions.—Speech of Sir Howard Vincent, A.D., 1907, vol. i, p. 827.

took the chair; the War Office representatives were Lord Roberts, Lord Methuen, Major-General Mackinnon, Major-General Stopford, Haig and Ellison. Lord Stanley also formed one of the 'official' group. Colonel Lucas was Secretary. There were fourteen Militia Colonels, headed by the Duke of Bedford, Lord Raglan, Lord Bathurst and Lord Hardinge.[1]

The official view was put very clearly. The main object of the meeting was to ascertain from the Militia Colonels 'whether in their opinion the Militia would be prepared to take a new form of enlistment, which would subject them to service overseas in the event of war, and, if so, what conditions, if any, should be attached to the new form of enlistment'. Sir Frederick Stopford as Director of Military Training explained the present War Office proposals.

'The Militia should not form part of the Territorial Army;[2] that the Militia should be drawn closer to the Regular Troops: that it should be made liable to service abroad in case of emergency; and that in the event of its being sent abroad, it was desirable that it should go out, as far as possible, in complete battalions or companies under their own officers, but that this should not preclude its being utilized to furnish drafts to the Regular Army in the field when necessary.'

The reply to this proposal was a flat refusal on the part of most of the Militia representatives.

'To these conditions the Militia Officers strongly demurred, on the ground that past experience showed that any attempt to use the Militia as drafts for the Line and especially for Line battalions

---

[1] The Report of this Meeting was published in 1907 as Command Paper 3513 of 1907. It is presumably due to the date of the publication that D. Haig is shown on the list of signatories as 'Major-General'. He was promoted to the rank on August 25, 1906.

With the candid approval of the King, Haldane had recalled Haig from India specially to assist in the work of reorganization at home.

[2] The phrase 'Territorial *Army*' actually occurs in the report, not 'Territorial *Force*'.

other than those of the territorial regiment, rendered service in the Militia highly unpopular with Officers and men, and that, if these conditions were expressed it would be impossible to enlist Militiamen for service overseas.'

The Militia Colonels did not like the project for overseas service at all; fourteen of them signed a Resolution 'A': 'If the Militia are to be enlisted for service oversea, the Infantry should go on foreign service with their battalion units.' Of the fourteen, four then qualified their refusal by adding the rider 'B': 'But should exceptional circumstances require it, drafts of not less than company units, under their own Officers, may be sent to join the Regular battalions of their territorial regiment.'

Not content with this rebuttal of the official suggestion, the Militia Colonels proceeded to draw up a further Resolution embodying eleven points, which they considered were just claims of the Militia. The official report somewhat drily observes that the claims of this Resolution 'give a clear idea of some of the privileges to which Officers of Militia believe the Force to be entitled'. Clause 1 claimed that 'the military rank of a Militia Officer should be in all respects equal to that of the equivalent rank in the Regular Army. Clauses 10 and 11 recommended that no one should be allowed to hold a Regular commission, or compete for an examination to the Indian Police, or for any foreign service of the Army, or in the Colonies, unless he had served for two trainings in the Militia'. These eleven resolutions were signed by all the Militia officers present.

This intransigent attitude created a problem for Haldane and his advisers. One further attempt, therefore, was made to obtain an agreed solution. In the autumn of 1906, Lord Derby, father of the present Earl, invited a number of Militia Commanding Officers to stay at Knowsley. 'They were to meet Mr. Haldane and have one last discussion on the future of the Constitutional Force.' The only other persons present were Lord Stanley (the present Earl of Derby), Douglas Haig, and Lieutenant-Colonel Ellison.[1] The Militia were given two alternatives. The first was that their units could take a leading place in the new Territorial Force. They would naturally be the senior units in the new organization, and, although the constitution, method of training, and control of the new Territorial Force would differ very considerably from the historical life of the Militia, it is permissible to-day to regret that the older force did not take the opportunity thus offered and bring its great history and local tradition to the aid of the new creation of Haldane's brain. At Knowsley the decision was no half-hearted one. The Militia were not going 'to join the Volunteers'.

Neither would it accept the other alternative, that of engagement for overseas service as drafts for the Regular Army. So the decision was taken that as the name of the Militia, with its age-old significance, could not be applied to either of the two new forms, the name should pass away, and the formation which Lord Haldane required to complete the machinery of the Regular Army should take a new appellation with a new meaning.[2]

In casual reference to this period, phrases will be found which imply that 'the Militia was converted into the Special Reserve'. Such expressions are inaccurate and incomplete. The historic Militia came to an end. Simultaneously an entirely new organization came into being. Individual Militia officers and men entered the new force. On occasions the complete strength of an old Militia unit went over as Special Reservists, but in gross and in detail the Special Reserve was something new; it was not the old Militia. There was little doubt in the minds of those responsible for the Official Chronology of the years succeeding 1907. Beside the return of strength of the

[1] Ellison, xvii.
[2] Colonel A. S. Barham, C.M.G., T.D., recounting conversations of this date with the Duke of Bedford, said: 'The Duke was quite honest; he said, "If we cannot be used in our present form you had much better bring the Militia to an end."' (Colonel Barham commanded at this date the Bloomsbury Rifles; the Duke of Bedford was Honorary Colonel of the Regiment.)

THE TERRITORIAL AND RESERVE FORCES ACT

Special Reserve may be found return of strength of 'the moribund Militia and Militia Reserve Division'.[1] These were the men who, having entered into Militia engagements, did not accept the invitation to transfer to the new formations. Therefore, they worked out the term of their service in the Militia unit of their first choice, and when the last such man came to the end of his allotted time of service, then the Militia, in its old form, ceased to be.

Haldane proposed to employ the machinery of the existing Army Reserve. Legislation would be introduced to allow for recruitment direct into the Reserve.[2] Thus this Reserve would be formed of two classes of men, those of the old style who went to the Reserve after a period of colour service, and those of the newer style, who would enlist direct into the Reserve, undergo a short period of training, and then return to civil life, subject to the Reservists' obligation of recall to the colours. They would not draw Reserve pay but would receive an Annual Bounty. They would be called up each year for Annual Training, at which time they would of course draw pay at Army rates. These would be called Special Reservists.[3] In peace-time, the two classes of Reservists would not normally meet. The Special Reservists would be carried on the strength of Special Reserve battalions, one to each Infantry Regiment of the Army List. The battalions would be based upon the Regimental depot. The Special Reservist recruits would do their recruit training at the depot; for Annual Training the battalion would train as a unit under its own officers. On mobilization the Special Reserve battalion would incorporate those men of the Regimental Army Reserve who were not required for the purpose of bringing up to strength,

---

[1] 'Chronology', 1911, p. 7.
[2] There was a precedent for direct enlistment with the Reserve. During the South African War the Post Office telegraphists and the railwaymen of the London and North-Western Railway were enlisted into the Army for one day, and then passed straight into the Reserve for twelve years.—Speech of Sir Charles Dilke, June 19, 1907. A.D., 1907, vol. ii, p. 215.
[3] Haldane first called this the 'Special Contingent'.

and providing first reinforcements for, the Line battalions of the Regiment.

In certain cases it was proposed to form, in addition, a second such Reserve Battalion for the Regiment; these were to be known as Extra Special Reserve Battalions.[1]

Lord Roberts was among the most influential of those who urged Haldane to proceed with his scheme by legislation, as soon as it was clear that alteration by agreement was not possible. In any case legislation was obviously necessary. The alteration to the strength of the Regular Army could be carried out by the mere fiat of the Secretary of State for War, subject to Parliamentary Control on the occasion of Army Estimates. The new formations of Haldane's plans on the other hand would involve changes in many matters at that time covered by the Army Act, the Reserve Forces Act, 1882, and the Reserve Forces and Militia Act, 1898.[2] The new County Associations would require statutory authority to hold lands and buildings and to administer public funds. To provide comprehensive legislation dealing with the whole scheme, Haldane turned to the Chancery lawyers who had, in the old days, devilled for him in Lincoln's Inn.[3] With one of these, John Kemp,[4] Haldane worked in Scotland during a Parlia-

---

[1] Twelve English Regiments and three Scottish Regiments had each one such Extra Special Reserve Battalion. The Royal Irish Rifles, the Leinster Regiment, the Royal Munster Fusiliers and the Royal Dublin Fusiliers had each two Extra Special Reserve Battalions; the Royal Irish Regiment, the Royal Irish Fusiliers, and the Connaught Rangers one each. (It will be remembered that there were no Territorials in Ireland.)—Command Paper 4497 of 1909.

These Extra Special Reserve Battalions were in some respects not very different from the old Militia units. It was expected that they might go abroad as units for garrison purposes.

[2] Command Paper 3361 of 1907.

'I am a lawyer and I own that to me the proposition that we could have carried through the reorganization of the Army without the Bill is an astounding one.'—Haldane, House of Commons, June 19, 1907. A.D., 1907, vol. ii, p. 246.

[3] Autobiography, p. 193.

[4] Later Sir John Kemp.

mentary recess. Frederick Liddell,[1] the Government draughtsman, gave the new measure its final shape.

While these men were engaged in drafting the Bill which was later to become the Territorial and Reserve Forces Act, Haldane was receiving powerful aid from Douglas Haig, Director of Training at the War Office. It was a fundamental part of Haldane's conception of the Territorial Force that it should be an Army complete in every respect. He wished every Territorial Force Division to have its full complement of artillery, engineers and other arms and services. In this project he met a great deal of opposition from senior officers. Lord Roberts himself was very sceptical as to the possibility of training Territorial soldiers to be efficient gunners within the limitations imposed by the civilian nature of the force.[2] Henry Wilson, from the Staff College, poured scorn on the scheme and employed all the resources of his mordant wit to belittle the Territorial Force.[3] Against such detractors Douglas Haig was a tower of strength. He made up his mind that the Territorial Force had to be an army of all arms, and regard for his technical ability convinced many waverers.

During the same waiting period there were other attacks to be staved off. Ellison tells how within the War Office an attempt was made, as late as September, to interpose the Militia, as a second echelon, between the Regular Army and the Volunteers. Haig's support stopped that attempt.[4] From certain sections of the Volunteers there came steady objections

[1] Now Sir Frederick Liddell, K.C.B.

[2] The Field-Marshal was very much in earnest on this subject; two years later he was still uttering his warnings. 'But I go further, my Lords, and say emphatically that the 196 Territorial batteries, by reason of their unsatisfactory composition, the want of proper organization, and their lack of anything approaching sufficient training and gun practice, would not, in spite of their numbers, be the slightest use in the field; and not only would not be of the slightest use, but they would be a positive danger. . . . Believe me, my Lords, to trust to amateur artillerists would be to court disaster.'
—House of Lords, March 15, 1908. A.D., 1908, p. 645.

[3] 'Journal of Field-Marshal Earl Haig', Duff Cooper, vol. i, pp. 110 and 111.

[4] Ellison, xviii.

to the County Associations. Haldane, anxious if possible to reach agreed solutions, was heavily pressed. Esher's support was, however, powerful. He was very pungent on the 'trades unionism' of the Volunteer C.O.s in the House of Commons, and strongly against any idea of whittling down the County Associations to mere advisory bodies.[1]

During the late winter of 1906, the final stages of the work were reached. The proposals were put before the Defence Committee, and through Esher to the King.[2] The realization that at long last a man had produced a coherent scheme was perhaps the vital factor commanding respect from all quarters. On January 12th Haldane was able to send the Monarch the final draft Bill.[3] Even so it was doubtful whether he would find an opportunity to present it to the House. The Liberal Party was busy with schemes of social reform. Haldane tells the story of the fortunate combination of circumstances which gave him his chance. A Bill which, according to the agreed programme for the session, should have been presented by one of his colleagues, was not ready for submission to the House. Haldane suggested that he had a small Bill of his own which might conveniently fill the gap. His Radical colleagues were slightly dismayed when the nature of the Bill was made clear. The reduction in Army Estimates of the previous year stood Haldane in good stead with his own party. He was assured of the support of the Prime Minister, while behind the scenes was the powerful influence of the veteran Liberal, Lord Haliburton.

There still remained the danger that prolonged opposition in the House of Commons might kill any chance of the Bill becoming law in the forthcoming session. Haldane interviewed Balfour and received a very reassuring reply. The Conservative Party, Balfour felt, had not managed to produce any satisfactory scheme for Army reform, and therefore it was only fair that they should give a chance to Haldane's measure.[4]

[1] Esher Journals, vol. ii, p. 196.
[3] Lee, vol. ii, p. 500.
[2] Esher Journals, p. 209.
[4] Autobiography, p. 193.

The King's Speech at the opening of Parliament on February 12, 1907, told of proposals which would be laid before the House 'for more clearly defining the functions of the Military forces of the Crown both regular and auxiliary, and for the improvement of their organization'.

On February 25, 1907, Mr. Haldane introduced his second Army Estimates. This time the result of his economies was plainly manifest; there was a total reduction of £2,036,000. In view of the debatable nature of some of the new proposals he was shortly to introduce, such a reduction was of the highest political value. He was careful to point out the means whereby the economies had been effected. He had been successful because he had taken the soldiers into his confidence and had asked them how the unnecessary expenditure could be avoided. This, he claimed, was the only sensible course and was infinitely superior to the older method of treating the soldier at the War Office, which was 'to set spies on him'. Haldane, moreover, went out of his way to pay a tribute to the reorganization of the War Office which had been carried out as a result of the recommendations of Lord Esher's Committee, and had been put into effect during the régime of his predecessor and political opponent, Mr. Arnold-Forster.

'Without the reform of the War Office which was made then . . . it would . . . have been impossible to get, at any rate in anything like the same degree, the economies which we have succeeded in getting this year.'[1]

With the Territorial and Reserve Forces Bill already on the Parliamentary threshold, it was of course impossible to refrain from some reference to the new proposals. The problem of the Militia was dealt with in a manner which left very little illusion as to his views.

'It is essential to the War Office to get recruits for the Regular Line. We get 12,000 recruits a year for the infantry of the Line

[1] A.D., 1907, vol. i, p. 63.

from the Militia at present, and without the Militia we could not get them. These recruits go into the Militia young and the Line takes them up when they reach the age at which they can go to the Line. The result is that under the existing system the War Office must control the Militia. It is impossible to get away from that, and if the Militia protests against it, the protest is met with the argument that the most important thing is to get the infantry of the Line sufficiently recruited and if one has to suffer the Militia must go under.'[1]

Turning to the Volunteers, he showed a full appreciation of the intolerable financial burden laid upon the officers in command of Volunteer units.

'The financial position of the Commanding Officers is deplorable. ... The unfortunate Commanding Officer of the Volunteer battalion is an even greater patriot than he is popularly supposed. He risks not only his life but his fortune.'

Therefore the proposed scheme for a Territorial or Home Army would contain financial provision for relieving Commanding Officers from these liabilities.

Mr. Haldane then proceeded to explain in fairly full detail the provisions of his new scheme. One passage was of particular interest in the light of future events. The Territorial Force would be enlisted for home service. If the country were engaged in a serious war outside the shores of these islands, the Regular Expeditionary Force would be sent abroad. The Territorial Force would be embodied, and would receive six months' training.

'And our belief is that at the end of that time ... not only would they be enormously more efficient than the Volunteers or Yeomanry forces at this present time, but that they would be ready, finding themselves in their units, to say, "We wish to go abroad and take our part in the theatre of war, to fight in the interests of the nation and for the defence of the Empire." '[2]

[1] A.D., 1907, vol. i, p. 63.   [2] A.D., 1907, vol. i, p. 73.

THE TERRITORIAL AND RESERVE FORCES ACT

On the same date, February 25th, Mr. Haldane issued a Memorandum upon the Military Forces in the United Kingdom.[1] This document opened with the definite statement:

'At present the numbers and organization of the Military Forces in the United Kingdom are based on no scientific standard, and these forces have been raised on no definite plan.'

The Memorandum set out the disadvantages of the three-line system of Regular Army, Militia and Volunteers, and pointed out the defects of each line as they existed at that date. The basis of the proposed reform was to reduce the three lines to two lines.[2]

'Its ground plan is to divide the forces of the Crown into two categories and two only, any attempt to organize in three lines must, I am convinced, end in leaving us weak and ill organized everywhere. The National Army will, in future, consist of a Field Force and a Territorial or Home Force. The Field Force is to be so completely organized as to be ready in all respects for mobilization immediately on the outbreak of a great war. In that event the Territorial or Home Force would be mobilized also, but mobilized with a view to its undertaking in the first instance, systematic training for war. The effect of such training, given a period of at least six months, would be, in the opinion of all military experts, to add very materially to the efficiency of this force. The Territorial Force will, therefore, be one of support and expansion, to be at once embodied when danger threatens, but not likely to be called for till after the expiration of the preliminary period of six months.'

The Memorandum, and the Secretary of State's opening speech, thus marked a further step in the gradual unfolding of the Haldane Scheme. They revealed the Territorial Force as an organization for 'support and expansion', and they explained the theory of a minimum period of post-mobilization training.

The door was not entirely closed to the Militia, for the last

[1] Command Paper 3297 of 1907.   [2] Paragraph 11.

sentence of paragraph 4 in the Memorandum, which told of the lamentable state of the Constitutional Force, gave a hint that there was still room for the Militia within the Territorial Force. 'The true role of the Militia is undoubtedly as a country force to be recruited locally, as are the Volunteers, from men whose service will be voluntary.'

The position and function of the Special Contingent was explained,[1] but it was not definitely stated that this organization would take the place of the Militia. Indeed, even at this late stage in events, it would have been entirely possible to base the Special Contingent upon the Depots, and leave the Militia units to take their place in the Territorial Force.

Both in his speech and in the Memorandum Mr. Haldane admitted that there had been a slight change of view since the first scheme for County Associations. It had been thought desirable to bring the work of Associations in closer touch with the Military authorities.

The debate was continued on February 27th and 28th without bringing forth many new points. The way was, therefore, in some measure prepared for the introduction of the Territorial and Reserve Forces Bill, which Mr. Haldane formally moved, in a poorly filled House, on March 4, 1907. Under the style of 7 Edward, cap. 9, the Act was to empower the Army Council to establish, (1) County Associations, (2) a Territorial Force, and (3) a new branch of the 1st Class Army Reserve to be called the 'Special Reserve'.

The County Associations were to administer, but not to command, the Territorial Force. They were to be constituted upon the terms of a model scheme which was to be laid before Parliament. Under the Presidency (as a rule) of the Lord Lieutenant of the County, the Associations were to be composed of representatives of the Territorial Force, representatives of County Councils, and other local bodies, of Universities and especially of representatives of the interests of employers and workmen.

[1] Paragraph 11.

The Territorial Force was to be liable for service anywhere in the United Kingdom, but not outside. Its numbers were to be voted by Parliament.[1]

The Special Reserve was to consist of men who enlisted directly into the Reserve and accepted the liability of members of the Army Reserve without having served first in the Regular Forces.

The Bill, a not overlong document of twenty-six pages, consisted of four parts. Part I authorized the establishment of County Associations: Part II provided for the terms of service of the new Territorial Force: Part III founded the new Special Reserve, and Part IV covered certain miscellaneous subjects.

Before the Second Reading of the Bill, there was a debate in the House of Lords on March 21, 1907, staged by supporters of the Militia. The Earl of Wemyss moved the resolution, but the most notable and important speech was that made by the Duke of Bedford.[2] He left no doubt in the minds of his hearers that the Militia would not, in his opinion could not, join the Territorial Army. He had, he said, sent to 121 Military Commanding Officers the question whether they thought it would be possible to continue their units upon Mr. Haldane's terms for the Volunteers; 104 had replied 'No', 3 had replied 'Yes', 14 had not replied at all.[3] His main point was that the poorer wage-earning class who went into the Militia could not afford to be Volunteers.

The Second Reading of the Bill was taken on April 9th, 10th, and 23rd, and then the measure passed into Committee stage. On May 6th, the Prime Minister at the opening of the Committee stage announced an agreed time-table for discussion. Even so the various sections of the Bill occupied a good deal of Parliamentary time. The House debated the Bill in Committee on nine different days.[4] The powerful Liberal

---

[1] It was proposed to fix the limit at 300,000. The Volunteers had not been controlled by Parliament in this way.
[2] A.D., 1907, vol. i, pp. 711 et seq.   [3] Ibid., p. 722.
[4] May 28th and 29th, and June 3rd, 4th, 5th, 10th, 17th, 18th, and 19th.

majority was irresistible, the various clauses were disposed of one by one, so that, in the House of Lords on June 10th, Earl Wemyss was constrained to refer with sadness to 'the Guillotine Bill which is passing through the House of Commons at a rapid rate'.

In the great mass of reported speech which was occasioned by the passage of the Territorial and Reserve Forces Bill through the House of Commons, there was not a great deal of fresh argument. The opposition was as a whole more vocal than those in support of the Bill.[1] Fortunately, perhaps, a great deal of the opposition arguments cancelled each other out. From Mr. Arnold-Forster and his allies came searching doubts as to the efficiency of the soldiery of the Territorial Force when opposed to 'Continental Armies'. The Militia element attacked with dogged persistency, while the Volunteers, led by Sir Howard Vincent, opposed the imposition of fines for non-fulfilment of obligations, and the stricter control of the new regulations. The Yeomanry saw with dismay the lower rates offered by the Territorial Force.[2] From the newly arrived Labour Party came a general protest against increased military strength, and a more impassioned attack on the clause relating to cadet corps. Indeed, in respect of this particular clause, there was some sign of dissension in the Government ranks.

Perhaps the most dangerous attack was from the Militia, and it was countered by Sir Edward Grey, who rose on the Second Reading to reply for the Government.[3] He utilized a much quoted saying of Lord Lansdowne and turned it against the opposition.

'The fact is that Lord Lansdowne really gave away the case as regards the Militia when he said that the Militia had been plun-

[1] Sir Charles Dilke put the same fact from the other side. 'In Committee they had not had the advantage of the presence of those who filled the Division lobbies whenever a division took place.'—Speech on the Third Reading, June 19, 1907. A.D., 1907, vol. ii, p. 210.
[2] 2s. 8d. a day in place of 5s. 6d. See A.D., 1907, vol. ii, p. 664.
[3] A.D., 1907, vol. i, p. 802.

dered at one end for the Line and encroached on at the other end by the Volunteers. Yes, and if you follow that question out, you get, in my opinion, the corollary that if you are to maintain the Militia on their old basis you can only do it by plundering the Line or encroaching on the Volunteers.'

The Third Reading of the Bill was taken on June 19th. During its passage through the House there had been little alteration in the phraseology of the text, but there had been one very important decision, largely due to the Duke of Bedford's speech in the House of Lords. The avenue which had been left open to the Militia in the Memorandum and in the Secretary of State's opening speech was not to be trodden.[1]

Arnold-Forster opened the debate with a rather pathetically cynical speech. He distrusted the whole principle of the Volunteer system. 'The fact is'—so ran his argument,—'that those who are engaged to come out and go to war come out, but those who are not engaged do not come.' It was the speech of a sick man; he did his best to minimize the work of the Bill, yet in the peroration he proclaimed the measure 'a direct reversal of everything I have attempted to do and a direct challenge to everything that I believe to be right'.

There was not much for Haldane to do,[2] and the measure passed to its final division. The vote was 286 to 63: the opposition consisted largely of the Irish Members who voted against the Government for reasons more connected with the Irish Council Bill, and of some of the Labour Party. Most of the Unionist Members abstained from the Division. Sir Charles

[1] As late as April 8th, in a Memorandum dealing with certain aspects of the Territorial and Reserve Forces Bill (Command Paper 3366 of 1907) Mr. Haldane had written: '. . . It certainly would have been a misfortune had the existing Militia units not found their place in the new Territorial Force. In this way, and in this way only, is it possible that the laudable ambition of the Militia to take the field in its units, each unit under its own officers, should be satisfied.'—A.D., 1907, vol. ii, p. 202.

[2] Except make one bon mot. He had been accused of 'murdering' Arnold-Forster's short-term army. Haldane protested: 'I own that I was under the impression that I found a deceased baby, and I decently interred it.'—A.D., 1907, vol. ii, p. 250.

Dilke and Sir Howard Vincent were among the very few who carried their dislike of the Bill to the Opposition Lobby. The Tellers for the Opposition were the Labour Members, Mr. Arthur Henderson and Mr. George Roberts.

So the Bill went to the House of Lords. Haldane might have had reason to be apprehensive of counts in the Upper House. The Militia question loomed large and the Militia Peers were influential. In the event the struggle was less severe than might have been expected. There was an air of defeatism in the Militia ranks. The Earl of Wemyss made a fair statement of the position when the Bill reached the Lords.

'Your Lordships are no doubt aware that in another place, by an arrangement between the two Front Benches, the Militia has been taken out of the Territorial Force and is no longer coupled with the Volunteers and the Yeomanry. But although the name of the Militia remains, its constitution has been completely altered. The Militia is now to be a reserve for the Army.'[1]

That was a true statement, and the Government took an early opportunity of driving the fact home. The Earl of Portsmouth, speaking for the Government, said of the 3rd and 4th Battalions of the proposed Special Reserve:

'The men in these battalions will have to accept liability to service abroad and their primary function will be drafting to supply the demands of the Regular Army in the field.'[2]

Thereafter the Opposition largely disintegrated into sections, each attempting to gain concessions for the particular forces in which they were interested. The Duke of Bedford and Lord Raglan fought for the status of Militia officers in the Special Reserve Battalions; Lord Harris fought for better terms for the Yeomanry. With the main battle won, the Government could afford to concede minor points.

Only in one instance was there a possibility of trouble. In order to placate the Radical element in his party, Haldane

[1] A.D., 1907, vol. ii, p. 351.   [2] A.D., 1907, vol. ii, p. 367.

had modified his first ideas about the support afforded by Associations to Cadet units. The relevant section as sent up to the Lords contained the proviso, 'provided that no financial assistance shall be given by an association in respect of any person or corps in a school in receipt of a Parliamentary Grant until such person has attained the age of sixteen'.

In the House of Lords on July 9th, Lord Methuen moved to omit this restricting clause. In spite of the fact that the Government declared that they could not accept the amendment, it was carried.[1] There was clearly a tense situation. The dispute between Lords and Commons was already acute, and it was clear that in the present temper of the Lower House no such amendment from the House of Lords would be acceptable.

Esher once more came to the rescue. On July 18th he moved another amendment which allowed Associations to support cadet corps for boys under sixteen, 'provided that no financial assistance out of moneys voted by Parliament should be given'.[2]

So finally the measure came back to the House of Commons. The Cadet Corps amendment was not liked by the Radicals. Mr. J. R. MacDonald spoke against it, but, as Mr. Haldane pointed out, it was an amendment reached by agreement and the Government would support it.

That was the end. The other Lords' amendments were agreed to, and the Territorial and Reserve Forces Act in due course received the Royal Assent and became law.

With the safe passage of the Territorial and Reserve Forces Bill, one stage of the road had been traversed. An onerous and difficult task lay ahead. Parliament might authorize new formations to take the place of traditional Militia, Yeomanry, and Volunteers. These new formations had to be filled by voluntary enlistment, and how successful the experiment was going to be, few would be bold enough to prophesy. At this juncture the King came to Haldane's assistance and did what no other man in the Kingdom could have done. He summoned

[1] A.D., 1907, vol. ii, p. 685.   [2] A.D., 1907, vol. ii, p. 825.

to a meeting at Buckingham Palace on October 21, 1907, the Lords Lieutenant of all the counties of England, Wales and Scotland.[1] In a speech to the assembly he made perfectly clear his hope and expectation that the Lords Lieutenant would throw their whole local influence behind the new Territorial Force and the system of County Associations.

The detailed work of organization was considerable and at the first introduction of the Bill, Haldane had explained that it would not be possible to start the new force in the year 1907. For the Territorial Force the appointed day was April 1, 1908. On that date the old Volunteer units came to an end, and the units and the members of the Force had to decide whether they would transfer their allegiance to the new Territorial Force. The start was fairly satisfactory. In order to be recognized by the War Office a unit had to reach 30 per cent of its Territorial Force establishment. By May 5th, the War Office had recognized 48 Yeomanry regiments out of 56, '287 Artillery units out of 369, 69 Engineering units out of 117; 172 Infantry units out of 204 . . . up to May 1st the number of men enlisted in the Yeomanry was 12,044 and in the Infantry 72,179'.[2]

By June 1st the total strength had risen to 144,620 out of an establishment of 302,199.[3] That year the Territorial Force went to camp as such for the first time; 4,765 officers and 99,982 other ranks performed the full fifteen days' annual training.[4]

Mr. Haldane worked indefatigably for the success of his scheme. He travelled the length and breadth of the country, often spending his nights in the train, in order to address meetings or visit units. Throughout 1908 the numbers grew steadily; even so, by the end of the year, the strength was only 207,000 all ranks.

At the commencement of 1909, however, the movement

[1] Lee, vol. ii, p. 501.
[2] Lord Lucas in House of Lords, May 27, 1908. A.D., 1908, p. 1240.
[3] A.D., 1908, p. 1271.   [4] Ibid., p. 1722.

received a powerful stimulus from the 'Daily Mail',[1] and from other influential supporters.[2] Numbers then began to rise rapidly and by June 1, 1909, the Territorial Force reached a strength of 9,313 officers and 259,463 other ranks. Seven months later it had grown to a total of 276,618 all ranks on February 25, 1910. This, as Mr. Haldane pointed out when he introduced the 1910 Estimates, was 88·5 per cent of the total establishments.[3]

The support of the King continued to be both wholehearted and practical. In June 1909, at Windsor Castle, he presented colours to 108 units of the Territorial Force. In July at Knowsley Park, the seat of Lord Derby, he reviewed the West Lancashire Division, and the next day at Worsley Park, Lord Ellesmere's seat, the East Lancashire Division.[4]

The Territorial Force as created by Mr. Haldane consisted of 14 Divisions, 14 Cavalry Brigades and Corps Troops. There were in all 204 Infantry battalions, which allowed a fairly large margin over those actually required for the Infantry Brigade. Some of the old Volunteer units disappeared in the conversion; on the other hand, many of the Royal Horse Artillery batteries, Territorial Force, which formed the Artillery of the Cavalry Brigades, were raised as new formations. With the exception of these Horse Artillery batteries, practically every unit of the Territorial Force traced a direct descent from a unit of the former Yeomanry or Volunteers. A feature of the organization was the inclusion of 10 cyclist battalions.

In connection with the formation of the two London Divisions, 27 Infantry battalions (including in the total one cyclist unit) changed their names, and whereas in the past they had been battalions of the Queen's, Royal Fusiliers,

---

[1] Haldane paid a tribute to the value of the 'Daily Mail's' campaign in the House of Commons, March 4, 1909, on the occasion of the Army Estimates.—A.D., 1909, p. 33.
[2] The play, 'An Englishman's Home', was a notable recruiting feature of the time.
[3] A.D., 1910, p. 21.   [4] Lee, vol. ii, p. 508.

Middlesex Regiment, East Surreys, Queen's Own Royal West Kents, King's Royal Rifles or Rifle Brigade, they now became battalions of a new Corps, the London Regiment.[1]

The Horse Artillery of the Territorial Force were armed with the 15-pounder Ehrhardt,[2] the Field Artillery with the old Boer War 15-pounder, converted by the addition of recoil mechanism,[3] and the Royal Garrison Artillery (Territorial Force) with the 4·7 gun.

Mr. Haldane gave a great deal of his own particular attention to the fitting of his new Divisional organization into the geographical conditions of the country. So far as was possible, artillery and mechanical units were placed in engineering districts.

A development of very great importance was the building up of a Territorial Medical Corps. This was achieved by the work of a special Committee under Surgeon-General Sir Alfred Keogh. The result of their deliberations was embodied in an Army Order 219 of 1908. There followed the establishment of a Territorial Association Nursing Service, and the organization of Voluntary Aid Detachments.[4]

The administration of the Territorial Force was conceived on entirely novel lines. The County Associations were charged with the recruitment, clothing and general maintenance of the units under their charge. For that purpose they were paid

[1] Mr. Haldane, House of Commons, March 12. A.D., 1908, p. 743.
[2] This was not completed till after 1910.—'Chronology', 1910, p. 5.
[3] There was a good deal of discussion about the efficacy of this gun, which was obviously a makeshift. The truth was that Haldane would certainly never have got past his Radical colleagues a proposal to arm the whole of the Territorial Force with the new 18-pounder. The pertinacity of Conservative members of the House of Commons on this subject led to practical demonstrations: 'I have already, at the request of the Honourable Member, blocked up the Star Chamber Court with field artillery.'—Mr. Haldane, March 16, 1908. A.D., 1908, p. 810.
536 such guns were handed over to the Territorial Force, equivalent to 134 four-gun batteries.—A.E., 1908.
[4] Army Order 194 of 1908. See Autobiography, p. 197. See also 'Report . . . as to the progress made in constituting the Medical Service of the Territorial Force', Command Paper 4056 of 1908.

War Office grants based upon the number of men they administered. Though these grants were divided under certain sub-headings, Associations had a very wide distribution in expenditure. Their accounts were subject, not to Treasury control, but to commercial audit. Moreover, surpluses which existed at the end of a financial year did not automatically revert to the Treasury but could be carried forward as Association funds.

On the other hand, Associations had nothing to do with training. This was under purely military control. This centralization was one of the fundamental tenets of the Haldane plan. In command of each Division was a Major-General, with staff officers to assist him. Moreover, he had allotted for his use a 'Training Grant'. This sum of money was for him to spend, the responsibility that it was wisely employed was his, and subject to that he was a free agent. This innovation was of the greatest importance. From January 1, 1908, the former Director of Auxiliary Forces became the Director-General of the Territorial Force, and his Directorate no longer formed part of the Department of the Adjutant-General, but became the special charge of the Civil Member, the Parliamentary Under-Secretary of State, who thus undertook the responsibility of representing the Territorial Force upon the Army Council.

Thus by the close of the year 1908, the whole machinery of the Territorial Force had been set in motion. There were two additions made in following years. In 1909, a circular announced the proposed formation of a Territorial Reserve, a Technical Reserve and the Veteran Reserve.[1] The actual formation of these Auxiliary bodies commenced the following year;[2] the first two groups did not attain great strength, but the third under the revised title of the National Reserve reached a strength on January 1, 1913, of 5,464 officers and 185,372 other ranks. On June 8, 1912, H.M. King George V held

[1] 'Chronology', 1909, p. 6. See also A.D., 1909, p. 933.
[2] 'Chronology', 1910, p. 7.

a review of the London Division of the National Reserve in Hyde Park.[1]

The initial stages of the development of the Special Reserve differed somewhat from those of the Territorial Force. Although recruiting for the Special Reserve opened on January 16, 1908, the 101 Militia Battalions which were being preserved trained in 1908 as Militia.[2] Thereafter 70 became 'amalgamated with the existing depots of Line Regiments, and will drill both Line and Special Reserve recruits, 4 will form a depot for Special Reserves of Rifle Regiments, and 27 will form Extra Reserve battalions'.[3]

Twenty-three Militia Battalions were disbanded and disappeared from the Army List. By December 31, 1908, there were 67,740 Special Reservists serving out of an Establishment of 80,300, and the strength of the force remained at much the same level for the next five years.

All these men had signed attestation papers as Special Reservists in the Regular Army. There remained a rapidly shrinking band of those who, not wishing to join the new force, were serving out their Militia engagements. On January 1, 1913, there remained only 636 of the 'moribund' Militia, and 64 of the Militia Reserve.[4] The end came soon after and the traditional terms of Enlistment of the Constitutional Force vanished from the British Army.

[1] 'Chronology', 1912, p. 9.
[2] A.D., December 23, 1908.
[3] Memorandum of Secretary of State, A.E., 1908–9.
[4] 'Chronology', 1912, p. 6.

CHAPTER 15

THE CREATION OF THE IMPERIAL GENERAL STAFF AND THE TRAINING OF THE ARMY

THE Expeditionary Force had been created and the Territorial and Reserve Forces Bill had been passed. It remained to give a central doctrine to the new Army organization of Haldane's creation, and to provide the means for its direction and command in War.

Douglas Haig became Director of Staff Duties on November 9, 1906. On his staff he had, among others, Colonel L. E. Kiggell, C.B.,[1] Colonel W. Adye, and, on January 1, 1908. these were joined by Major F. B. Maurice.[2] It was this group which undertook the responsibility of providing a central doctrine for the training for war, and the organization in war, of the whole British Army. A certain amount of the work had already been done. 'Combined Training' of 1902 was, as has been seen, the forerunner of a new conception of military textbooks. The Report of Lord Esher's Committee had sketched out a plan for a dual series of training manuals. One set was to deal with the aspects of military training applicable to all arms.[3] Another set would be specialized, and would be confined to certain training peculiarly the responsibility of the arms concerned.

Before the issue of the Report, there had been an addition to the original form of 'Combined Training'. In 1903, Parts VI

---

[1] Now Lieutenant-General Sir Launcelot Kiggell, K.C.B., K.C.M.G. (Chief of Staff to Sir Douglas Haig when Commander-in-Chief, British Expeditionary Force).

[2] Now Major-General Sir Frederick Maurice, K.C.M.G., C.B.

[3] Report of the War Office (Reconstitution) Committee, Part II, Section iv, paras. 20 and 21.

and X had appeared in a separate Volume. These parts had dealt with Training in the Field, with Staff Duties in connection with marches, and the like.

To these two volumes had succeeded in 1905 a small work which still bore on its outer cover the title, 'Combined Training', but inside had, for the first time, the style, 'Field Service Regulations. Part I. Combined Training'.

In the same way, the first steps had been taken to provide a publication which should take the place of Lord Wolseley's 'Soldier's Pocket Book', and should perform in an official manner what had been done for so many years past by this famous work of private enterprise. An experimental 'Field Service Pocket Book' appeared in the War Office in 1906. Only 100 copies were printed, bound in red boards, and it is probable that it was never intended for public issue. The following year, 1907, enlarged from 166 pages to 190 pages, and in the familiar pocket-book form, it was issued as 'Field Service Pocket Book, 1907 (Provisional)', and was put on sale. A year later as 'Field Service Book, 1908,' of 204 pages, it had taken the form which was to endure with little change to the present day.

By 1909 the whole position had been codified. In that year there appeared the booklet which bore as its title, 'Field Service Regulations, Part I—Operations—1909'. Thus was the final form given to the training manual for all arms, conceived by Colonel Henderson and approved by Lord Esher's Committee.

With Part I there had been little difficulty. 'Combined Training' had shown the way, and a general agreement upon Strategical and Tactical principles had grown up as a result of the South African War.

With regard to the companion volume, 'Field Service Regulations—Part II—Administration', the situation was entirely different. Douglas Haig in the Directorate of Staff Duties was convinced of the necessity of providing a manual which should cover the whole organization of an Army in

THE CREATION OF THE IMPERIAL GENERAL STAFF

the field, that the duties and functions of officers, units, and commands in the Lines of Communication and at the base should be as clearly defined as those of a Division or a Brigade in the Field Army. This was a new departure, and it aroused considerable opposition. The branches of the Adjutant-General and Quartermaster-General could not see the necessity for a detailed organization of this nature, and, above all, they could not see why such an organization should be imposed upon their branches by a directorate from the General Staff side. With the Adjutant-General and Quartermaster-General in definite opposition, the Chief of the General Staff was but lukewarm in his support of the new idea. Fortunately Haig was able to count upon the support of Haldane, and it was the powerful backing of the Secretary of State which carried along the preparation and final issue of 'Field Service Regulations—Part II—Organization and Administration, 1909'.

The existence of this series of authoritative manuals was of the greatest value for the inculcation of one central doctrine, not only in the Regular Army but also in the Territorial Force, in the Officers' Training Corps, and, as a result of the Imperial Conference, in the Dominion Forces.

When, at the end of the victories of 1918, Sir Douglas Haig, in his letter to General Rawlinson, referred to the value of leaders trained in the principles of Field Service Regulations he was touching upon a subject very dear to his own heart. It was with the same thought that the Commander-in-Chief wrote to his old Chief on the day following the Armistice:

'... And where would we be today without the Imperial General Staff which was your creation and the Field Service Regulations (Part II Organization) which you forced through in spite of opposition from Army Council and Treasury.'[1]

[1] Autobiography, p. 289.

THE OFFICERS' TRAINING CORPS

In 1906 the Secretary of State appointed a Committee under Sir Edward Ward, the Permanent Under-Secretary of State, to consider the best means of providing officers (*a*) for the Regular Army in time of War, (*b*) for the Auxiliary Forces. Other members of the 'Ward Committee' were Professor Hudson Beare of Edinburgh University, Professor Bourn from Oxford, Colonel Edwards from Cambridge, Rev. Mr. David, Headmaster of Clifton, Lord Lovat, Major-General Ewart, D.M.O. at the War Office, and Brigadier-General Henry Wilson, Commandant of the Staff College.[1]

The Committee issued an interim report in February 1907: this had chiefly to do with the supply of officers to the Regular Army in time of war. A system of Officers' Training Corps was to be set up, a Senior Division in the Universities, a Junior Division in the Schools. A later report dealt with the supply of officers to the Special Reserve. This second report was not published, though many of its recommendations were embodied in the Army Order which created the Special Reserve.

The whole of the proposals of the Ward Committee were, in general terms, accepted by the Army Council. A special branch of the Directorate of Staff Duties was therefore established. This branch, now S.D. 3, had the particular task of working out the functions and the organization of the Officers' Training Corps. What had in the past been a series of disconnected Cadet Corps or Rifle Corps in the schools and Universities, trained according to the whims of their Commanding Officers, for the time being, were by this measure of centralization to be watched over by the War Office, and their training was to be on the lines laid down in official manuals, and reviewed at regular intervals by the results of a standard system of examinations.

The plan was set in motion by Army Order 160 of 1908. Contingents of the Senior Division were established in 19

[1] A.D., 1907, p. 93.

Universities and contingents of the Junior Division in 152 Public Schools.[1] The Regulations for the Officers' Training Corps, which followed in Army Order 178 of the same year, laid down that the purpose of the scheme was to provide a standardized degree of elementary military training with a view to providing candidates for commissions in the Supplementary Reserve and Territorial Force, and in the Regular Army in time of war.

By January 1, 1912, the last year of Haldane's tenure of office, the Officers' Training Corps had expanded to 55 contingents of the Senior and 155 of the Junior Division. The total strength was 630 officers and 23,701 other ranks; 3,809 cadets held certificate A, 425 certificate B. From the Officers' Training Corps already 264 commissions had been taken in the Special Reserve and 566 in the Territorial Force. On July 3, 1911, King George V held a review of the Corps in Windsor Great Park, at which 477 officers and 15,868 cadets were present.

THE CREATION OF THE IMPERIAL GENERAL STAFF

The Dominions were obviously destined to play an ever more important part in the Defence Scheme of the Empire. Dominion contingents had contributed to the final success in South Africa. Moreover, since the middle of the nineteenth century, there had been a steady development in the policy whereby the Dominions not only assumed the responsibility for their own defence, but also assumed the responsibility for the important naval bases which, though situated within territories of the Dominions, had a value for the whole system of Empire Defence.

If Imperial Defence were to be regarded as a whole, then it was obviously desirable that local divergencies of organization or equipment should be limited where possible.

An Imperial Conference of Premiers was held in London

[1] These were the figures on December 31, 1910.—'Chronology', 1910, p. 6.

in 1907. In readiness for this meeting, the General Staff at the War Office had prepared a Memorandum on the 'Possibility of Assimilating War Organization throughout the Empire'. This, dated March 14, 1907, and signed by General Lyttelton as Chief of the General Staff, is printed as an appendix to the Memorandum, shortly to be quoted.

The suggestions thus put forward to the assembled Empire Statesmen were, in brief, that there should be one basic organization for the forces of all the component parts of the Empire, that so far as possible the same military terms should be used for the same units or formations, and that orders should so far as possible be couched in the same military phraseology. Instances were given to show how already there was a tendency, in the various Dominions, for formations to assume local shape. In Canada the Infantry unit was the Regiment not the battalion, in Australia and New Zealand the organization of hospital work in the field was not that which had been adopted for War Establishments.

The Memorandum suggested that the basis for all the Empire Forces might be the organization of Divisions, Brigades, Mounted Brigades, etc., with their administrative Field units, as adopted for the British Army. It was pointed out that this organization had already been decided for the Six Divisions of the Regular Army, and the Fourteen Divisions of the Territorial Force, and that in India the Division of three Brigades was also in process of adoption.

This Memorandum came before the Conference and in their deliberations on the subject they carried the matter a very considerable stage further. They decided that it was necessary to form a General Staff 'selected from the forces of the Empire as a whole', and that the staff should be charged with the duty 'to study military science in all its branches; to collect and disseminate to the various governments military information and intelligence; to undertake the preparation of schemes of defence as a common principle, and (without in the least interfering in questions connected with command

THE CREATION OF THE IMPERIAL GENERAL STAFF

and administration) at the request of the respective governments, to advise as to the training, education, and war organization of the military forces of the Crown in every part of the Empire'.

The question thus put forward was taken up by the General Staff with the result that, on December 15, 1908, a letter was sent, over the signature of Sir Edward Ward, to the Colonial Office:

'I am commanded by the Army Council to forward for the information of the Earl of Crewe the enclosed statement of their views on the subject of the Imperial General Staff and to request that—should his Lordship think it advisable—this statement may be submitted to the Ministers of the respective self-governing Dominions.'[1]

The Memorandum which accompanied the letter, after reviewing the above-quoted decision of the 1907 Conference, made suggestions as to the best method of carrying out the scheme for an Imperial General Staff. Camberley, it was thought, must for some years to come be regarded as the centre of the Staff Organization of the Empire. The creation of Staff Colleges in the self-governing Dominions was envisaged, and a system of interchange was recommended whereby officers from the Dominions would attend at Camberley, and British Staff Officers would be sent to the Dominions. Terms were carefully laid down to govern the responsibility of the Staff Officers of the Dominions to the Government of the Dominion. Although the General Staff should be an entity throughout the Empire, the authority of the Chief of the Imperial General Staff over the Staff of the Dominion was limited to 'guidance'. 'This full control' of the local Chief of Staff by his own government 'must be accepted from the outset. The solution of this difficulty would appear to be that, while the Chiefs of the local sections of the General Staff keep in close communication with the Chief of the Imperial General Staff they cannot receive orders from him.'[2]

[1] Printed as 33/Gen./No. 306.   [2] Page 8 of Memorandum.

It was this careful consideration for the quite justifiable susceptibilities of the Dominion Governments which was to prove a potent factor in the success of the scheme.

The further paragraphs of the Memorandum worked out in detail the type of Staff organization and Staff training that would be requisite. From the evidence of Haldane himself, it is clear that the credit of this preliminary work must go to Douglas Haig, as the Director of Staff Duties, and to General Sir W. G. Nicholson, as Chief of the General Staff.[1]

Armed with the memoranda prepared by the General Staff at the War Office, an Imperial Defence Conference met in London in July 1909. Prominent among the statesmen present were Sir Wilfrid Laurier, the veteran Premier of Canada, and General Louis Botha from South Africa. The decisions of this conference were embodied in a Blue Book.[2] In brief they confirmed the organization of the Imperial General Staff and the principle of 'the standardization of the Military Forces of the Empire without impairing the autonomy of the self-governing Dominions'.[3]

To mark the Government's acceptance of the new principle an Order in Council dated November 22, 1909, changed the style of the First Member of the Army Council from that of the Chief of the General Staff to the larger title of the Chief of the Imperial General Staff.

VISCOUNT HALDANE OF CLOAN

In July 1912, Lord Loreburn, the Lord Chancellor, fell suddenly ill, and considered it his duty to resign at once. The position was communicated to Mr. Asquith, the Prime Minister, who was on a cruise in the Mediterranean, and the cabled reply was: 'Consult Haldane as to who should succeed him at the War Office.'[4]

---

[1] Autobiography, p. 200. General Nicholson had succeeded General Lyttelton as Chief of the General Staff on April 2, 1908.
[2] Command Paper 4948.
[3] 'Chronology', 1909, p. 8.
[4] Autobiography, p. 237.

THE CREATION OF THE IMPERIAL GENERAL STAFF

Thus closed the longest tenure of office by any Secretary of State for War. Haldane held the post from November 11, 1905, to June 14, 1912, a period of six and a half years. His closest competitor in length of service was his fellow reformer, Mr. Cardwell, who was Secretary of State for War from December 9, 1868, to February 21, 1874.

During that long period Haldane had never spared himself. It was indeed his amazing physical health and capacity for long hours of work that enabled him to carry on his self-imposed task. Even he, in the latter years, began to feel tired, and there can be small wonder at that fact.[1]

The most spectacular part of his work had been done in the first four years. By the close of 1909 the Expeditionary Force had been created, the Special Reserve, the Territorial Force and the Officers' Training Corps were in being, and the major portion of the work had been done towards the establishment of an Imperial General Staff.

The succeeding years were less dramatic, but the strain on Haldane's time and energy continued. After the low level of the Army Estimates of 1908–9 there commenced an upward trend.

1908–9	£26,859,299
1909–10	£27,234,825
1910–11	£27,549,491
1911–12	£27,652,342
1912–13	£28,023,138

When Mr. Asquith became Prime Minister in 1908, he was succeeded as Chancellor of the Exchequer by Mr. Lloyd George. The same Cabinet reshuffle brought Mr. Winston Churchill, now a member of the Liberal party, into the Cabinet. Neither of these colleagues was likely to view with equanimity rising military budgets, and Haldane had constantly to fight the Army battle in the Ministry.

The main tussle, however, had come in 1908. The pressure

[1] Esher Journals, vol. ii, pp. 428–32.

on Haldane then was very heavy, but he was steadily supported by Esher,[1] and by the King, and in the end his refusal to carry through any further reduction in the Army was accepted by the Cabinet.

In another direction, another set of figures might have seemed to move against Haldane. After the peak of 1910 there followed a steady decline in the strength of the Territorial Army.

1st January, 1911—9,696 officers, 257,156 other ranks.
1st January, 1912—9,403 officers, 256,508 other ranks.
1st January, 1913—9,294 officers, 254,039 other ranks.

The decline was, however, probably chiefly due to the fact that a proportion of the recruits obtained in the enthusiasm of the 'Daily Mail' campaign had lacked staying power, and that the force was reaching its natural level of members.

The fall in strength was, for what it was worth, ammunition for the arguments of the National Service League, but in truth while the Territorial Force lost a few of the less ardent spirits, the training of the troops progressed well. It is worth recalling the verdict of a German historian. Paul Kluke writes of this period:

'Damit gelang es, jahrlich gegen 90 % der Territorialsoldaten ins Lager zu ziehen und davon wieder rund ¾ fur 15 und mehr Tage zusammenzuhalten, fur eine freiwillige Truppe eine erstaunliche Leistung. Da wuchs dann selbst eine so schwierig auszubildende Waffe wie die Feldartillerie uber erwarten gut in ihre Aufgabe hinein. Geflissentlich suchte man die Grenzen zwischen regularen und Territorialtruppen zu verwischen.'[2]

In his resistance to the campaign for Compulsory Service, Haldane was fortified by the decision of the General Staff itself. In 1910, they had asked his consent to produce their own scheme. Having studied the problem, they reported to him the considered War Office view that in the existing

[1] Esher Journals, June 26, 1908, pp. 324, 327.
[2] 'Heeresaufbau und Heerespolitik Englands', p. 120.

THE CREATION OF THE IMPERIAL GENERAL STAFF

European situation any change-over of our military system from its traditional form to an army recruited by compulsion in time of peace was out of the question. 'Our General Staff, therefore, rejected their own idea, and I was clear in my own mind that they had done so wisely.'[1]

For the international situation was indeed deteriorating. The annexation by Austria of Bosnia and Herzegovina, decided upon on August 18, 1908, and carried into effect on October 7th, brought about a dangerous period of tension.[2] To this event succeeded the German Emperor's 'Daily Telegraph' interview of October 28, 1908, and the Casablanca incident of the same year. A period of uneasy quiescence followed, to be broken by an event of first-class international importance. In July 1911, the German Government sent the cruiser 'Panther' to Agadir. Much of the history of the summer of 1911 belongs to the nature of Foreign policy rather than to a discussion upon military development.

Two facts, however, need to be mentioned. Giving as an excuse the intense drought of that summer, Haldane cancelled the Army Manœuvres in East Anglia.[3] With the money thus saved, the final arrangements for mobilization were completed.[4] The occasion was for Haldane the proof of the completeness of his plans:

'If the country decided on such a step, I was in a position to mobilize the Expeditionary Force and send it straight off to the Continent.'

The Expeditionary Force, as a fighting machine, was ready. The Agadir crisis was also to confirm the plans for its employment, for in the discussions at the Committee of Imperial Defence which of necessity took place at this time of tension, it quickly appeared that a vital and fundamental difference existed between the plans of the seamen and the soldiers. The decisive conference took place on August 23,

[1] Autobiography, p. 196.
[2] Lee, vol. ii, pp. 627–33.
[3] 'Chronology', 1911, p. 13.
[4] Autobiography, p. 224.

1911. While the War Office asked of the Admiralty that the Navy should be able to safeguard the passage of the Expeditionary Force to the Continent of Europe, the Naval plan was to use the Army as a projectile to be fired by the Fleet, as Fisher used to say.[1] The Admiralty had the conception of landing the Army, in small packets, along the northern German coasts.

Such a fundamental difference of opinion had to be solved, and on this occasion it was solved by Haldane's insistence upon a Governmental adoption of the military plan, and upon a complete change of directing personnel at the Admiralty.[2]

The first was quickly achieved. Asquith accepted the military view of co-operation with the French; the second was achieved after a few days of vigorous discussion, Winston Churchill replacing McKenna at the Admiralty.

The story of the conference of August 23rd, the part played by Henry Wilson, and the subservience to French plans and French doctrine that followed, belong rather to the History of the Great War. In retrospect, it may be felt that the tragedy of the event was the completeness of the defeat of the Navy case. The military thesis, because it was fairly simple, was accepted as the plan to be followed:

'We put the whole power of the British Empire behind France and never made it plain what that power was.'[3]

On March 27, 1911, the Secretary of State had proceeded to the House of Lords with the dignity of Viscount Haldane of Cloan; a few days earlier Colonel the Rt. Hon. J. E. B. Seely, D.S.O., had succeeded Lord Lucas as the Parliamentary Under-Secretary of State for War.

Therefore, when Haldane a year later proceeded to the Woolsack, he was in the natural course of things succeeded at the War Office by Colonel Seely.

---

[1] See Esher Journals, March 15, 1909, vol. ii, p. 357.
[2] Autobiography, pp. 226–232.
[3] Major-General Sir Frederick Maurice, Lecture Notes.

THE CREATION OF THE IMPERIAL GENERAL STAFF 303

Before the close of his term of office, Haldane had few illusions as to the danger of German policy. More than any other British Minister, he had done his best to study and to explain to his own countrymen German thought, and German aspirations. He had laboured incessantly to improve the relations between the two countries. Yet, as was his duty, he had created the military machine which, if events moved to push of pike, would save the world from the dominance of German hegemony.

He had embarked upon no scheme of grandiose expansion; his contribution was efficiency. At a period of time when the British Naval Budgets under the pressure of German building rose from £32,911,046 in 1907-8 to £46,309,300 in 1913-14, the Army Estimates rose by less than 5 per cent.

'After the Esher reorganization of the War Office, the preparation of Army Estimates was put on a basis enabling responsibility for the alteration of funds, within the total, to be definitely assigned. The relative priority of different forms of expenditure was determined by the members of the Army Council (other than the Secretary of State) sitting as a formal Estimate Committee with the C.I.G.S. in the chair, and the Estimates so prepared were presented to Parliament over the signatures of all the members of Council. They show that the actual regimental establishments of the Regulars in 1908 totalled 177,366 officers and men, and in 1914, 177,271, the main difference in details being that in the latter year room had been found within the total for a Flying Corps of 1,005. As regards money, while the expenditure on Territorial Forces rose from £2,243,000 in 1908-9 to £3,086,000 (estimates), in 1914-15 the total expenditure on the Army rose from £26,859,000 to £28,845,000 (estimated), the latter figure including £1,000,000 for aviation; so that the whole provision for that new service and the increase for the Territorials were found without taking a penny from the rest of the Army.'—Sir Charles Harris, 'The Times,' May 1925.

CONCLUSION

FIFTEEN years have been passed in review. Many men laboured, some in high places, some in obscurity, to make the British Army fit for war. When the test came, that Army was, within the terms of its then duty, apt and ready for battle. It was on August 3, 1914, that Haldane, acting for Mr. Asquith, ordered the mobilization of the army to take place on the morrow. Immediately six divisions of regular troops were in full stride towards battle. Behind them the Special Reserve battalions were assembling the necessary drafts, and behind again stood fourteen divisions of the Territorial Force. Moreover, in those fourteen divisions every man had a rifle, every battery had its guns, and every division had its full complement of services. 'In every respect the Expeditionary Force of 1914 was incomparably the best trained, best organized, and best equipped British Army which ever went forth to war.'[1]

Among those who toiled that this might be, there are some whose names stand out. At this distance of time, regarding the passing stage with the eye of history, the observer may select for notice some to whom the contemporary world denied great prominence. First, however, in station, and not last in importance stands the Monarch. The Army as a whole, the Territorial Army in particular, owes a great debt to King Edward VII. It was his steady support of Lord Esher which made possible War Office reform; it was his upholding of Haldane which carried forward the Territorial Force. Arthur James Balfour, by his creation of the Committee of Imperial Defence, gave the central inspiration to all the military might

---

[1] 'Military Operations France and Belgium', vol. i, p. 10.

'To Germans, Britain appeared to be a powerful and prosperous country in the throes of a disabling convulsion. Yet the country had never been better equipped for War.'—'A History of Europe', vol. iii, 'The Liberal Experiment', p. 1105, H. A. L. Fisher.

of the nation. Haldane's work to-day is known, and rightly honoured. Esher's part, less known, was hardly inferior. Himself disdainful of place, and perhaps distrustful of responsibility, he had a great faculty for clear thinking, and he was in deadly earnest about Army Reform. His unique social position, and his independence of character, made him a most valuable worker behind the scenes. Among the soldiers, Wolseley's best work had been done before the period under our review, when he was, with few to help him, fighting the battle of progress against a reactionary circle of aged warriors. Douglas Haig provided Haldane with the staff officer of his dreams. To these must be added the name of Ellison, a man to whom history has perhaps paid scant tribute.

There were two occasions within the fifteen years when, as it were, a great wind bore down from heaven upon the ship of military state, and drove it with ever quickening speed upon a steady course. One such occasion was in the early spring of 1904 when Lord Esher's Committee in three concise reports recast the whole organization of the War Office. The second was the winter at Cloan, in the first days of 1906, when Haldane, pacing his library, reviewed the British Army in the light of his question: 'What must be our objective, and what was required for its attainment.' With both these occasions Lieutenant-Colonel G. F. Ellison was intimately connected, first as Secretary to Lord Esher's Committee of Three, secondly as personal Military Secretary to Mr. Haldane. Such things do not come by coincidence.

Yet, when all is said and done, the one man to whom, above all others, was due the resurgence of the British Army, was a rugged uncouth figure named Stephanus Johannes Paulus Kruger, sometime President of the Transvaal Republic. For England to have been surprised by a Continental War in her 1899 state of unreadiness would have been a national tragedy that to-day barely allows contemplation. The South African War was a lesson, a bitter one, but to the credit of the entire nation the lesson was learnt and was not ignored.

APPENDIX A

STANHOPE MEMORANDUM

PAPER BY THE SECRETARY OF STATE, LAYING DOWN THE REQUIREMENTS FROM OUR ARMY, DATED JUNE 1, 1891

Her Majesty's Government have carefully considered the question of the general objects for which our Army is maintained. It has been considered in connection with the programme of the Admiralty, and with knowledge of the assistance which the Navy is capable of rendering in the various contingencies which appear to be reasonably probable, and they decide that the general basis of the requirements from our Army may be correctly laid down by stating that the objects of our military organization are:—

(a) The effective support of the civil power in all parts of the United Kingdom.
(b) To find the number of men for India, which has been fixed by arrangement with the Government of India.
(c) To find garrisons for all our fortresses and coaling stations, at home and abroad, according to a scale now laid down, and to maintain these garrisons at all times at the strength fixed for a peace or war footing.
(d) After providing for these requirements, to be able to mobilize rapidly for home defence two Army Corps of Regular troops and one partly composed of Regulars and partly of Militia, and to organize the Auxiliary Forces, not allotted to Army Corps or garrisons, for the defence of London and for the defensible positions in advance, and for the defence of mercantile ports.
(e) Subject to the foregoing considerations and to their financial obligations, to aim at being able, in case of necessity, to send abroad two complete Army Corps, with Cavalry Division and Line of Communication. But it will be distinctly understood that the probability of the employment of an Army Corps in the field in any European war is sufficiently improbable to make it the primary duty of the military authorities to organize our forces efficiently for the defence of this country.

E. S.

1st June, 1891.

APPENDIX B

E.C., p. 32, 'Normal War Establishments, 1898'

STRENGTH AND COMPOSITION OF AN ARMY CORPS

	Officers	Other Ranks	Total
Staff	34	137	171
[1] 3 Infantry Divisions	978	29,124	30,102
1 Cavalry Regiment	25	506	531
Headquarters 1 Cavalry Regiment	7	44	51
[2] Corps Artillery	60	1,639	1,699
Ammunition Park	20	672	692
Regimental Staff Corps Engineers	2	6	8
1 Pontoon Troop	5	208	213
1 Telegraph Division	6	238	244
1 Balloon Section	3	51	54
1 Field Company	7	205	212
1 Field Park	1	44	45
1 Railway Company	5	153	158
1 Battalion	29	981	1,010
Supply Column	6	145	151
Supply Park	9	531	540
Field Bakery	5	312	317
Field Hospital	5	56	61
Total in the Field	1,207	35,052	36,259
Excess numbers at the Base	37	3,299	3,336
	1,244	38,351	39,595

An Infantry Division consisted of:—
Staff, two Infantry Brigades each of four battalions, one Squadron Cavalry, one Brigade Division Royal Field Artillery, Ammunition Column, Regimental Staff Division Engineers, one Field Company, Supply Column, Field Hospital.

[2] Corps Artillery included:—
One Brigade Division Royal Horse Artillery, two Brigade Divisions Royal Field Artillery, and Ammunition Column.
(A Brigade Division consisted of three batteries.)

APPENDIX C

DISTRIBUTION OF CAVALRY REGIMENTS AND INFANTRY BATTALIONS OF THE BRITISH REGULAR ARMY IN 1899, 1906, 1914, 1935

(The upper figures of two are those of Cavalry Regiments)

	1899	1906	1914	1935
Home	19 Cavalry	18	19	14
	71 Infantry	81	83	70
India	9 Cavalry	9	9	5
	52 Infantry	52	52	45
MEDITERRANEAN				
Egypt	1 Cavalry	0	1	3
	2 Infantry	4	5	6
Malta	8	7	5	2
Gibraltar	3	3	2	2
Palestine	—	—	—	2
AFRICA				
South Africa	2 Cavalry	4	2	—
	6 Infantry	14	4	—
Mauritius	1	1	1	—
AMERICA				
Canada	1	—	—	—
West Indies	2	1	1	1
ASIA				
Ceylon	1	$\frac{1}{2}$	—	—
China: Hong Kong	2	$1\frac{1}{2}$	3	5
Malaya	—	1	1	2
Total Cavalry	31	31	31	22
Total Infantry	153	166	157	136

NATIVE REGIMENTS

There were native regiments in the pay of the British Government as follows:—

1906. 2 Battalions Indian at Mauritius; 4 Battalions Indian and 1 Battalion Chinese at Hong Kong and North China; 1 Battalion West India Regiment and 1 Battalion West African Regiment at Sierra Leone; 1 Indian Battalion at Straits Settlements; 1 Battalion West India Regiment at Jamaica. Total, 11.

1914. 2 Battalions in West Africa; 1 Battalion West India Regiment in Jamaica; 1 Battalion in Ceylon; 1 Battalion in Straits Settlements; 2 Battalions Hong Kong; 1 Battalion North China (all Indian). Total, 8.

1935. 1 Indian Infantry Battalion in China.

APPENDIX D

THE MILITIA IN 1899

Army Estimates, 1899–1900, Vote 3

ESTABLISHMENT
Grand total . . . . Permanent Staff, 4,630. Militia, 131,670 (including Militia Reserve, 30,000).

DETAIL	Permanent Staff			Militia			
	Officers	Sergeants	Buglers, Drummers, etc.	Officers	Sergeants	Trumpeters, Buglers, and Drummers	Rank and File
Artillery . . .	51	488	180	521	360	—	16,920
Engineers . . .	—	75	22	99	83	—	1,781
Infantry . . .	232	2,432	966	2,753	1,932	6	100,064
Militia Medical Staff Corps .	—	13	—	15	24	—	555
Channel Islands Militia .	9	75	—	192	150	50	3,520
Malta Militia . .	4	32	42	66	63	—	2,117
Bermuda Militia .	2	7	—	9	12	6	372
Total . .	298	3,122	1,210	3,655	2,624	62	125,329
Present at Training, 1898	291	3,106	1,186	2,655	2,269	52	93,893

Militia (less Channel Isles, Malta, and Bermuda)—Establishment All Ranks 125,113
                                Present at Training . . . 93,606
Total Vote 3. Militia Pay, Bounty, etc., 1898–99 . . . . £568,600
                                1899–1900 . . . . £586,600

APPENDIX E

VOLUNTEER CORPS

Army Estimates, 1899–1900

Establishment All Ranks

THE HONOURABLE ARTILLERY COMPANY
Horse Artillery . . . 166
Field Artillery . . . 162
Infantry 562
Total, 890

LIGHT HORSE
1st Fifeshire
1st Forfarshire } Total, 304

ARTILLERY CORPS
Sixty-six corps (each one to three batteries) . . . . . Total, 47,646, with P.S. 48,048

ENGINEER CORPS
Twenty Engineer Units
Seven units of Submarine Miners (Tyne, Severn, Clyde, Tees, Forth, Tay, Mersey)
Electrical Engineers Corps
Engineer and Railway Staff Corps Total, 14,948, with P.S. 15,044

INFANTRY
Two hundred and thirteen Rifle Corps (including two weak Middlesex Corps attached to other units), includes one Cyclist Corps 26th Middlesex . Total, 196,804, with P.S. 198,198
Organized in Thirty-three Brigades.

Note.—(i) The Bermuda Rifle Corps of 319 all ranks and including the Permanent Staff was carried in Army Estimates but is not here considered.

(ii) The establishment of independent Volunteer Rifle Corps varied from 402 all ranks to 2,273 (3rd Volunteer Battalion Welsh Regiment).

APPENDIX F

THE COMMITTEE ON THE ORGANIZATION, ARMS, AND EQUIPMENT OF THE YEOMANRY FORCE

The Committee consisted of:—

Lord Harris, Colonel Royal East Kent Mounted Rifles (Chairman).
Major-General the Earl of Dundonald.
Colonel Viscount Galway, Notts. Yeomanry.
Colonel A. G. Lucas, D.A.G. Imperial Yeomanry.
Colonel L. Rolleston, South Notts. Yeomanry.
Major the Marquis of Bath, Royal Wiltshire Yeomanry.
Captain Sir J. Dickson-Poynder, M.P., Royal Wiltshire Yeomanry.

The Committee called no witnesses, in view of the fact that so many of their number had long and intimate knowledge of the Yeomanry.

The main recommendations of the majority were:—

The force to retain its title of Yeomanry Cavalry, or if His Majesty pleases of Imperial Yeomanry Cavalry. . . . The arms to be a rifle and bayonet, and if the sword is withdrawn for drill purposes then a revolver to be added. . . . Camp to be for 18 days, 14 compulsory, musketry done locally; or 21 days, 17 compulsory, musketry done at camp. . . . Men's pay to be 10s. per day. Five pounds horse allowance to men producing a horse approved by the C.O. . . . Formation of Yeomanry Staff Corps and enlistment of yeoman for foreign service to be tried. . . .

Three members did not agree with the suggestions as to arms (and drill): they thought that the Yeomanry were the cavalry of the reserve forces, and should be armed, equipped, and trained as were the Regular Cavalry.

Two other members, on the contrary, thought that there should 'be no temporizing with the arme blanche'. The word Cavalry should be dropped from the title. They thought the suggested period of training too long and recommended a week with a further week of voluntary training.

'Army and Navy Gazette', 1901, p. 288.

APPENDIX G

UNITS IN THE AREAS OF THE SIX ARMY CORPS COMMANDS

THE 1ST ARMY CORPS

Cavalry Regiments	5	All Regulars
Artillery Batteries	27	
Infantry Battalions	24	

THE 2ND ARMY CORPS

	Regular	Militia	Yeomanry	Volunteers
Cavalry Regiments	2	—	13	—
Artillery Batteries	45	43	—	129
Infantry Battalions	20	15	—	35

THE 3RD ARMY CORPS

	Regular	Militia	Yeomanry	Volunteers
Cavalry Regiments	4	—	2	—
Artillery Batteries	25	70	—	—
Infantry Battalions	20	28	—	—

THE 4TH ARMY CORPS

	Regular	Militia	Yeomanry	Volunteers
Cavalry Regiments	4	—	—	—
Artillery Batteries	22	12	—	87
Infantry Battalions	8	25	—	65

THE 5TH ARMY CORPS

	Regular	Militia	Yeomanry	Volunteers
Cavalry Regiments	1	—	18	—
Artillery Batteries	19	29	—	162
Infantry Battalions	4	43	—	77

THE 6TH ARMY CORPS

	Regular	Militia	Yeomanry	Volunteers
Cavalry Regiments	—	—	5	—
Artillery Batteries	5	30	—	$125\frac{1}{2}$
Infantry Battalions	2	13	—	48

Command Paper 1413 of 1903.

APPENDIX H

EXTRACT FROM REPORT OF THE NORFOLK COMMISSION, p. 19

Schedule B
VOLUNTEERS

Financial Administration

1. Pending the rearrangement of grants recommended in paragraph 58, iii, it would be advisable, in the case of corps whose financial situation has been rendered precarious by a falling off in numbers, that a total grant equal to the average received during the past five years should be given. This average should be granted only on the recommendation of a duly constituted board appointed by the General Officer Commanding the District.

Officers

2. The post of Brigadier and all staff posts in the Volunteer cadres should be open to Volunteer officers possessing the requisite qualifications.

3. A Volunteer officer attached for instruction to a line regiment should be attached during its annual course of company training.

4. The accommodation for Volunteer officers at schools of musketry should be largely increased.

5. Volunteer officers should be permitted to attend, and should receive allowances for attending schools, lectures, and staff rides, such as would prepare them to perform the duties of staff officers.

6. Volunteer officers before promotion to field rank should be required to pass the examination in tactics for that rank.

7. A grant should be given for each subject in the voluntary examinations in addition to the grant for tactics.

8. The same grant as is given for tactics should be given to Volunteer submarine miner officers passing in Part III.

9. The Public School Corps should be grouped into permanent administrative battalions, each, if possible, with an Adjutant, educated at one of the schools of the group. These Adjutants and those of the

University Corps, should be required periodically to supply to the Volunteer Department of the War Office the names of Cadets or Volunteers suitable for commissions as Volunteer officers.

10. Candidates for commissions as Volunteer officers should be allowed to attend schools of instruction, and on passing the examination of the school should receive the same grants for attendance as are given to officers.

11. The privilege of being allowed to compete for army commissions recently given to officers of the Imperial Yeomanry who have fulfilled certain conditions, should be extended to Volunteer officers.

12. Field officers of Volunteers should be permitted to obtain chargers on the terms specified for regular officers in the Allowance Regulations.

Training

13. All brigades and units allotted to positions or garrisons should, where the conditions are suitable, have their camp training as often as possible at these stations, and should visit them at other times. The officers should be given opportunities of attending and studying the ground, under the guidance of a staff officer, and should know the exact positions to which they are allotted.

14. The training of Royal Engineer Volunteers should be confined to the special duties they have to perform on mobilization and all the requisite stores should be provided.

15. The camp allowances should be on the scale of 2s. 6d. per man per day, with an additional allowance of £2 for each officer and £1 for each man completing twelve, not necessarily consecutive, days.

16. Regimental camps should be discouraged. In cases where for special reasons they are considered necessary the allowances should be on the same scale as for brigade camps. Class II allowances should be discontinued.

17. Heavy batteries should go into camp only at places where suitable ranges and manœuvre ground are available. The necessary travelling allowances and cost of carriage to enable them to do this should be granted.

18. Each heavy battery should receive a camp allowance calculated to cover the cost of the conveyance of horses to and from camp.

19. Compensation should be allowed for horses injured on duty.

Musketry

20. The annual allowance of rifle ammunition should be considerably increased, chiefly with a view to the improvement of the less proficient shots.

21. The Musketry Regulations for the Volunteers should be revised

by means of a conference between the Commandant of the school of musketry and Volunteer officers of experience, and should provide that no Volunteer should fire at the longer ranges until fully proficient at the shorter ones.

Gunnery

22. The amount of ammunition allowed for practice should be increased.

Mounted Corps

23. Sufficient financial provision should be made to enable all mounted corps to learn their mounted work.

Travelling Allowances

24. Travelling allowances should be given for company training, for training at war stations, and for officers and non-commissioned officers visiting those stations.

Guns

25. Modern guns should be issued to all heavy batteries not already armed with them.

Permanent Staff

26. Good service as an Adjutant of Volunteers should count towards accelerated promotion and staff employment. The tenure of these appointments should be for five years, and they should not necessarily be vacated on promotion to field rank.

27. The selection of thoroughly good non-commissioned officers as sergeant instructors is of great importance. The number of sergeant instructors allowed by the present scale, while meeting the requirements of scattered corps, is insufficient for units concentrated at one centre. In such cases one per two companies should be allowed, in addition to the Sergeant-Major and Quartermaster-Sergeant, and the present Volunteer Quartermaster-Sergeants should gradually be replaced by regular Sergeant Instructors.

28. The employment of Sergeant Instructors as recruiters for the Line is undesirable.

Royal Engineer Volunteers

29. Field Companies of Engineer Volunteers should have an increased allowance.

30. The Volunteer submarine miners should be given a regular Adjutant and two regular Sergeant Instructors per division.

31. Opportunities should be given to Volunteer submarine miners to practice by searchlight.

Medical Arrangements

32. Brigade bearer companies should be units of the Royal Army Medical Corps (Volunteers), and be combined with the Field Hospitals. The bearer companies and Field Hospitals should, however, not be parts of the brigades, but attached to them.

33. The titles of regimental medical officers should be assimilated to those of the Royal Army Medical Corps (Volunteers) and of the Brigade bearer companies.

34. The Senior Medical Officer of the brigade should have the same camp allowance as other staff officers of his rank.

Volunteer Army Service Corps

35. A Volunteer Army Service Corps is urgently required in addition to the skeleton companies attached to brigades.

Mounted Infantry and Cyclists

36. The special allowances for mounted infantry and cyclists should be maintained at the present amounts, and the minimum number of efficients per company required by the existing regulations as a condition of earning those allowances should be abolished.

Special Recommendations Concerning Artillery Corps

37. Every composite artillery corps should be transformed into a corps entirely of one kind.

38. It is unnecessary to maintain all the existing companies of Volunteer Garrison Artillery, many of which are at unsuitable places.

EXTRACT FROM REPORT OF NORFOLK COMMISSION ON THE STATUS OF MILITIA COMMANDING OFFICERS, p. 33

'(He) goes out of active existence so far as his battalion is concerned (after the training) for the rest of the year. That is what I think is such a bad system.'

He is not allowed to select his adjutant, quartermaster, or permanent staff, though they form the cadre of his unit, he cannot promote a sergeant of the permanent staff to colour-sergeant, nor a colour-sergeant to staff-sergeant, no matter how great their merit; he is not even consulted in their promotions, transfers, or retirements, all of which are done over his head. He 'may come up during the preliminary drill to inspect the recruits belonging to his unit, but he will not assume direct command unless specially authorized to do so by the general officer commanding' (Militia Regulations, para. 189). At other times if he enters his own barrack-square or his own orderly-room he does so on the sufferance of his own adjutant. Some of our Regular witnesses appeared to think that his military aspirations in the non-training period ought to be amply gratified by an occasional stroll into barracks in plain clothes, a look at his recruits, culminating in lunch with the colonel of the depot.

APPENDIX I

ORDER IN COUNCIL OF THE 10TH DAY OF AUGUST, 1904

At the Court of Buckingham Palace the 10th day of August, 1904

Present:

THE KING'S MOST EXCELLENT MAJESTY IN COUNCIL

Whereas an Army Council has been constituted under His Majesty's Letters Patent, and it is expedient to make such provision as is hereinafter contained with respect thereto:

Now, therefore, His Majesty, by and with the advice of His Privy Council, is pleased to order, and it is hereby ordered, as follows:—

1. The Secretary of State is to be responsible to His Majesty and Parliament for all the business of the Army Council.

All business other than business which the Secretary of State specially reserves to himself, is to be transacted in the following principal divisions:—

(a) The first military member of the Army Council (the Chief of the General Staff), the second military member of the Army Council (the Adjutant-General), the third military member of the Army Council (the Quartermaster-General), and the fourth military member of the Army Council (the Master-General of Ordnance) to be responsible to the Secretary of State for the administration of so much of the business relating to the organization, disposition, personnel, armament, and maintenance of the Army as shall be assigned to them or each of them from time to time by the Secretary of State.

(b) The finance member of the Army Council to be responsible to the Secretary of State for the finance of the Army, and for so much of the other business of the Army Council as may be assigned to him from time to time by the Secretary of State.

(c) The civil member of the Army Council to be responsible to the Secretary of State for the non-effective votes, and for so much of the other business of the Army Council as may be assigned to him from time to time by the Secretary of State.

2. The Secretary of the War Office will act as Secretary of the Army Council, and will be charged with the interior economy of the War Office, and the preparation of all official communications of the Council and with such other duties as the Secretary of State may from time to time assign to him.

A. W. FITZROY

APPENDIX J

DIARY OF CERTAIN MEETINGS, ETC., DECEMBER 1905 TO MARCH 1906

Prologue

November 9th, 1905.—'At the present time, diplomatic relations between France and Germany are neither more nor less than the relations between outposts' (p. 309).

December 16th.—Grierson meets Huguet

Major-General J. H. Grierson to Lord Sanderson.

> WINCHESTER HOUSE,
> ST. JOHN'S SQUARE,
> S.W.
> *January 11th.*
>
> DEAR LORD SANDERSON,
> As I told you to-day in our conversation, I have had no communication with the French Military Attaché on the subject of British Military co-operation with France except, to a certain extent, about the 16th or 18th December when I rode with him in the Row (a chance meeting) and he told me of the French fears as to an attack by Germany. . . . (B.D., No. 211, p. 172.)

December 20th.—M. Cambon sees King Edward VII (Ibid., p. 313).

December 27th.—Repington's article in 'The Times' (R., p. 2).

December 28th.—Huguet dined with Repington (R., p. 2).

December 29th.—Repington's express letter to Sir Edward Grey.

December 30th.—Repington's luncheon with Esher; afterwards met Fisher at Admiralty.

Sir Edward Grey's letter from Fallodon to Repington. (Quoted P., p. 8.)

APPENDICES

January 3rd.—Grierson and Repington dined together.

January 5th.—Huguet lunched with Repington. Repington saw Lord Esher and Sir George Clarke at Whitehall Gardens. Arranged that Repington should see Huguet again.

January 7th.—Huguet left for Paris. Saw that evening M. Rouvier, the Prime Minister, and M. Etienne, Minister of War. Later General Brugère, Generalissimo, and General Brun, Chief of Staff.

January 10th.—M. Cambon sees Sir Edward Grey.

January 11th.—Huguet returns from Paris.

January 13th.—Sir Edward Grey's talk with Haldane.

January 14th.—Haldane sees Campbell-Bannerman.

January 15th.—Grierson instructed to open official conversations.

January 16th.—Grierson sees Huguet and writes to Barnardiston.

Epilogue

The end of this particular period of tension is marked by an unofficial letter of thanks to General Ducarne of the Belgian General Staff dated April 30th. (B.D., No. 221, p. 14.)

References are as follows:—

    B.D.   'British Documents of the Origin of the War', vol. iii.
    P.   'The Turning Point', Maurice Paléologue.
    R.   'The First World War', Repington.
    A.   'Autobiography', R. B. Haldane.

APPENDIX K

FIRST PARAGRAPH OF THE QUESTIONNAIRE GIVEN BY LIEUTENANT-COLONEL REPINGTON TO COLONEL HUGUET ON JANUARY 6, 1906, AND THE REPLY BROUGHT BACK BY HUGUET FROM PARIS

1. Have the Conseil Supérieur de la Guerre considered British co-operation in case of war with Germany? In what manner do they consider this co-operation can best be carried out (*a*) by sea, (*b*) by land?

Reply

1. La question de la cooperation de l'armée britannique sur terre a été etudiée — on estime que, pour être le plus efficace, son action devra:—

(*a*) Être liée à celle de l'armée française, c'est-à-dire, être placée sous la même direction, soit que les deux armées agissent sur le même théâtre d'opérations, ou sur des théâtres différents; (*b*) se faire sentir dès le début des hostilités, en raison de l'effet moral considerable que en résultera. Il serait à désirer qu'un certain nombre de corps anglais, quels que soient leur nombre et leur effectif (1 ou 2 divisions si possible) puissent être débarqués vers le 5me ou 6me jour.

. . . .

Le reste de l'armée executerait sa mobilisation régulièrement et partirait quand il serait achevée.

'The First World War', pp. 6 and 7.

BIBLIOGRAPHY

OFFICIAL PUBLICATIONS

The Armaments Year Book. Geneva, 1935.
Army Debates. Vols. 1898–1912. (Abbreviated A.D.)
Army Estimates. 1896–1912, and 1936. (Abbreviated A.E.)
Army Lists.
British Documents on the Origin of the War. Vol. III. (Abbreviated B.D.O.)
Chronology of Events connected with Army Administration. 1858–1907, and 1908-9-10-11-12. (Abbreviated 'Chronology'.)
General Annual Returns of the British Army. 1898, 1899, 1934.
Military Operations France and Belgium. Vol. I.
Queen's Regulations.
Life in the Ranks of the British Army (pamphlet). 1883.

REPORTS

Report of the Royal Commission appointed to enquire into the Civil and Professional Administration of the Naval and Military Departments. 1890. (Abbreviated Hartington Commission.)
Report of the Committee appointed to enquire into War Office Organization. 1901. (Abbreviated Dawkins Committee.)
Report of the Royal Commission on the South African War. 1903. (Chairman Lord Elgin.)

> *Note.*—This Commission is often incorrectly referred to as the 'Esher' Commission. Lord Esher himself always uses the style 'Elgin' Commission, as does the German historian Paul Kluke. In this work the abbreviation Elgin Commission or E.C. is used.

Report of the Committee on the Organization, Arms and Equipment of the Yeomanry Force. 1902. (Cd. Paper 886 of 1902.)
Report of the Royal Commission on the Militia and Volunteers. 1904. (Abbreviated Norfolk Commission.)

Report of the War Office (Reconstitution) Committee. 1904. Published in three Parts.
>   Part I. Cd. Paper 1932 of 1904. January 18, 1904.
>   Part II. With map. Cd. Paper 1968 of 1904. February 25, 1904.
>   Part III. Cd. Paper 2002 of 1904. March 7, 1904.
>   This is the 'Esher Committee' properly so called. The official 'Chronology' speaks of Lord Esher's Committee. (Abbreviated Esher Committee.)

MEMORANDA, ETC.

Memorandum of Secretary of State (The Stanhope Memorandum). Cd. Paper 607 of 1901.

The State of the Six Army Corps Commands. Cd. Paper 1413 of 1903.

Particulars regarding the Proposed Army Organization Scheme. Cd. Paper 1910 of 1904.

Summary of the Speech of Secretary of State for War. Cd. Paper 1907 of 1904.

Yeomanry Cavalry Training Returns. 1900–1.

Imperial Yeomanry Cavalry Training Returns. 1901–2–3.

Returns showing the Establishment of each Regiment of Militia. 1902–7.

Army (Volunteer Force) Comparative Statement showing Increase, Decrease, etc. Cd. Paper 966 of 1902.

Army (Volunteers) Copy of Circular Letter Addressed, etc. Cd. Paper 2437 of 1905.

Army (Volunteers) Copy of Circular Letter Addressed, etc. . . . in substitution. . . . Cd. Paper 2439 of 1905.

Return showing Annual Cost of Royal Garrison Regiments, etc. Return No. 239 of 1903.

Army Summary of the Recommendations of the Interdepartmental Committee, etc., on Reserves of Guns and Stores. Cd. Paper 1908 of 1904.

Order in Council defining the Duties of the Army Council. Cd. Paper 2251 of 1904.

Order in Council defining the Duties of the Inspector-General. Cd. Paper 2252 of 1904.

Order in Council defining the Duties of the Director of Army Finance. Cd. Paper 2253 of 1904.

Memorandum by the Director-General Army Medical Service on the Physical Unfitness, of Men offering themselves for Enlistment. Cd. Paper 1501 of 1903.

Army Statement showing Extensions of Service, etc. Cd. Paper 1905 of 1904.
Army Statement showing basis on which the Estimated Extra Cost . . for Conscription was made. Cd. Paper 1909 of 1904.
Memorandum by the Secretary of State for War on Army Reorganization, July 30, 1906. Cd. Paper 2993 of 1906.
Memorandum on the Military Forces in the United Kingdom. Cd. Paper 3297 of 1907.
Army. Territorial and Reserve Forces Bill. Memorandum by the Secretary of State for War. Cd. Paper 3366 of 1907.
Memorandum showing how various Enactments are affected by the T.F. and R.F. Bill. Cd. Paper 3361 of 1907.
Memorandum showing the Amendments proposed to the Army Act, Cd. Paper 3359 of 1907.
Territorial Force Annual Trainings. 1908. M.T.2. W.O. July 6, 1908.
Territorial and Reserve Forces Bill. Bill 197.
Army Statement showing (1) Number of Special Reservists Recruited . . . (2) Dispersal of Militiamen . . . etc. Cd. Paper 3935 of 1908.
Army (Special Reserve). Statement showing strengths, etc. March 1, 1909. Cd. Paper 4497 of 1909.
Report dated July 18, 1908, by the Director-General of the Army Medical Service as to the . . . Medical Service of the T.F. Cd. Paper 4056 of 1908.
Report of the War Office Committee appointed to discuss certain Militia Questions. Cd. Paper 3513 of 1907.
The Imperial General Staff. W.O. Letter.
And others of less importance.

TRAINING MANUALS, ETC.

Infantry Drill. 1892.
Combined Training. 1902.
Treatise on Service Ordnance. 1908.
The Soldier's Pocket Book.

JOURNALS, ETC.

Journal of the Royal United Service Institution. 1898–1912. (Abbreviated as 'R.U.S.I. Journal'.)
The Army and Navy Gazette.

The Times.
Punch.
And others.

HISTORICAL

Army Book of the British Empire.
Brassey's Annual.
The History of the British Army. Hon. J. W. Fortescue. Vol. XIII.
Fifty Years of Europe. J. A. Spender.
A Short History of Our Own Times. J. A. Spender.
The River War. Winston Churchill.
With Kitchener to Khartoum. G. W. Steevens.
With the Flag to Pretoria. Harmsworth.
World Crisis. Winston Churchill. Vol. I.
The First World War. Repington. Vol. I.
The Turning Point. Maurice Paléologue.
The Origin of the World War. Sidney Bradshawe Foye.
Recent Revelations of European Diplomacy. G. P. Gooch.
The War Office Past and Present. Capt. Owen Wheeler.
The War Office. Hampden Gordon.
Heeresaufbau und Heerespolitik Englands. Paul Kluke.
Outline of the Development of the British Army. Lt.-Gen. Sir Hastings Anderson.
Annals of the King's Royal Rifle Corps. Vol. III.
 and other Regimental Histories.

MILITIA

The Constitutional Force. Col. Jackson Hay, C.B., C.M.G.
An Army without a Reserve (pamphlet). Militia Club.
History of the Royal Monmouthshire Militia. Capt. R. E. Sargeaunt.
History of the 4th Battalion Norfolk Regiment, late East Norfolk Militia.
The Essex Militia. Vol. 4.
And others.

VOLUNTEERS AND TERRITORIAL FORCE

History of Volunteer Infantry. R. P. Berry.
History of the Volunteer Forces. C. Sebag-Montefiore.
The Volunteers from Wimbledon to Bisley. The British Volunteer Force 1859-89. By 'The Ancient'. (Abbreviated as 'The Ancient'.)
The Territorial Force. H. Baker.
What is the Territorial Army. Col. G. R. Codrington.
Fifty Years of It. The Experiences and Struggles of a Volunteer of 1859. J. H. A. Macdonald.
The Honourable Artillery Company. G. Goold Walker.
The History of Queen Victoria's Rifles. Keeson.
The Rangers' Historical Records.
And other Regimental Histories.
Order Books of the XIX Middlesex R.V. Bloomsbury Rifles.
Order Books of the XX Middlesex R.V. Artists Rifles.
Order Books of the XL (later XXII) Middlesex R.V. Central London Rangers.

BIOGRAPHY

King Edward VII. A Biography. Vol. II. Sir Sidney Lee. (Abbreviated Lee.)
Autobiography. Richard Burton Haldane. (Abbreviated Autobiography.)
Before the War. Viscount Haldane.
Journals and Letters of Reginald Viscount Esher. Vols. I and II. (Abbreviated Esher Journals.)
Reminiscences by Lt.-Gen. Sir Gerald Ellison, K.C.B., K.C.M.G., published in 'The Lancashire Lad', July 1934 et seq. (Abbreviated Ellison.)
    (*Note.*—By the kindness of General Ellison the two concluding chapters of these important memoirs were read in typescript form before publication.)
Twenty-five Years. Sir Edward Grey.
Fifty Years of Parliament. Asquith. Vol. II.
Life of Lieut.-General Sir James M. Grierson. D. S. Macdiarmid. (Abbreviated Macdiarmid.)
Field-Marshal Earl Haig. J. Charteris.

Journal of Field-Marshal Earl Haig. Duff Cooper.
Memoirs of H. O. Arnold-Forster.
Field-Marshal Sir Henry Wilson, His Life and Diaries. Sir C. E. Callwell.
From Midshipman to Field-Marshal. Evelyn Wood.
Life of Wolseley. F. Maurice.
Trooper 8008 I.Y. Hon. Sidney Peel.
Lord Grenfell's Memoirs.

INDEX

Acklom, Capt. J. E., 57
Acts of Parliament—
  Army, 274
  Army Enlistment, 1870, 4
  Naval Defence, 1889, 12
  Reserve Forces, 1882, 274
  Reserve Forces and Militia, 1898, 274, 277
  Territorial and Reserve Forces, 1907, 224, 275, 280, 282 et seq., 291
Adye, Col. W., 291
Airy, Sir R., 37
Akers-Douglas, Rt. Hon. R. (later Viscount Chilston), 162, 164
Albemarle, Earl of, 38
Allenby, Brig.-Gen. E. H. H. (later F.-M. Viscount), 218, 262, 263
Amery, Rt. Hon. L. S., 253
Ampthill, Lord, 268
Ardagh, Col. J. C. (later Maj.-Gen. Sir John), 11, 175, 204
Armament—
  Guns—
    12-pdr., 155, 225
    12½-pdr., 97
    13-pdr., 155
    15-pdr., 123, 153, 256, 288
    18-pdr., 154, 225, 256, 288
    4.5-in. Howitzer, 225
    4.7-in., 123, 139, 140, 155, 288
    40-pdr., 64
    64-pdr. M.L., 64
    9.45-in. Howitzer, 154
    Ehrhardt, 153, 154, 288
    75-mm. French, 153, 154
  Rifles—
    Lee-Enfield, 107

Armament—*continued*
  Rifles—*continued*
    Short Rifle, 155, 224
    Carbine, 105, 155
  Sword, 105, 225
  Lance, 105, 225
Armed Associations, 56
Armstrong and Vickers, Messrs., 154
Army Council, 22, 147, 185, 193, 194, 198, 206, 208 et seq., 227, 231, 234, 254, 255, 266, 280, 289, 293, 294, 297, 298, 303, 320, 321
Army Reserve, 3, 7, 18, 19, 29 et seq., 40, 69, 70, 73, 78 et seq., 89, 124, 133, 140, 141, 180 et seq., 258, 260, 281
Arnold-Forster, Rt. Hon. H. O., 27, 73 et seq., 88, 124, 147, 153, 154, 161 et seq., 208, 213, 220 et seq., 233, 242, 259, 277, 282, 283
Asquith, Rt. Hon. H. H. (later Earl of Oxford and Asquith), 126, 148, 151, 158, 165, 170, 231 et seq., 243, 298, 299, 302, 305
Aston, Col. G. (later Maj.-Gen. Sir George), 227

Badcock, Lt.-Gen. Sir A. R. (later General), 112
Bagot, Capt. the Hon. W. L., 106
Balfour, Rt. Hon. A. J. (later Earl of Balfour), 148, 150, 158 et seq., 191 et seq., 206, 207, 213 et seq., 233, 236, 242, 248, 276, 305
Balfour of Burleigh, Lord, 162

Balfour, Col. E., 94, 100
Ballard, Admiral G. A., 240
Banbury, Sir F. (later Lord). 176
Barham, Col. A. S., 61, 272
Barnardiston, Lt.-Col. N. W. (later Maj.-Gen.), 240, 243, 323
Bath, Marquis of, 313
Bathurst, Lord, 270
Beare, Professor T. H., 294
Becket, Mr. E. W., 178
Beckett, Lt.-Col. E. W., 105
Bedford, Duke of, 124, 186, 201, 247, 260, 267, 268, 270, 272, 281 et seq.
Bellairs, Mr. Carlyon (later Commander), 134
Bertie, Sir F. L. (later Viscount, of Thame), 237, 239
Bingham, Lord (later Earl of Lucan), 267
Borrett, Maj.-Gen. H. C., 90, 91
Bossat, General, 101
Botha, Gen. Louis, 112, 140, 298
Bourn, Professor, 294
Boyle, Mr. A., 60
Brabazon, Maj.-Gen. Sir J. P., 111
Brackenbury, Maj.-Gen. H. (later Gen. Rt. Hon. Sir Henry), 11, 12, 17, 19, 36, 84, 86, 87, 163, 167
British Central African Regiment, The, 41
British Expeditionary Force, 243, 244, 246, 250, 251, 254, 256, 259, 262, 266, 278, 291, 299, 301, 302, 305
Broadhurst, Mr. H., 122
Brodie, Mr. H. C., 13
Brodrick, Rt. Hon. St. John (later Earl of Midleton, q.v.), 5, 16, 17, 29, 30, 83, 85, 109, 128 et seq., 198, 202, 203, 214, 218, 219, 233, 255
Bromley-Davenport, Mr. W. (later Brig.-Gen. Sir William), 208
Brugère, Gen., 323
Brun, General, 323

Buller, Lt.-Gen. R. H. (later Gen. Rt. Hon. Sir Redvers), 33, 74, 75, 93, 104, 105, 142
Burls, Mr. E. G. (later Sir Edwin), 87
Busk, Capt. H., 56
Byng, Brig.-Gen. Hon. Julian (later Viscount, of Vimy), 218, 262

Cambon, M. Paul, 236 et seq., 241, 322, 323
Cambridge, H.R.H. the Duke of, 4, 15, 21, 22, 47, 69, 129, 199, 200, 201, 209
Campbell-Bannerman, Mr. H. (later Rt. Hon. Sir Henry), 19, 28, 122, 126, 133, 135, 136, 168, 188, 196, 199, 231 et seq., 276, 281, 323
Capper, Lt.-Col. J. E. (later Maj.-Gen. Sir John), 227
Cardwell, Viscount, 3, 5, 27, 28, 39, 44, 69, 70, 169, 202, 253, 268, 269, 299
Carson, Rt. Hon. Lord, 190
Cave, Col. Sir T. Sturmy, 122, 123
Chamberlain, Rt. Hon. A. (later Rt. Hon. Sir Austen), 162
Chamberlain, Rt. Hon. Joseph, 151, 162, 211
Chelmsford, Lord, 24
Chesham, Lord, 109, 110, 113, 267
Chief of the Imperial General Staff, Office of, 209, 210, 303
Childers, Mr. H. C. E., 5, 69, 70
Chinese Regiment, The, 41, 220, 249, 310
Churchill, Lord Randolph Spencer, 19.
Churchill, Mr. W. S. (later Rt. Hon.), 37, 152, 157, 158, 162, 183, 184, 190, 197, 241, 299, 302
City Imperial Volunteers, 94, 96 et seq., 103, 110
Clarke, Mr. G. S. (later Lord Sydenham), 19, 22, 167, 203 et seq., 210, 234, 323

INDEX

Cole, Major G. H., 253
Colley, Sir G., 35
Colomb, Sir J., 193
Commander-in-Chief, Office of, 20 et seq., 70, 198 et seq., 203, 204, 207, 209, 212, 215
Commissions—
  Harris, 134
  Hartington, 19 et seq., 167, 198, 199, 205, 207
  Norfolk, 93, 151, 173 et seq., 191
  Royal, on South African War (Elgin Commission), 14, 69, 71 et seq., 145, 148, 149, 163, 165 et seq., 179, 200, 203 et seq., 214
Committees, etc.—
  1895 Board, 201, 202
  1899 Board, 202
  Lord Brownlow's, 54
  Clothing, 1901, 153
  Dawkins, 167, 202, 203, 205
  Lord Dunraven's, 116
  Sir C. H. Ellice's, 5
  Imperial Defence, 174, 175, 179, 192, 198, 206 et seq., 227, 240, 276, 301, 305
  Imperial Defence Conference, 1909, 298
  Imperial Yeomanry, 105 et seq.
  Sir A. Keogh's, 288
  Lord Mayor's, 1899–1900, 97, 98
  Col. Lucas's, 112 et seq.
  Gen. MacDougall's, 4
  Mowatt, 16, 86 et seq., 153, 188, 225
  National Defence, 213
  Lord Raglan's, 134
  Stanhope, 12
  Col. Stanley's, 51
  Gen. Stopford's, 225, 226
  Territorial Force (The Duma), 267, 269
  Gen. Vetch's, 153
  Ward, 294
  War Office, for Mobilization, 202
  War Office Council, 202, 203

War Office Reconstitution (Esher), 6, 16, 22, 163, 170, 179, 204 et seq., 235, 277, 291, 292, 306
Congleton, Maj. Sir R., 37
Connaught, H.R.H. the Duke of, 129, 142, 209
County Associations, 258, 266, 269, 274, 276, 280, 285, 286, 288, 289
Crewe, Earl of, 297

Dalmahoy, Lt.-Col. J. A., 173
Darley, Rt. Hon. Sir F. M., 149
Dashwood, Gen. R. L., 5
David, Rev. A. A., 294
Dawkins, Mr. C. E. (later Sir Clinton), 202, 203, 205
Deane, Col. T., 112, 115
Delcassé, M., 195, 237, 241
Denbigh and Desmond, Earl of, 97
Derby, Earl of, 173, 271, 287
Devonshire, Duke of, 162, 174, 198, 213, 214
Dickson-Poynder, Capt. Sir. J., 313
Dilke, Rt. Hon. Sir C. W., 17, 28, 135, 136, 282, 284
Donoughmore, Earl of, 185, 186, 192, 208, 255
Douglas, Maj.-Gen. C. W. H. (later Gen. Sir Charles), 208, 261
Ducane, Gen. Sir E. F., 4, 227
Ducarne, Gen., 323
Duncombe, Hon. H. V., 95
Dundonald, Maj.-Gen., the Earl of, 313
Dunraven, Lord, 116, 117

Edge, Sir J., 149
Edmonds, Maj. J. E. (later Brig.-Gen. Sir James), 227
Edward VII, H.M. King, 145, 147, 149 et seq., 159, 162 et seq., 167, 168, 176, 177, 208, 231, 235, 251, 252, 266 et seq., 276, 277, 285, 300, 305, 320 et seq.

Edwards, Col. H. J., 294
Elcho, Lord, 60
Elgin, Earl of, 148, 149
Ellice, Sir C., 5
Elliott, Rt. Hon. A. R. D., 162
Ellison, Capt. G. F. (later Lt.-Gen. Sir Gerald), 15, 204, 205, 211, 226, 234, 235, 245, 266, 267, 270, 272, 275, 306
Esher, Viscount, 20, 148, 149, 162, 163, 167 et seq., 196, 198, 203 et seq., 231, 234, 251, 266, 267, 269, 276, 277, 285, 300, 305
Etienne, M., 323
Ewart, Maj.-Gen. J. S. (later Lt.-Gen. Sir John), 294

Fanshawe, Brig.-Gen. H. D. (later Lt.-Gen. Sir Hew), 263
Field Force, The, 17, 72, 74, 79, 96, 122, 131, 224, 264
Fisher, Admiral Sir J., 163, 167, 204, 206, 215, 239, 302, 322
Franklin, Maj.-Gen. W. E. (later Lt.-Gen. Sir William), 263
Freeman-Thomas, Mr. F. (later Earl of Willingdon), 267
French, Lt.-Gen. Sir J. (later Earl of Ypres), 218, 227, 234, 240, 251
Furse, Major (later Lt.-Gen. Sir W. T.), 227

Galway, Earl of, 50, 313
George V, H.M. King, 289, 295
Gibb, Mr. G. S. (later Sir George), 203
Gibson, Mr. H. J. (later Sir Henry), 203
Gladstone, Capt. G. A., 60
Gladstone, Viscount, 231
Goschen, Rt. Hon. G. J. (later Viscount, of Hawkhurst), 213
Gough, Lt.-Col. H. (later General Sir Hubert), 227, 262
Granby, Marquis of, 46

Grenfell, Lord, 157, 167, 173
Grey, Rt. Hon. Sir E. (later Viscount, of Fallodon), 157, 158, 170, 231, 232, 236 et seq., 252, 282, 322, 323
Grierson, Maj.-Gen. J. (later Lt.-Gen. Sir James), 162, 196, 227, 239 et seq., 246, 262, 322, 323
Griffith-Boscawen, Mr. A. (later Rt. Hon. Sir Arthur), 184
Groves, Sir C., 173
Grosvenor, Lord, 60
Guest, Mr. F. E. (later Capt. Rt. Hon. Frederick), 197
Gunter, Lt.-Col. E., 36

Haig, Maj.-Gen. D. (later F.-M. Earl), 212, 227, 231, 234, 242, 270, 271, 275, 291 et seq., 298, 306
Haking, Col. R. C. R. (later Gen. Sir Richard), 227
Haldane, Lt.-Col. J. A. L. (later Gen. Sir Aylmer), 227
Haldane, Mr. R. B. (later Viscount, of Cloan), 13, 126, 127, 140, 147, 151, 178, 197, 217, 220, 225, 227, 231 et seq., 323
Haliburton, Lord, 276
Hamilton, Lt.-Gen. Sir B. M. (later General), 262
Hamilton, Lt.-Gen. Sir Ian (later General), 93, 99
Hamilton, Lord George, 162, 184
Hamley, Sir E., 13
Harcourt, Lt.-Col. E. W., 60
Harcourt, Sir W., 136
Hardinge, Viscount, 186, 270
Harris, Mr. C. (later Sir Charles), 85, 245, 247, 249, 256, 265, 303
Harris, Col. Rt. Hon. Lord, 106, 134, 284, 313
Hartington, Marquis of (later Duke of Devonshire, q.v.), 19
Henderson, Mr. A. (later Rt. Hon.), 284

INDEX

Henderson, Col. G. F. R., 32, 33, 205, 225, 226, 292
Herbert, Capt. E. A., 33
Hildyard, Gen. Sir H. J. T., 17
Holland, Mr. B., 149
Hopkins, Admiral Sir J. O., 149, 175
Huguet, Col., 239 et seq., 322 et seq.
Hyslop, Lt.-Col. W. C., 220

Jackson, Sir J., 149, 167
James, Capt. W. H., 9, 35, 36
Jarvis, Lt.-Col. W. (later Col. Sir Weston), 116, 117

Kelly-Kenny, Gen. T. (later Gen. Sir Thomas), 79, 89, 92, 201
Kemp, Lt.-Col. G., 108, 110, 157
Kemp, Mr. J. (later Sir John), 274
Keogh, Surg.-Gen. Sir A., 288
Kiggell, Col. L. E. (later Lt.-Gen. Sir Launcelot), 227, 291
Kitchener, Lord (later F.-M. Earl), 9, 24, 34, 112, 113, 140, 143, 209, 217
Knight, Mr. W. C. (later Maj.-Gen. Sir Wyndham), 106, 107, 110
Knollys, Viscount, 163, 176, 198, 254
Knox, Rt. Hon. Sir R., 86, 173
Kruger, President, 110, 126, 306

Labouchere, Rt. Hon. H., 30, 158
Lake, Col. P. H. N. (later Lt.-Gen. Sir Percy), 71, 175
Lansdowne, Marquis of, 38, 51, 80, 82, 84, 86, 87, 90, 97, 105, 124, 126, 128, 142, 186, 193, 199 et seq., 213, 236 et seq., 242, 257, 282
Laurie, Lt.-Gen. J. W., 29
Laurier, Rt. Hon. Sir W., 298
Liddell, Mr. F. (later Sir Frederick), 275
Llewellyn, Lt.-Col. E. H., 173
Lloyd George, Mr. D. (later Rt. Hon.), 126, 299
Lobell, Herr von, 36, 154, 226, 227

Londonderry, Marquis of, 190
Long, Mr. W. (later Viscount), 109
Lonsdale, Earl of, 106
Loreburn, Earl of, 298
Lovat, Lord, 267, 294
Lucas, Col. A. G., 105, 109 et seq., 270, 313
Lucas, Lord, 134, 286, 302
Lyttelton, Lt.-Gen. Hon. Sir N. G. (later Gen. Rt. Hon. Sir Neville), 208, 296, 298

McCrae, Mr. C. C., 172
Macdonald, Col. J. H. A. (later Brig.-Gen. Rt. Hon. Sir John), 62, 104, 223
MacDonald, Mr. J. R. (later Rt. Hon.), 236, 285
McKenna, Rt. Hon. R., 302
Mackinnon, Maj.-Gen. W. H. (later Gen. Sir William), 96, 97, 269, 270
March, Earl of, 173
Mather, Mr. W. (later Rt. Hon. Sir William), 203
Maurice, Major F. B. (later Maj.-Gen. Sir Frederick), 291
Maurice, Maj.-Gen. Sir J. F., 51
Mercier, Gen., 126
Methuen, F.-M. Lord, 146, 267, 270, 285
Midleton, Earl of (see Brodrick), 131, 140, 141, 153, 164
Miles, Col. H. G. S. (later Lt.-Gen. Sir Herbert), 203
Militia, 3, 5, 14, 16, 18, 42 et seq., 64, 71, 75 et seq., 85, 86, 89 et seq., 122 et seq., 132 et seq., 144, 151, 156 et seq., 162, 166, 173, 175 et seq., 182, 184, 186 et seq., 190, 193, 197, 219 et seq., 247, 254 et seq., 267 et seq., 290, 307, 311, 318, 319
Militia Reserve, 18, 19, 48 et seq., 89 et seq., 134, 145, 171, 190, 268, 273, 290

Milne, Lt.-Col. G. F. (later F.-M. Lord), 227
Morley, Rt. Hon. Viscount, 165, 231
Morocco, Sultan of, 195
Mowatt, Rt. Hon. Sir F., 87
Murray, Maj.-Gen. Sir J. W. (later Lt.-Gen.), 208

N.A.R.A., Founding of, 59, 60
Newton, Lord, 223, 233
Nicholson, Lt.-Gen. Sir W. G. (later F.-M. Lord), 77, 82, 91, 214, 298
Norfolk, Duke of, 173, 174
Norman, F.-M. Sir H., 149
Norton, Capt. C. W., 136, 154, 190

Officers' Training Corps, 294, 295, 299
Ottly, Rear-Admiral Sir C. L., 240
Oxford and Asquith, Earl of (see Asquith).

Parsons, Maj.-Gen. L. W. (later Lt.-Gen. Sir Lawrence), 263
Pearse, Maj. H. (later Col.), 35
Pearson, Col. M. B., 223
Plumer, Maj.-Gen. H. C. O. (later F.-M. Lord), 116, 208, 227, 263
Portland, Earl of, 222
Portsmouth, Earl of, 257, 259, 284
Pryce-Jones, Lt.-Col. E., 121

Radolin, Prince, 195
Raglan, Lord, 47, 50, 134, 222, 270, 284
Rasch, Sir C., 221
Rawlinson, Col. H. S. (later Gen. Lord), 227, 293
Redmond, Mr. J. E., 195
Reid, Sir R., 231
Reitz, Joubert, 146
Repington, Lt.-Col. C. à C., 238, 244, 245, 322 et seq.
Ritchie, Mr. C. T. (later Rt. Hon. Lord), 135, 162

Ritzenhofen, Lt. F.-M. Gustavus, 129
Robb, Col. F. S., 100, 101
Roberts, Maj.-Gen. F. (later F.-M. Earl), 7, 24, 33, 75, 76, 91, 99, 112, 126, 129, 131, 141, 152, 155, 159, 205 et seq., 214, 225, 226, 253, 267, 270, 274, 275
Roberts, Mr. G. H. (later Rt. Hon.), 284
Robertson, Col. W. (later F.-M. Sir William), 227, 241
Rolleston, Col. L. (later Col. Sir Lancelot), 313
Romer, Maj. C. F. (later Gen. Sir Cecil), 227
Rosebery, Earl of, 125, 126, 163, 232, 233
Rouvier, M., 195, 237, 323
Royal Flying Corps, Formation of, 265, 303
Royal Garrison Regiments, 83, 161, 171, 220, 247, 255, 268, 288
Royal Reserve Battalions, 78, 82, 83, 124
Russell, Mr. G. (later Sir George), 60
Rutley, Capt. J. L., 60

St. Quintin, Col. T. A., 106
Salisbury, Marquis of, 126 et seq., 143, 148, 149, 150, 213
Samuel, Mr. H. (later Viscount), 176
Sandars, Mr. J. S., 207
Sanderson, Lord, 258
Sargeant, Col. W. C. E., 221
Sargeaunt, Capt. R. E., 45
Satterthwaite, Lt.-Col. E., 173
Seely, Major J. E. B. (later Lord Mottistone), 156, 187, 191, 197, 265, 267, 302
Selborne, Earl of, 134, 164, 214
Shee, Mr. G., 151
Sirdar, The (see Kitchener)
Smith, Mr. F. E. (later Earl of Birkenhead), 258
Smith-Dorrien, Lt.-Gen. H. L. (later Gen. Sir Horace), 227

INDEX

Special Reserve, 272 et seq., 280, 281, 284, 290, 294, 295, 299, 305
Spencer, Earl of, 60, 148, 185
Staff College, 23, 227, 275, 294, 297
Stanhope, Rt. Hon. E., 12, 14, 60, 61
Stanhope Memorandum, 14, 16, 18, 74, 85, 127, 243
Stanley, Lord (later Earl of Derby), 267, 270, 271
Steevens, Col. J. (later Maj.-Gen. Sir John), 15
Stephenson, Maj.-Gen. T. E., 263
Stewart, Col. H. A. A., 123
Stopford, Col. L. A. M. (later Maj.-Gen. Sir Lionel), 70, 71, 72, 226, 227, 267, 270
Strathcona, Lord, 149

Taubman-Goldie, Sir G. D., 149, 167
Taylor, Capt. W., 60
Territorial Army, 52, 53, 57, 62, 104, 134, 178, 269, 270, 278, 281, 300, 305
Territorial Force, 147, 155, 178, 244, 250, 252, 266, 269 et seq., 275, 278 et seq., 293, 295, 296, 299, 300, 303, 305
Tirpitz, Admiral von, 130
Treves, Sir F., 145, 163
Tully, Lt.-Col. T., 32, 33
Turner, Maj.-Gen. Sir H. E., 175

Valentia, Viscount, 106, 108, 109, 110
Vetch, Maj.-Gen. W. F., 153
Vickers & Maxim, Messrs., 98, 154
Victoria, H.M. Queen, 8, 20, 57, 60, 73, 74, 82, 129, 145, 148
Vincent, Col. Sir H., 94 et seq., 102, 187, 192, 197, 267 et seq., 282, 284
Vivian, Mr. H., 242, 252
Volunteers, 3, 5, 7, 9, 18, 42, 46, 54 et seq., 71, 75 et seq., 86, 89, 93 et seq., 112, 121 et seq., 132 et seq., 142 et seq., 153, 157, 158, 172, 173, 175, 176, 179, 182, 183, 187, 188, 190 et seq., 219, 222 et seq., 256 et seq., 267 et seq., 272, 275 et seq., 312, 315 et seq.

Wantage, Lord, 50, 52
Ward, Col. Sir E. W. D., 208, 294, 297
Warren, Gen. Sir C., 74
Welby, Sir C., 203
Wemyss, Earl of, 42, 51, 57, 125, 183, 186, 281, 282, 284
West, Major Marshall, 43
West African Regiment, The, 41, 310
West Indian Regiment, The, 41, 220, 310
Westrop, Lt.-Col. O'Callaghan, 173
White, Maj.-Gen. Sir G. S. (later F.-M. Sir George), 33
Widdows, Mr. A. E., 233, 245, 266
Wilkinson, Mr. Spencer, 13, 167, 173
Wilson, Brig.-Gen. H. (later F.-M. Sir Henry), 227, 246, 275, 294, 302
Wilson, Sir G. F. (later Rt. Hon. Sir Guy), 245
Wolseley, Lord (later F.-M. Viscount), 6, 11, 14 et seq., 21, 22, 24, 31, 33, 36, 69, 70, 73, 74, 80, 82, 84 et seq., 97, 129, 142, 175, 200, 201, 209, 292, 306
Wood, F.-M. Sir E., 8, 26, 32, 33, 35, 142
Wyndham, Mr. G. (later Rt. Hon. George), 52, 73, 87, 90, 95, 122 et seq., 128

Yeomanry, 3, 5, 18, 42, 43, 52 et seq., 64, 71, 75 et seq., 86, 89, 96, 102, 104 et seq., 122 et seq., 134 et seq., 144, 153, 157, 158, 192, 256 et seq., 278, 282, 284 et seq., 313, 316

PRINTED IN GREAT BRITAIN
BY UNWIN BROTHERS LIMITED
LONDON AND WOKING

For Product Safety Concerns and Information please contact our EU
representative GPSR@taylorandfrancis.com
Taylor & Francis Verlag GmbH, Kaufingerstraße 24, 80331 München, Germany

www.ingramcontent.com/pod-product-compliance
Lightning Source LLC
Chambersburg PA
CBHW071152300426
44113CB00009B/1175